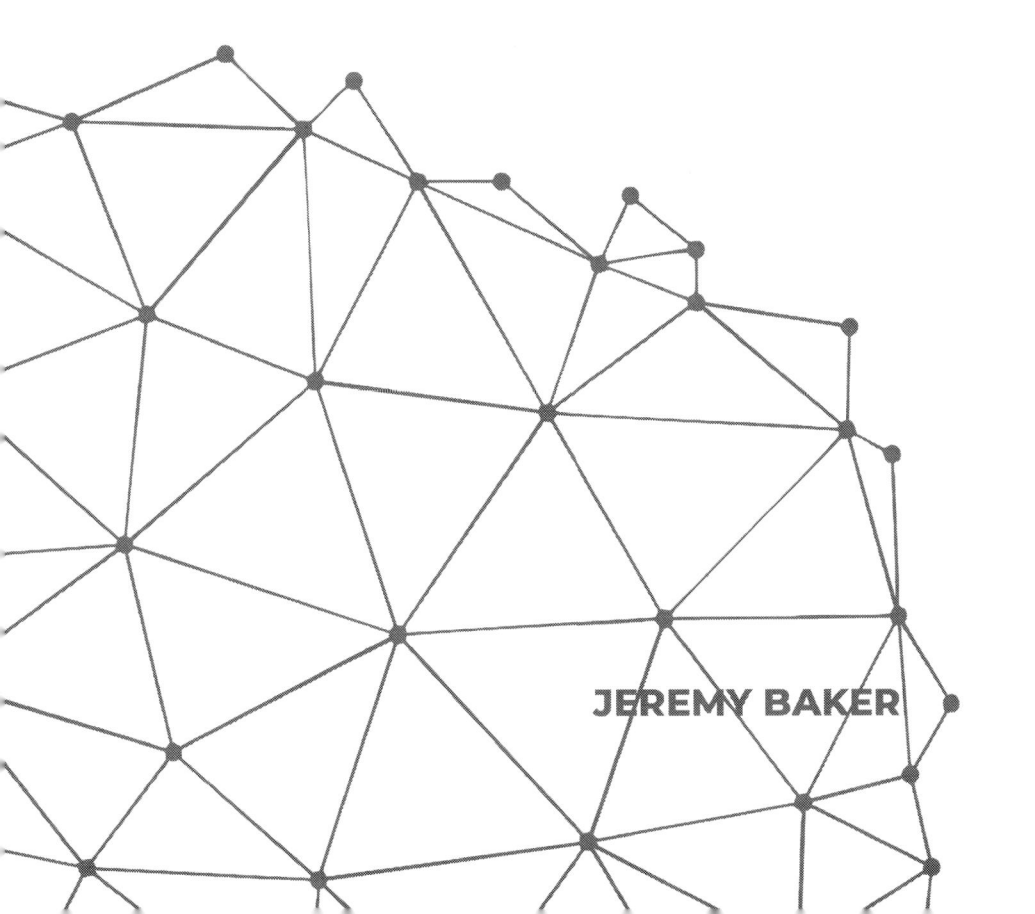

101 DEVOTIONALS
PART TWO

MAKE YOUR DAY COUNT

JEREMY BAKER

101 DEVOTIONALS PART TWO
Copyright © 2025 by Jeremy Baker

First Edition.
January, 2025

All rights reserved. No part of the book may be reproduced in any form or by any means graphic, or electronically including but not limited to photocopying, recording, scanning, digitizing, web distribution, or any manner whatsoever without permission in writing from the author except in the case of brief quotations embodied in critical articles and reviews.

Interior Design: Carolina Bunta
Cover Design: Yilbin Araujo

101 DEVOTIONALS
PART TWO

Jeremy Baker

101 DEVOTIONALS — PART TWO

TABLE OF CONTENTS

INTRODUCTION 11

THE REAL DEAL 15

WITH GOD ANYTHING IS POSSIBLE 23

THE WINNING HAND PT. 1 29

THE WINNING HAND PT. 2 35

PLAN ACCORDINGLY 41

AT THE END OF MY ROPE 47

DON'T JUST SIT THERE 53

YOU CAN'T BE DEFEATED 59

WHAT ARE YOU LOOKING FOR? 65

TRAPPED IN THE DRAPES 71

DO YOU SEE ANYTHING? 77

WHAT IS YOUR LIFE BUILT ON? 83

101 DEVOTIONALS — PART TWO

HOPE	89
COMMITMENT	95
DREAM BIG	101
FORWARD	107
MINDSET	113
THANKFULNESS	119
FAITH	125
GOD FIRST	131
FEAR NOT	137
WORDS	143
ATTITUDE	149
CHOICES	155
PERSEVERANCE	161
I AM'S	167
LEADERSHIP	173
LIFE	179
GROWTH	185
FRIENDS	191
FOCUS	197
PRAYER	203
EVANGELISM	209
WHAT IF?	215

TABLE OF CONTENTS

IDENTITY 221

TRUST 227

PASSION 233

COURAGE 239

LOVE 245

OBEDIENCE 251

WINNING 257

POSITIVE 263

GIVING 269

BURN THE PLOWS, EMBRACE THE GREATER 275

STAND FIRM IN THE STORM 281

VISION FOR MORE 287

VISION BEYOND THE VISIBLE 293

BREAK THE CYCLE 299

BETWEEN THE ROCKS 305

MADE NEW 313

GREATER THINGS 319

PRAYER OF SALVATION 325

APPENDIX 327

REFERENCES 329

101 DEVOTIONALS — PART TWO

INTRODUCTION

This second installment in the two-part devotional series—featuring 51 devotionals—has been thoughtfully created to inspire, motivate, and encourage you to grow deeper in your relationship with God. Building upon the foundation laid in the first book, this collection continues to offer practical steps for developing intentional habits that lead to lasting spiritual transformation. In a culture where settling for average is easy, those who commit to intentional growth will experience a life of greater purpose, fulfillment, and success.

Growth is a journey, not a destination, and it requires ongoing effort and consistent action. The choices you make today will shape your tomorrow. As you embark on this next step in your journey, consider: How far have you come since you began? What new areas is God calling you to explore? How will you continue to pursue the dreams and goals He has placed in your heart? The key lies in staying committed to growing each day, allowing God to equip you for the extraordinary future He has planned for you.

Hebrews 11:6 reminds us, "God is a rewarder of those who diligently seek Him." With 51 new devotionals to guide you, this book is designed to help you deepen the life-changing habits you've begun. Dedicate time each day to engage with these devotionals, listen for the Lord's voice, and follow His leading. As you open your heart to His guidance, you'll be empowered to take intentional steps toward becoming all He created you to be. Whether you take the stairs or the elevator, the choice to grow and move forward is always yours. Let this book be your daily companion as you continue pressing into God's presence and pursuing the extraordinary purpose He has for your life.

—Jeremy Baker

101 DEVOTIONALS — PART TWO

DAY 51
THE REAL DEAL

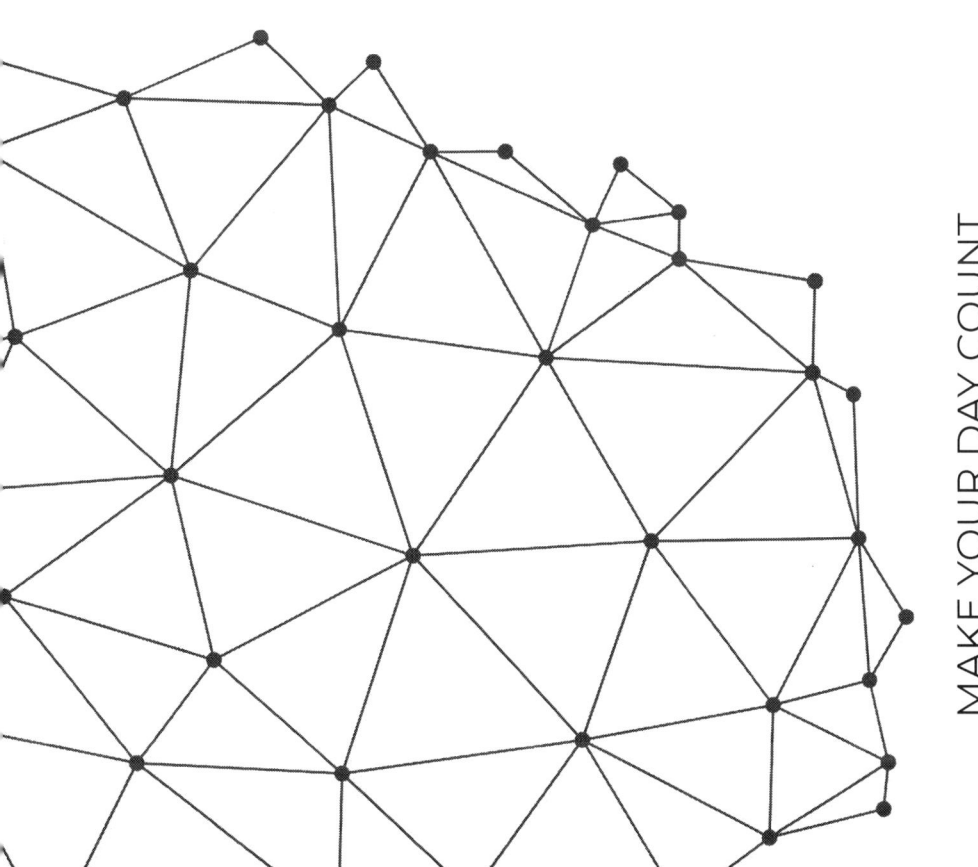

MAKE YOUR DAY COUNT

101 DEVOTIONALS — PART TWO

THE REAL DEAL

BIG THOUGHT
The real deal is always going to win in the end.

> "If you don't live the authentic you, you will live a fake reality."— Jeremy Baker

So many times, we find ourselves wearing masks, pretending to be something we're not. But the problem with masks is they don't just hide our true selves—they change who we are. We begin to act like the person we are pretending to be. We wear masks because we're afraid that the "real us" won't be accepted. We fear rejection. But the truth is, God can't bless fake. To be blessed, we must be authentic. We must be the real deal.

God made you uniquely and wonderfully. You are fearfully and wonderfully made by God. He created you to be the person you are, and you don't have to wear a mask to fit in. If you want to be loved and accepted, you must be real. The more real you are, the more freedom you will experience. Let go of the masks and trust God with who you truly are.

101 DEVOTIONALS — PART TWO

REMEMBER WHO MADE YOU

> *"I praise you, for I am fearfully and wonderfully made. Wonderful are your works; my soul knows it very well. My frame was not hidden from you, when I was being made in secret, intricately woven in the depths of the earth. Your eyes saw my unformed substance; in your book were written, every one of them, the days that were formed for me, when as yet there was none of them."*
> — Psalm 139:14-16

You were created by God with purpose and intentionality. He knows you, loves you, and has a plan for your life. You don't have to pretend to be someone else because you are enough as you are. God designed you, and His creation is good. You were made to be the real deal.

> *"For everything created by God is good, and nothing is to be rejected if it is received with thanksgiving."* — 1 Timothy 4:4

You are a work of God's art—fearfully and wonderfully made. You don't need to be anything more or less than who you are in Christ. Have confidence in that.

> *"For the Lord will be your confidence and will keep your foot from being caught."* — Proverbs 3:26

Trust that God will help you stand firm in who you are. Be confident, not in your own ability, but in God's ability to strengthen you. The more we understand that our identity is rooted in Christ, the more we can let go of the fear of rejection and stop pretending to be someone we are not.

THE COST OF FAKE: THE FLUTE PLAYER

There's a story of a wealthy man who wanted to play in the prestigious Imperial Orchestra, despite not knowing anything about music. He had the influence and money to get into the orchestra, so he sat in the second row and pretended to play the flute. He raised the flute, moved his fingers, and made no sound at all—but no one noticed because the orchestra's sound was so large.

After two years, a new conductor came to the orchestra, determined to ensure every musician played at their best. The new conductor announced that everyone would be auditioned, and if they couldn't play, they would be removed. The fake flutist, terrified, faked illness twice to avoid the audition. But eventually, he had to face the music. When he did, the conductor saw right through the mask, and he was immediately dismissed from the orchestra.

This story illustrates why pretending can only last so long. Eventually, we all have to face the music. The real deal will always be revealed. In life, authenticity will always win in the end. When we try to fake it, we are only deceiving ourselves and others, and eventually, the truth comes out.

BEING REAL IN A WORLD OF COUNTERFEITS

In 1 Corinthians 13, Paul teaches us that even the greatest spiritual gifts, like speaking in tongues or prophecy, are meaningless if they are not rooted in love. Without love, we are just noise, a clanging cymbal. It is love—true, authentic love—that proves the real deal.

> *"If I speak in the tongues of men and of angels, but have not love, I am a noisy gong or a clanging cymbal. And if I have prophetic powers, and understand all mysteries and all knowledge, and if I have all faith, so as to remove mountains, but have not love, I am nothing."— 1 Corinthians 13:1-2*

To be real is not just about being true to yourself, but being true to God's love and His calling in your life. Being real means living authentically, acting in love, and staying grounded in the truth of who God says you are.

KNOW WHO YOU ARE

To be the real deal, you have to first know who you are. If you don't know your true identity, you'll be vulnerable to trying to impress others, seeking validation in the wrong places, or wearing a mask. You must also know who you belong to—God. And most importantly, you need to know your why—your purpose in life. Without purpose, life can feel hollow, and it's easy to get lost in pretending.

Jesus said, "Abide in me, and I in you. As the branch cannot bear fruit by itself, unless it abides in the vine, neither can you, unless you abide in me." — John 15:4

When we stay connected to the true source—Christ—we bear fruit. Without Him, we wither. So, don't let the fake things of life—the pressures, expectations, or masks—take you away from your true purpose in Christ.

THE SUCKER SHOOTS

In life, there are things that try to drain us of our vitality—what I like to call sucker shoots. These are the distractions and fake things in our life that suck away our time, energy, and life-giving purpose. Just like the sucker shoots on a vine that suck the sap from the branches, these distractions prevent us from producing good fruit. They might look appealing for a while, but they won't bring life.

If you allow these distractions to stay in your life, they'll drain your energy and keep you from being who God created you to be. Don't let anything fake or counterfeit rob you of the real fruit God has for you. Be authentic. Be the real deal.

REFLECTION QUESTIONS

◊ Are you ready to be the real deal?

It's time to stop pretending. Know who you are, whose you are, and what your purpose is. Live authentically and be confident in the person God created you to be.

◊ What are the "sucker shoots" in your life that are keeping you from being the real deal?

Identify the distractions, fakes, and things that are draining you of your energy. Cut them off, stay connected to Christ, and bear good fruit.

THINK ON IT

The world may tempt us to wear masks, but God calls us to authenticity. He created you fearfully and wonderfully, designed with purpose and intention. There is no need to pretend or be anything other than who He made you to be. True freedom comes when you let go of the masks and embrace the identity God has given you.

> *"I praise you, for I am fearfully and wonderfully made. Wonderful are your works; my soul knows it very well." — Psalm 139:14*

Authenticity doesn't just honor who you are—it glorifies the One who created you. The real deal always wins in the end because God blesses what is genuine. Stay connected to Christ, prune away the distractions, and let His truth define you. When you live authentically, rooted in love and grounded in His purpose, you'll not only bear fruit but thrive in the freedom of being exactly who He made you to be!

101 DEVOTIONALS — PART TWO

DAY 52
WITH GOD ANYTHING IS POSSIBLE

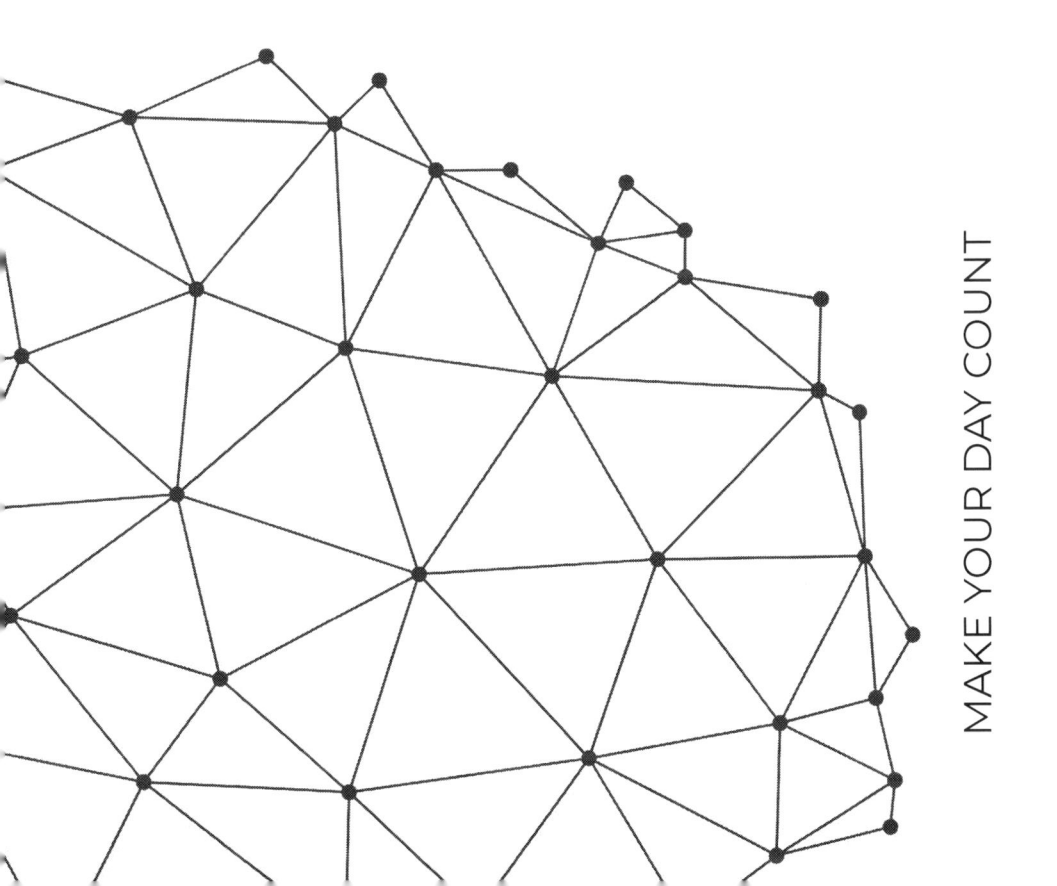

MAKE YOUR DAY COUNT

101 DEVOTIONALS — PART TWO

WITH GOD ANYTHING IS POSSIBLE

BIG THOUGHT
The fact that with God all things are possible is proven by the fact that God created the entire universe out of nothing.

Luke 1:37 –"For nothing will be impossible with God."

Matthew 19:26 –"But Jesus looked at them and said, 'With man this is impossible, but with God all things are possible.'"

Do you ever find yourself facing an impossible situation? Perhaps a relationship that seems beyond repair, a financial struggle that feels overwhelming, or a health issue that seems unfixable. We all face moments that test our faith and leave us wondering if anything can change. But with God, there is always hope—no matter how impossible it may seem.

The Word of God is clear: nothing is impossible with God. When we look to God, we are reminded of His infinite power and His ability to work miracles in our lives.

This is the heartbeat of God's Word—ALL things are possible with God. It doesn't say some things, or a few things, but all things. God is a good God. He is love. He is the God of restoration and revival. He can do what we think is impossible, and that's the hope we carry with us. God has no limitations. He is all-powerful. That means there is nothing He can't do, no person He can't save, and no situation He can't turn around. There is nothing impossible for God!

GOD IS BIGGER THAN YOUR IMPOSSIBLE

Think about this: when you read that all things are possible with God, what comes to mind? Are you filled with hope? With expectation? With faith and power? If not, let this truth fill you with confidence: God is bigger than your situation. He's bigger than your fear, bigger than your struggle, and bigger than any obstacle you face. Nothing is beyond His reach.

- ◊ No marriage is too broken for God to restore.
- ◊ No financial situation is too tangled for God to untangle.
- ◊ No sickness is too severe for God to heal.
- ◊ No mountain is too high for God to move.
- ◊ Whatever you're facing today, God can do the impossible.

A LIFE-CHANGING ENCOUNTER

There's a story of a young man, raised as an atheist, who was training to be an Olympic diver. His only real exposure to faith came through a friend who was an outspoken Christian. The diver had always ignored his friend's sermons, never really taking them seriously. One night, while practicing on an empty indoor pool under the bright light of the moon, he climbed to the highest diving board. As he extended his arms, he saw his shadow cast on the wall—and it was in the shape of a cross.

Overcome with emotion, he knelt down and asked God to come into his life. When he stood up, he saw that the pool had been drained for repairs—the very thing that could have cost him his life. The very thing he didn't believe in saved him, both spiritually and physically. What seemed impossible became a life-changing moment, proving that God can intervene in the most unexpected ways.

God can do the impossible in your life, too, if you trust Him. No situation is beyond His power.

KEEP BELIEVING—DON'T GIVE UP

Every day, people stop believing. They give up on their dreams, their hopes, and even on God. But the Bible tells us to keep believing.

Don't stop. Don't give up. God is working, even when we can't see it. Stay faithful.

> *"And let us not grow weary of doing good, for in due season we will reap, if we do not give up." — Galatians 6:9*

Put your hope, faith, and trust in the God of the impossible. Trust that He can turn things around, no matter how hopeless they may seem. Stay in the game of life, and keep fighting. God has more in store for you than you can imagine.

THE CHESSBOARD OF LIFE: "THE KING STILL HAS ONE MORE MOVE"

A fascinating story illustrates this point. Two friends were visiting a museum when they came across a famous painting titled "Checkmate" by Friedrich Moritz August Retzsch. The painting showed a man sitting across from a devil-like figure, with the game of chess in a dire situation for the man. The pieces on the board showed that his king was in a losing position—his opponent had won. The devil in the painting was jubilant, shouting "Checkmate," believing the game was over.

But one of the men—a former chess champion—wasn't convinced. He studied the painting closely, and after a while, he turned to his friend and said, "I've figured it out. This painting is titled wrong. The king still has one more move."

In the game of life, when it feels like everything is over, God still has one more move. The devil may think he's won, but God is the ultimate champion. When things look impossible, God is always working behind the scenes, ready to make that final, game-changing move. God can turn things around at any moment.

THINK ON IT

Nothing is impossible with God. No matter how overwhelming or hopeless your situation may seem, remember that God is bigger. He created the universe from nothing, restored the broken, healed the sick, and saved the lost. His power has no limits, and His timing is perfect.

> *"For nothing will be impossible with God." — Luke 1:37*

Even when life feels like it's in checkmate, trust that the King still has one more move. Keep your faith alive, don't give up, and let the God of the impossible lead the way. Whatever mountain you face, God can move it. Whatever brokenness you carry, God can heal it. Place your trust in Him, and watch Him do the miraculous. With God, anything is truly possible!

DAY 53
THE WINNING HAND PT. 1

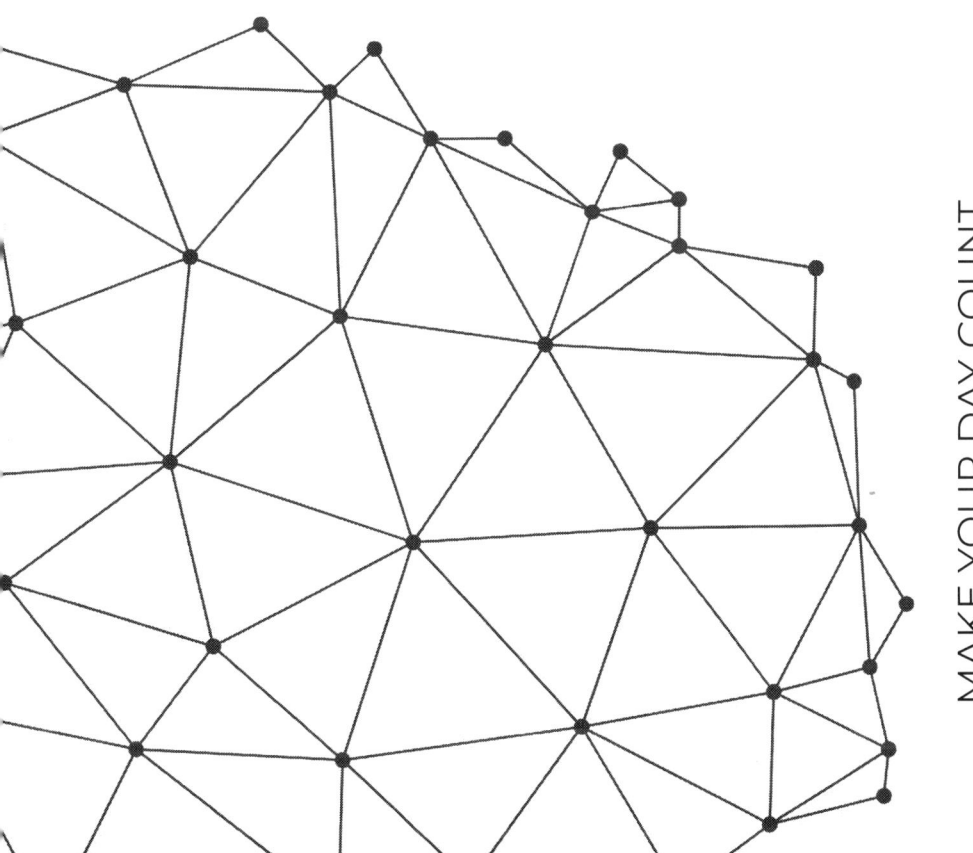

MAKE YOUR DAY COUNT

101 DEVOTIONALS — PART TWO

THE WINNING HAND PT. 1

BIG THOUGHT
I'm not where I need to be, but thank God I'm not where I used to be.

> **Proverbs 3: 5–6** – "Trust in the Lord with all your heart, and do not lean on your own understanding. In all your ways acknowledge him, and he will make straight your paths."

God has given you the winning hand. He has a plan and purpose for your life, and nothing is going to stop you. Even if it feels like you've been dealt a tough hand, you are a winner in God's eyes, and with Him on your side, you will never be defeated. Don't quit—keep going, and trust that the victory is already yours.

TRUST IN GOD'S PLAN

We all face challenges and setbacks. The road isn't always easy, but it's important to remember that God has a plan for us, even when things don't go as expected. When we place our trust in Him, He promises to guide us and make our paths straight.

> *"Trust in the Lord with all your heart, and do not lean on your own understanding. In all your ways acknowledge him, and he will make straight your paths." — Proverbs 3:5-6*

No matter how hard the journey may seem, God is always with us. He has a purpose for every step we take, and He will never leave us alone. Trust Him, because He has already given you the winning hand.

THE MARATHON RUNNER'S EXAMPLE: JOHN STEPHEN AKHWARI

On October 30, 1968, the Olympic Marathon in Mexico City was coming to an end. Mamo Wolde from Ethiopia had already claimed the gold medal, and the stadium was beginning to empty out. But then, as the last few spectators gathered by the marathon gates, they heard sirens and whistles. A lone figure wearing the colors of Tanzania limped into the stadium—his name was John Stephen Akhwari.

Akhwari had been severely injured in a fall earlier in the race, and he was limping around the track, his leg bloodied and bandaged. But despite the pain and the fact that he was far behind, he refused to quit. The crowd stood and applauded him as he crossed the finish line. His story wasn't one of victory in the race, but a victory of perseverance. He was asked afterward why he hadn't given up. He replied, "My country did not send me 5,000 miles to start the race. They sent me 5,000 miles to finish it."

John Stephen Akhwari may not have won the gold medal, but he became a symbol of determination and courage. He finished the race, even when it seemed impossible. In the same way, God has called you to finish your race, no matter the obstacles you face.

NEVER GIVE UP

Jesus didn't die on a cross for you to quit. Whatever you're facing right now, whether it's trouble in your health, your relationships, or your finances, don't quit. Remember, God is for you. He didn't bring you this far to leave you stranded in the middle of your struggle. He is fighting for you.

> "But thanks be to God, who gives us the victory through our Lord Jesus Christ." — 1 Corinthians 15:57

> "For the Lord your God is he who goes with you to fight for you against your enemies, to give you the victory." — Deuteronomy 20:4

THE WINNING HAND PT. 1

When you are facing trials, remind yourself of this truth: If God is for you, who can be against you? (Romans 8:31). No weapon formed against you will prosper (Isaiah 54:17). God has promised to fight for you, and He will not allow you to be defeated.

THE POWER OF PERSEVERANCE: WILMA RUDOLPH'S STORY

Wilma Rudolph was a woman who didn't have the best start in life. As a child, she contracted polio, which left her with a twisted leg and foot, requiring her to wear leg braces. But Wilma didn't give up. After seven years of painful therapy, she learned to walk without the braces. At age 12, she tried out for her school's basketball team but didn't make the cut. She didn't quit; instead, she practiced hard every day, eventually making the team the following year.

At 14, a college coach noticed her and convinced her to become a track runner. By the time she was in her 20s, Wilma was the fastest sprinter in America. In 1960, she competed in the Rome Olympics and made history by winning three gold medals—the most ever won by a female athlete at that time.

Wilma's journey was one of perseverance. She didn't allow her setbacks to define her. It's not how you start the race of life, it's how you finish. Wilma had been dealt a tough hand, but she didn't let it stop her. She kept going, and in the end, she became an Olympic champion.

THE KEY TO VICTORY: DOING YOUR BEST WITH WHAT YOU'VE GOT

People often find themselves in situations where they feel they've been dealt a bad hand. But it's not the hand you've been dealt, it's what you do with it that matters. Every single person has obstacles to overcome, but those who thrive are the ones who choose to do the best with what they have.

Whether you're facing financial hardship, health challenges, or personal struggles, doing the best you can with what you have will always be your best path forward. Just like Wilma Rudolph, you have the ability to overcome your circumstances—but you must keep going, no matter how tough it gets.

> *"But thanks be to God, who in Christ always leads us in triumphal procession, and through us spreads the fragrance of the knowledge of him everywhere." — 2 Corinthians 2:14*

THINK ON IT

God has already given you the winning hand, even when life feels difficult or unfair. Trust in His plan, persevere through challenges, and refuse to give up. Like a marathon runner pushing through pain or an athlete overcoming the odds, your race isn't about how you start but how you finish.

The journey may not always be easy, but with God on your side, you can face anything. Remember, He has already secured your victory. Keep pressing forward, lean on His strength, and trust that He is working all things for your good.

DAY 54
THE WINNING HAND
PT. 2

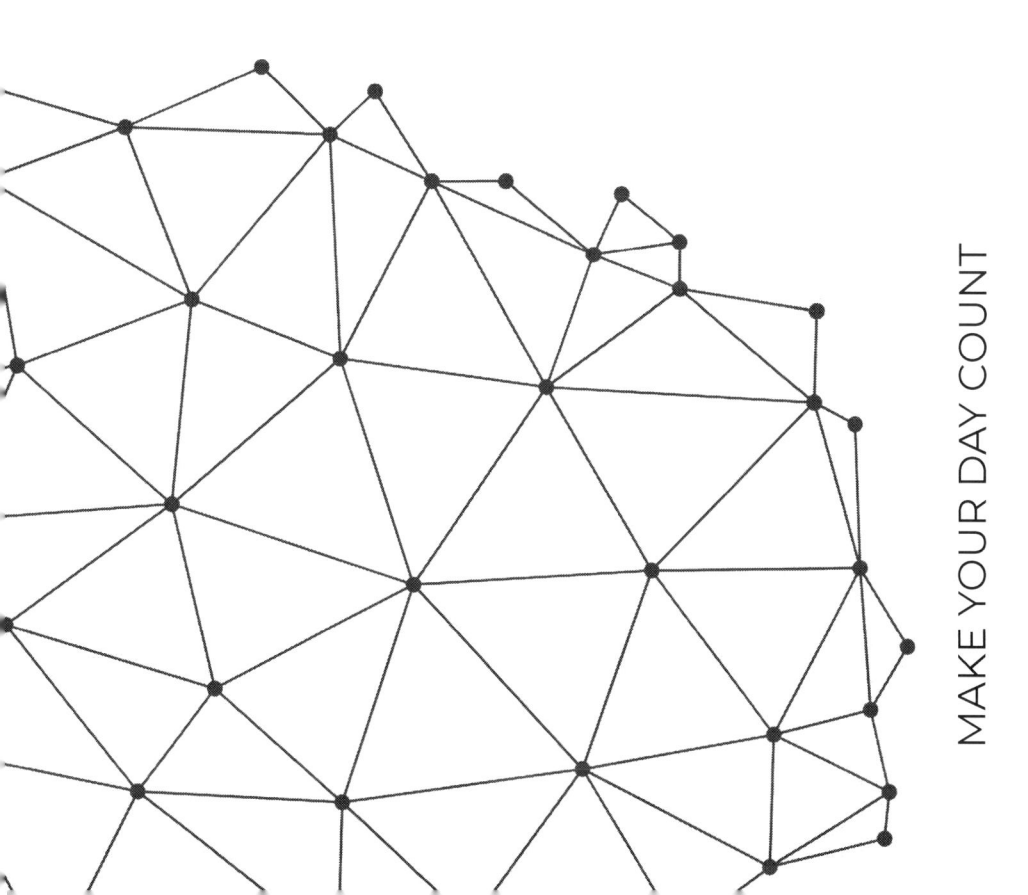

MAKE YOUR DAY COUNT

101 DEVOTIONALS — PART TWO

THE WINNING HAND PT. 2

BIG THOUGHT

In life, there are things we have control over and things we have no control over. You can't control the hand you've been dealt, but you can control how you play it.

> **Luke 1:37** – "For nothing will be impossible with God."

Life often throws challenges our way that are out of our control—where we were born, who our parents are, or the mistakes others have made that affect us. We don't always get to choose the circumstances, but we do get to choose how we respond. The key to success, joy, and fulfillment in life is not in controlling everything around us, but in trusting God and making the most of the hand we've been dealt. With God, we can always have a winning hand.

GEORGE FOREMAN'S COMEBACK

George Foreman, a two-time heavyweight boxing champion, faced an incredible comeback in his career. At the age of 45, he became the oldest man in history to win the heavyweight title. But Foreman's victory wasn't just physical—it was a victory of the mind.

When he stepped back into the ring for his comeback, the announcer would introduce him as the "former heavyweight champion." But George didn't see himself as "former" anything. He would silently say to himself, "I am the next heavyweight champion of the world." How could he win if he didn't believe he could?

It's a powerful reminder: every hand, no matter how bad, has the potential to be a winning hand, as long as you believe you can make the most of it and trust God to guide you through it. Your belief in what God can do through you is the key to your victory.

THE MAN WITH THE WITHERED HAND

In Mark 3:1-5, we find a man with a withered hand. He was in the synagogue—a place of worship and prayer—when Jesus approached him. His hand, once full of potential, was withered and useless, yet he was still in the right place, trusting that God could make a difference.

Jesus asked the man to stretch out his hand, and when he did, his hand was miraculously restored. This man's healing wasn't just about his physical hand; it was about the restoration of his hope. The withered hand represents anything in our lives that seems broken, lost, or beyond repair.

Maybe your hand isn't physically withered, but perhaps there are areas in your life that feel like they're withered—your joy, your marriage, your family, or your purpose. Whatever it is, know that God can restore and make something beautiful out of any situation. You may not be able to change the hand you've been dealt, but you can trust God to make it a winning hand.

LETTING GO OF THE PAST

In the story of the monkey trap, the people in India used a clever technique to catch monkeys: they placed something sweet inside a bottle and tied it to the ground. When the monkey grabbed the sweet treat, he couldn't pull his hand out of the bottle because his fist was too big to fit through the opening. The monkey was caught because he refused to let go of what he had in his hand.

This is what happens when we refuse to let go of bitterness, unforgiveness, or fear. When we hold on to past hurts, regrets, or disappointments, we become trapped, unable to move forward and embrace the future God has for us. If you are holding on to something from your past, it's time to let it go. It's time to trust that God can heal your wounds and turn your pain into victory.

TRUSTING GOD WITH YOUR HAND

No matter what hand you've been dealt, it's never too late for God to do something incredible with it. The man with the withered hand thought he would live with that affliction forever, but when Jesus

THE WINNING HAND PT. 2

showed up, he got a new hand. God can take your brokenness and make it whole.

Maybe you feel like you've been dealt a hand of fear, stress, anxiety, rejection, or sickness. But remember, God can take any situation and turn it around. Every hand, no matter how bad, has the potential to be a winning hand in God's hands.

TAKE A DEEPER LOOK

Shadrach, Meshach, and Abednego were thrown into the fiery furnace because they refused to bow down to false gods. But in the fire, God showed up and gave them a winning hand. Daniel was thrown into a lion's den for his faith, but God delivered him from the lions. Lazarus was dead and buried, but God raised him to life.

God is in the business of turning bad hands into winning hands. No matter how desperate your situation may seem, God can bring life and victory to it.

THINK ON IT

You may not have control over the hand you've been dealt in life, but you do have control over how you respond. Trust that God can take what seems broken or impossible and turn it into a testimony of His power and grace. Like the man with the withered hand, stretch out your faith and allow God to restore what feels lost.

> *"For nothing will be impossible with God."* — Luke 1:37

Let go of past hurts, disappointments, or fears that keep you trapped. Instead, place your life in God's hands. Remember, every hand has the potential to be a winning hand when you trust in the One who holds it all. Stay faithful, stay hopeful, and let God bring victory out of your situation.

101 DEVOTIONALS — PART TWO

DAY 55
PLAN ACCORDINGLY

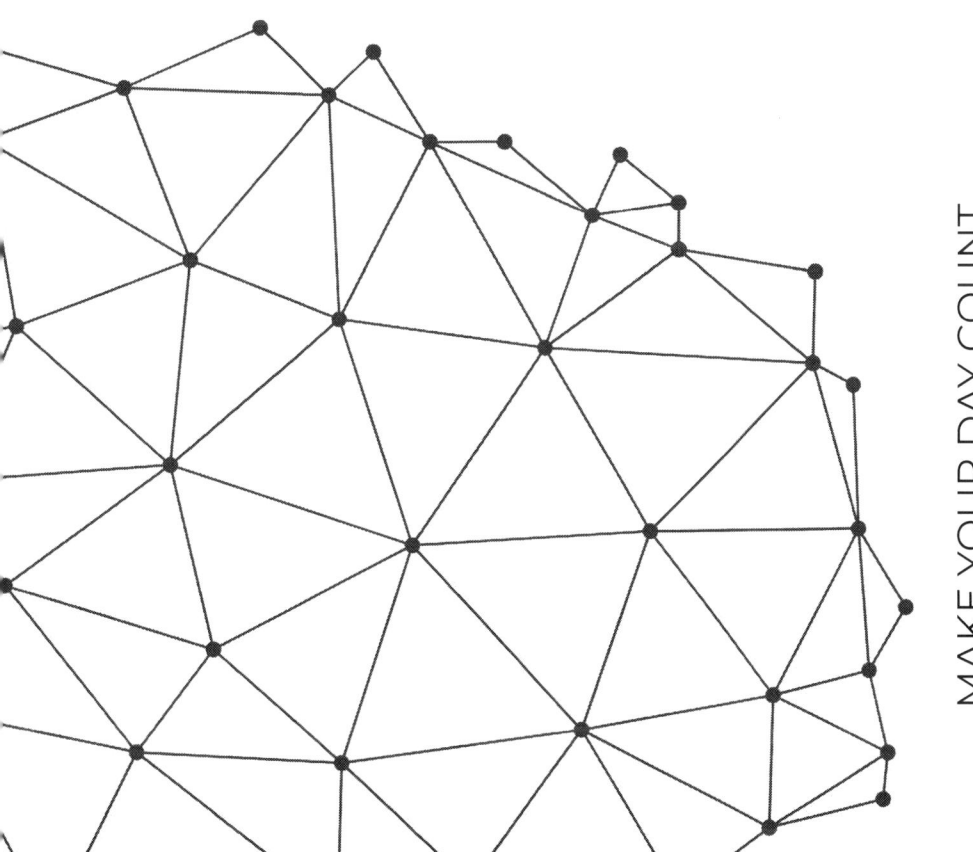

MAKE YOUR DAY COUNT

101 DEVOTIONALS — PART TWO

PLAN ACCORDINGLY

BIG THOUGHT

You have to have a plan!

> **Jeremiah 29:11** – "For I know the plans I have for you, declares the Lord, plans for welfare and not for evil, to give you a future and a hope."

In life, having a plan is essential for success. You can't just work hard and hope for the best—you need a clear vision of where you want to go, and the steps you'll take to get there. Planning allows you to be intentional, focused, and prepared, which are all crucial components for achieving any goal.

THE STORY OF THE YOUNG LUMBERJACK

A young man once approached the foreman of a logging crew and asked for a job. The foreman said, "Let's see you fell this tree." The young man skillfully chopped down a large tree, and the foreman was impressed. He hired the young man and he began work on Monday.

But by Thursday afternoon, the foreman approached the young man and said, "You can pick up your paycheck today." The young man was shocked. "I thought you paid on Friday," he said.

The foreman explained, "We normally do, but we're letting you go today. Our daily felling charts show that you've gone from first place on Monday to last place on Wednesday."

The young man was confused. "But I'm a hard worker! I arrive first, leave last, and even work through my breaks!"

The foreman, sensing the boy's integrity, asked, "Have you been sharpening your ax?"

The young man replied, "I've been working too hard to take the time."

THE LESSON: It's important to realize that hard work alone is not enough. You can't just focus on the tasks at hand without taking time to plan and prepare. Whether it's sharpening your ax or taking time to develop a strategy, preparation is key. If you don't plan accordingly, you'll work harder than necessary, but you won't achieve the level of success you're capable of.

THE WEDDING AT CANA: A LESSON IN PREPARATION

In John 2:1-11, we find the story of a wedding in Cana where the hosts ran out of wine—a serious mistake considering weddings in Jewish tradition could last 2-3 weeks. The family didn't plan properly and underestimated how much wine they would need. Thankfully, Mary, the mother of Jesus, was there, and she knew exactly what to do.

Mary approached Jesus and asked Him to perform a miracle. This was Jesus' first recorded miracle, and it was done because Mary aligned herself with God's will and took action.

Jesus took jars of water and turned them into wine, performing a miracle that not only saved the day but also demonstrated the importance of planning and preparation—and the power of Jesus' intervention in our lives.

GOD'S PLAN FOR YOUR LIFE

The Bible tells us that God has a plan for each of us. In Jeremiah 29:11, God says, "For I know the plans I have for you, declares the Lord, plans for welfare and not for evil, to give you a future and a hope." God's plan is always good, and He gives us hope and a future. However, we must also remember that the enemy has a plan to steal, kill, and destroy (John 10:10). But with God on our side, we can overcome any obstacle and stay on track with His plan.

PLAN ACCORDINGLY

THE IMPORTANCE OF HAVING A PLAN

There are countless opinions about the keys to success in life—hard work, discipline, sacrifice, and perseverance are all important. However, the most crucial factor for achieving success is having a plan. A vision or goal will keep you focused and determined, and it will guide your steps along the way.

If you ask people what they want in life, you'll likely hear answers such as:

- ◊ To make more money
- ◊ To be happier
- ◊ To be healthier
- ◊ To travel more
- ◊ To have better relationships
- ◊ To stop worrying
- ◊ To feel valued

These goals are great, but the real question is: How do you plan to get there?

A MUSEUM OF FAILED PRODUCTS

At the Museum of Failed Products in Ann Arbor, Michigan, 90% of all products created fail. The museum houses over 140,000 failed products—from cans of hairspray to bags of candy. The museum is not open to the public but is used by companies to help them avoid their competitors' mistakes.

This illustrates an important point: failure happens when there's no clear plan or when the plan isn't followed through. But just because a product fails doesn't mean it's the end. In life, failure is often a stepping stone to success. If your plan doesn't work out the first time, don't give up. Learn from your mistakes, adjust your plan, and keep moving forward.

💡 THINK ON IT

No matter what goal you're pursuing, having a plan is essential. You need a clear vision, along with the discipline and focus to follow through. Whether it's sharpening your ax, preparing for challenges, or trusting in God's plan, preparation is key to success.

With God's help, your plan will come to fruition—but you must take the first step and create that plan. Life might throw curveballs, but with a solid plan and trust in God, you can stay on track and achieve the success He has prepared for you. Keep sharpening your ax, stay focused, and trust in God's timing.

> *"For I know the plans I have for you, declares the Lord, plans for welfare and not for evil, to give you a future and a hope."*
> *— Jeremiah 29:11*

Don't underestimate the power of a solid plan. Whether it's sharpening your skills or trusting God in moments of uncertainty, preparation is the key to growth and success. Align your efforts with God's purpose, adjust when needed, and move forward with confidence.

DAY 56
AT THE END OF MY ROPE

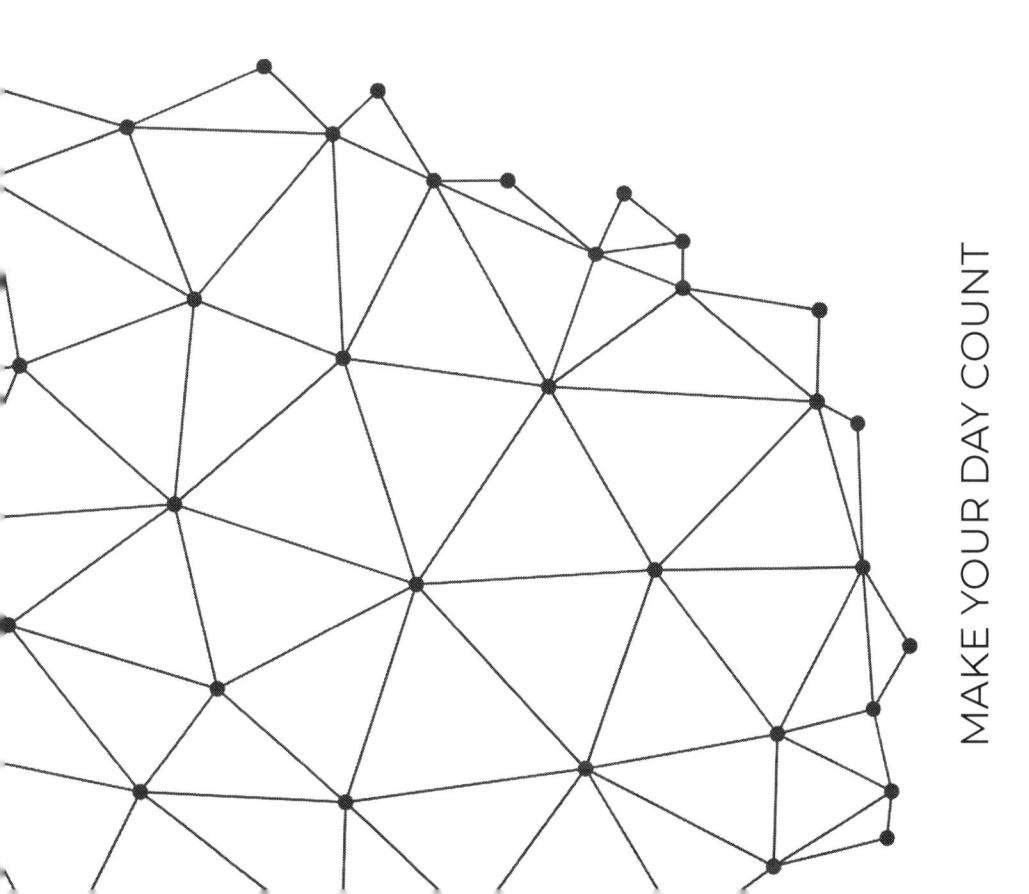

MAKE YOUR DAY COUNT

101 DEVOTIONALS — PART TWO

AT THE END OF MY ROPE

BIG THOUGHT
The minute you think of giving up, think of the reason why you held on so long.

> **Psalm 18:31–32** – "For who is God, but the Lord? And who is a rock, except our God— the God who equipped me with strength and made my way blameless."

We all experience moments when we feel like we're at the end of our rope. It's that point when we have no more strength, no more patience, and no more energy to keep going. Life's challenges—emotional, physical, financial—can weigh so heavily on us that it feels like giving up is the only option.

But when you find yourself at the end of your rope, don't just think about giving up. Remember why you've held on for so long. Think about the reasons you've made it this far and trust that you can go even further. Sometimes, the key is not trying to hold on with your own strength but letting God hold on to you.

THE DIRIGIBLE STORY: A LESSON IN HOLDING ON

During the 1930s, 250 men were holding ropes to a dirigible (an airship similar to a blimp) to prevent it from floating away. Suddenly, a strong gust of wind caught the dirigible, lifting it high off the ground. Some of the men immediately let go of their ropes, falling safely to the ground. Others, panic-stricken, clung tightly to their ropes as the dirigible rose higher.

Several men lost their grip and fell, injuring themselves severely. But one man remained dangling in the air for 45 minutes before being rescued. When reporters later asked him how he managed to hold on for so long, he replied, "I didn't hold on to the rope. I just tied it around my waist, and the rope held on to me."

This story is a reminder: when we are at the end of our rope, it's not about our own strength. Instead of desperately trying to hold on to God, let God hold on to you. He is the one who gives us the strength to keep going, even when we feel like we can't take another step.

WHEN YOU'RE AT THE END OF YOUR ROPE

Have you ever felt like you were at the end of your rope? Maybe you felt like you had no more patience, no more hope, or no more strength to face the challenges of life. When you reach that point, it's easy to feel alone, abandoned, or defeated.

But here's the good news: When you are at the end of your rope, remember that God is at the end of your rope. He hasn't forgotten about you. He promises to never leave you and to be with you until the very end (Matthew 28:20). When everything seems hopeless, God is with you, providing strength and hope.

DON'T STAY IN THE PIT

At times, life's difficulties can feel like a deep pit—emotional despair, financial hardship, physical pain, mental anguish, or some other trial. But staying in the pit is not an option. Your life and your destiny depend on you choosing to trust God and change your thinking.

The temptation is to stay stuck in the pit, overwhelmed by your circumstances. But God's word assures us that He is our rock and refuge, and He will deliver us from the depths. You don't have to stay there. God can pull you out, restore you, and give you new hope and strength.

TAKE A LOOK

These verses remind us that God is our strength and our rock in times of trouble. When we feel like we can't go on, we can trust that God will deliver us from all afflictions. Like Job, we may face trials, but God will use those trials to refine us and make us stronger. We don't have to rely on our own strength, because God is the one who holds us up and carries us through.

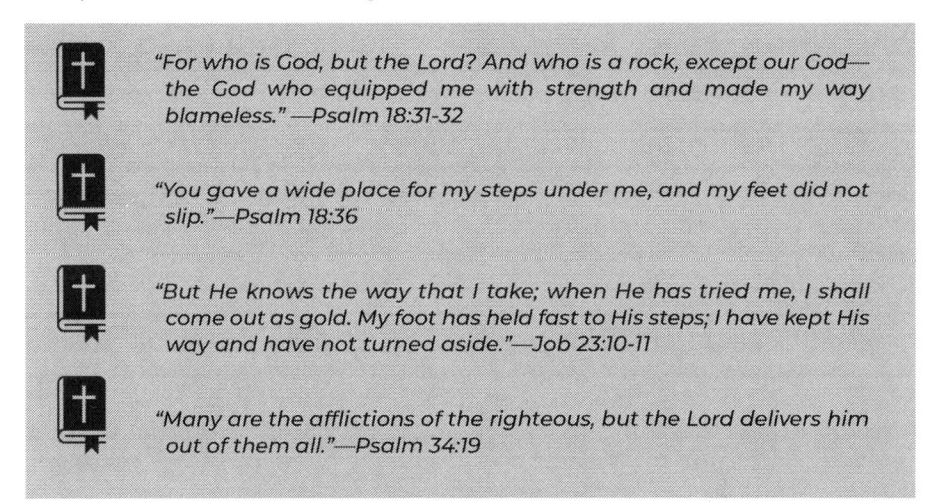

> "For who is God, but the Lord? And who is a rock, except our God—the God who equipped me with strength and made my way blameless." —Psalm 18:31-32

> "You gave a wide place for my steps under me, and my feet did not slip."—Psalm 18:36

> "But He knows the way that I take; when He has tried me, I shall come out as gold. My foot has held fast to His steps; I have kept His way and have not turned aside."—Job 23:10-11

> "Many are the afflictions of the righteous, but the Lord delivers him out of them all."—Psalm 34:19

THE MAP FOR LIFE

When I was younger, I didn't like using a GPS system when traveling. Instead, I would study a paper map before I left so I could find my way. But if I didn't study the map, I was sure to get lost. The map guided my journey, helping me get where I needed to go.

Life is the same way. The Word of God is our map. When we're at the end of our rope, we need to turn to God's word. The Bible is full of promises and truths that can guide us through life's difficulties and show us the way to victory.

THE TRUTH WILL SET US FREE

The truth of God's Word is what sets us free from despair. We can trust that no matter how hopeless our situation may feel, God will deliver us. The rope of hope—His promises—will never let us down.

> "And you will know the truth, and the truth will set you free." —John 8:32

THE ROPE OF HOPE

It's easy to place our hope in things that can fail us—money, jobs, people, our talents, etc. But the Bible tells us that our hope must be in the Lord. People and circumstances will sometimes fail us, but God's Word will never fail.

When you're at the end of your rope, trust in the Lord. He is the one who gives strength and hope to those who choose to rely on Him. Choose hope, even when the road feels long and the journey seems impossible. God will give you the strength to keep moving forward.

THINK ON IT

When you feel like you're at the end of your rope, remember that God is holding on to you. It's not about your own strength but about trusting in His unfailing promises. Like the man who tied the rope around his waist, allow God to carry you through the trials and challenges of life.

> *"For who is God, but the Lord? And who is a rock, except our God—the God who equipped me with strength and made my way blameless." — Psalm 18:31-32*

God's Word is the rope of hope that never lets us down. Even in your darkest moments, trust that He is with you, pulling you out of the pit and setting your feet on solid ground. Stay anchored to His truth, and let Him guide you through life's storms.

DAY 57
DON'T JUST SIT THERE

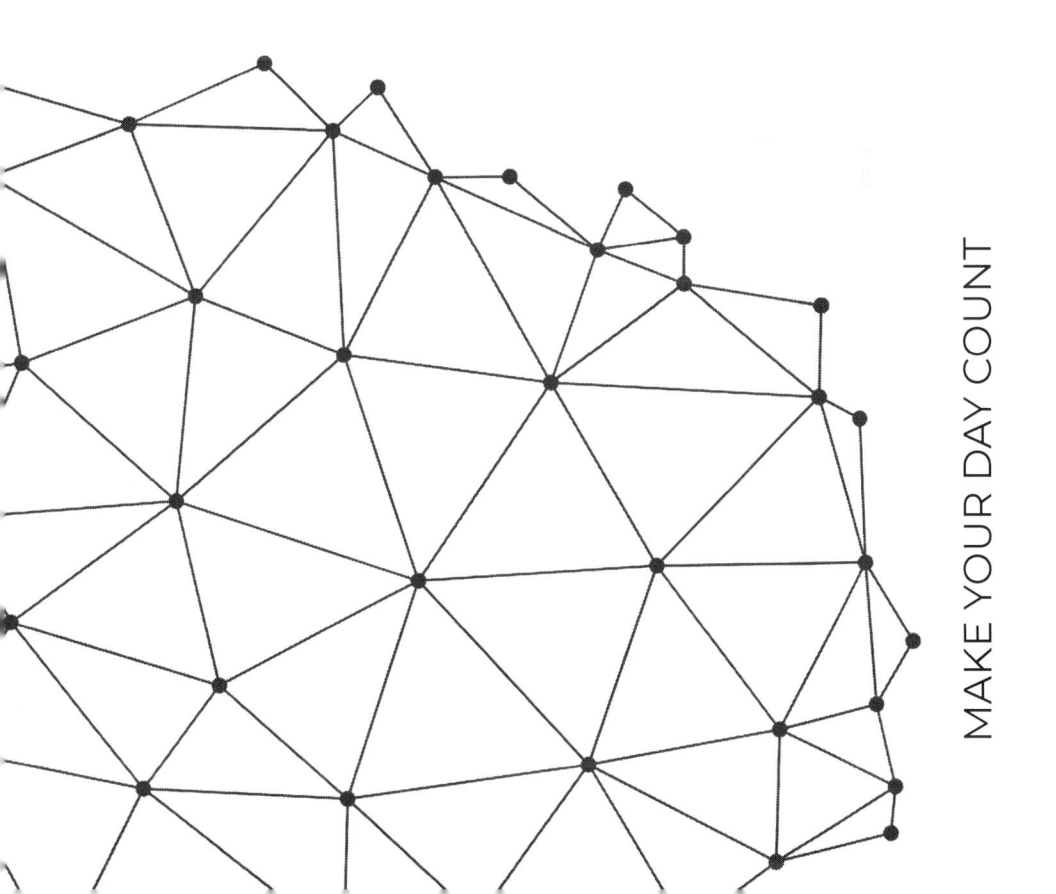

MAKE YOUR DAY COUNT

101 DEVOTIONALS — PART TWO

DON'T JUST SIT THERE

BIG THOUGHT
Don't just sit there. Do something. The answers will follow.

Romans 8:31 – "What then shall we say to these things? If God is for us, who can be against us?"

In the Bible, there is a story of four lepers who were sitting at the gate of a city, waiting for death. They were starving, suffering from their disease, and had no hope left. The city was under siege, and there was no food or help to be found. These men were stuck—sitting, waiting, and dying. But then, they had an epiphany: "Why are we sitting here until we die?"

They realized that doing nothing meant certain death, but taking action—no matter how risky—might offer them a chance to survive. So, they decided to get up and head towards the enemy camp. In the end, God worked a miracle: He made the enemy army hear the sound of a great army, and they fled, leaving behind tents filled with food, riches, and supplies. The lepers walked into the camp and were saved, not by their own strength, but by their decision to take action. (2 Kings 7:3-8).

This story serves as a reminder: Don't just sit there, waiting for things to change. Do something. Move forward, and trust that God will guide your steps.

THE LEPERS' BOLD DECISION

The four lepers were in a desperate situation. The city was under siege, the famine was severe, and they were stuck between the option of certain death within the city or the unknown possibility of survival by going to the enemy. Their bold decision to move forward turned out to be their deliverance.

These men had nothing to lose. If they stayed, they would die. If they moved, there was a chance of survival. So, they decided to take action, and when they did, God worked on their behalf. God didn't wait for them to have all the answers. He didn't need them to be perfect. He just needed them to move. Faith requires action—taking the first step even when the path ahead isn't clear.

DON'T WAIT FOR PERFECT CONDITIONS

In life, many of us are waiting for the perfect moment, the perfect circumstances, or the perfect condition to move forward. But waiting for everything to be just right often leads to stagnation. The four lepers didn't wait for their situation to change or for the enemy to retreat. They took action, trusting that God would meet them in their steps.

Faith isn't about waiting for things to align perfectly—it's about stepping out, even when things seem uncertain, and trusting that God is in control. Just like the lepers, you don't have to have all the answers. You just need to do something.

AN AIRPLANE, A BICYCLE, AND A CHRISTIAN

What do an airplane, a bicycle, and a Christian all have in common? If they stop moving forward, they're in trouble.

Just like an airplane needs to keep moving to stay in the air, or a bicycle needs to keep moving to stay upright, you need to keep moving forward in life to thrive. If you stop moving, you risk losing momentum. Your faith requires movement.

DON'T LET FEAR HOLD YOU BACK

Fear often keeps us stuck. We worry about what others will think or whether we'll fail. But just like the story of the bumblebee, sometimes things that seem impossible are only impossible because we're too afraid to try.

Dr. Jack Fraser, a physicist, pointed out that according to the laws of aviation, a bee shouldn't be able to fly. Its wings are too small for its body. But the bee doesn't care about the laws of physics—it just keeps flying. In the same way, don't let fear or doubt stop you. Keep moving forward, no matter what people say or what seems impossible.

THE MANNEQUIN CHALLENGE

The mannequin challenge was a viral internet trend in which people froze in place, like mannequins, while music played in the background. While it was a fun and creative challenge, it also serves as a metaphor for many people's lives. So many people are "frozen" in their circumstances—too afraid to move, too comfortable to take risks. But in life, you can't afford to stay frozen. You can't afford to just sit there, waiting for change. You have to move.

THE GOLD DOORSTOP: A LESSON IN VALUE

In 1799, Conrad Reed found a 17-pound rock while fishing in Little Meadow Creek. His family used it as a doorstop for three years because they didn't know its value. In 1802, they discovered it was gold, worth $3,600 (equivalent to a small fortune at the time).

Just like that lump of gold, your potential may be hidden. Until you decide to take action, you may not realize how much God has placed inside you. Move forward, step out in faith, and you will begin to discover your value and purpose. God has placed treasures within you—but you won't find them by sitting still.

THINK ON IT

Don't just sit there—step out in faith! Like the four lepers who chose action over despair, your first step forward can lead to God's miraculous intervention. The perfect conditions may never come, but faith requires movement, even when the path is unclear.

> *"What then shall we say to these things? If God is for us, who can be against us?"* — Romans 8:31

God has placed incredible potential within you. Don't let fear or uncertainty keep you frozen. Take action, trust His plan, and watch as He guides your steps and reveals the treasures He has placed inside you. Keep moving forward—God is with you!

DAY 58
YOU CAN'T BE DEFEATED

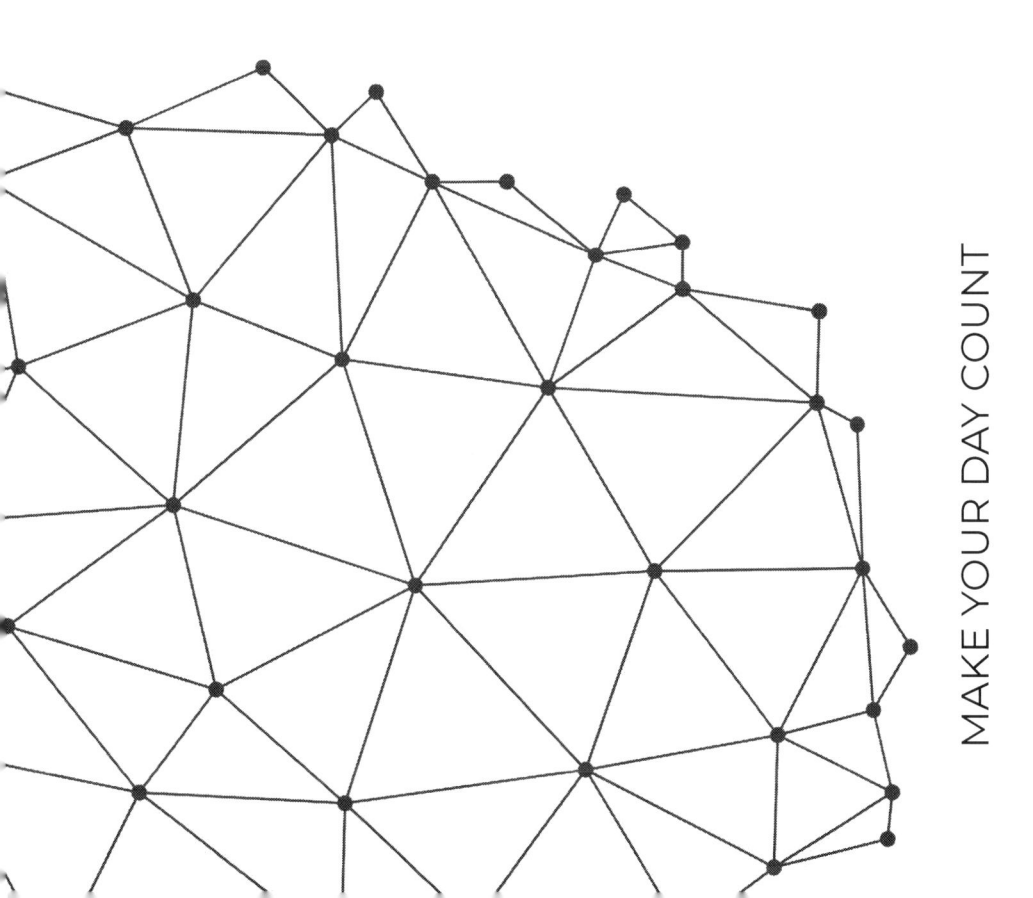

MAKE YOUR DAY COUNT

101 DEVOTIONALS — PART TWO

YOU CAN'T BE DEFEATED

BIG THOUGHT
You are only defeated when you quit.

Romans 8:31 – "If God is for us, who can be against us?"

Psalm 118:6 – "The LORD is on my side; I will not fear. What can man do to me?"

General George Patton, a famed World War II tank commander, once said, "Courage is fear holding on a minute longer. If you give into your fears, you are on the path to defeat. If instead you stand strong in spite of your fears, you are on the path to victory." This powerful statement reminds us that defeat is not determined by how hard the battle is, but by whether or not we quit. As long as we keep standing and keep fighting, we cannot be defeated.

When you face challenges, remember that you are never alone. With the power of God on your side, there is no battle you cannot win, no obstacle you cannot overcome. The Bible assures us of this:

> *"Therefore do not throw away your confidence, which has a great reward. For you have need of endurance, so that when you have done the will of God you may receive what is promised."*
> *— Hebrews 10:35-36*

When life gets tough, never forget that with God on your side, you cannot be defeated.

GOD IS ALWAYS WITH YOU

It's easy to feel defeated, to feel as though you're fighting alone, but as a Christian, you are never truly alone. God is always with you. Even in the most difficult times, you can rely on His presence and His power. Jesus Himself faced moments of deep sorrow and fear, but He never gave up. He trusted God, and God showed up in powerful ways.

In the story of Lazarus (John 11), Jesus didn't just perform a miracle; He demonstrated that even death could not defeat Him. Lazarus had died, and Mary and Martha were devastated. But when Jesus arrived, He called out, "Lazarus, come out!" And Lazarus walked out of the tomb alive!

In the same way, when you feel like you're at the end of your rope, remember that nothing is impossible with God. Trust in Him, and He will show you His power. When you are afraid, trust in God. When you are weary, trust in His strength. With God, you can't be defeated.

> *"When I am afraid, I put my trust in you."* — Psalm 56:3

YOU ARE IN GOOD HANDS

There's a story of a young boy and a group of scientists who were exploring the Alps. The scientists spotted a rare flower deep in a ravine and needed someone to be lowered down on a rope to retrieve it. A young boy volunteered, but only after bringing along his father to hold the rope. The boy trusted his father's strength and reliability—he knew that with his dad holding the rope, he was safe.

In the same way, you can trust God to hold the rope in your life. No matter how deep or dangerous the ravine may seem, God will never let you fall. He has a firm grip on your life, and with Him, you are secure.

> *"Let us hold fast the confession of our hope without wavering, for He who promised is faithful."* — Hebrews 10:23

God is faithful. He will never let you go, no matter how difficult life gets. You are in good hands with God, and He will see you through every challenge.

GOD IS UNDEFEATED

In sports, an undefeated team is a rare and extraordinary achievement. There may only be one undefeated NFL team or a handful of undefeated NCAA basketball teams, but God is the ultimate undefeated champion. He has never lost a battle, and He never will.

No matter what forces come against Him, God will always emerge victorious. The enemy may try, but God will never be defeated.

> *"But thanks be to God, who gives us the victory through our Lord Jesus Christ." — 1 Corinthians 15:57*

This victory is not just for God; it's for you too. Through Jesus Christ, you have been given the victory. You cannot be defeated, because Christ has already won the battle for you. When you feel defeated, remember this truth—you are on the winning side. With God's power, you will always overcome.

THINK ON IT

Defeat only comes when you quit. With God on your side, you are never truly alone, and no battle is beyond His power to win. Remember, God is undefeated, and His strength holds you firm in every challenge you face.

Trust that God's hands are holding your life securely. No matter how hard the journey may seem, He will never let you go. Stay confident, stay faithful, and keep moving forward—you can't be defeated because the victory is already yours in Christ!

101 DEVOTIONALS — PART TWO

DAY 59
WHAT ARE YOU LOOKING FOR?

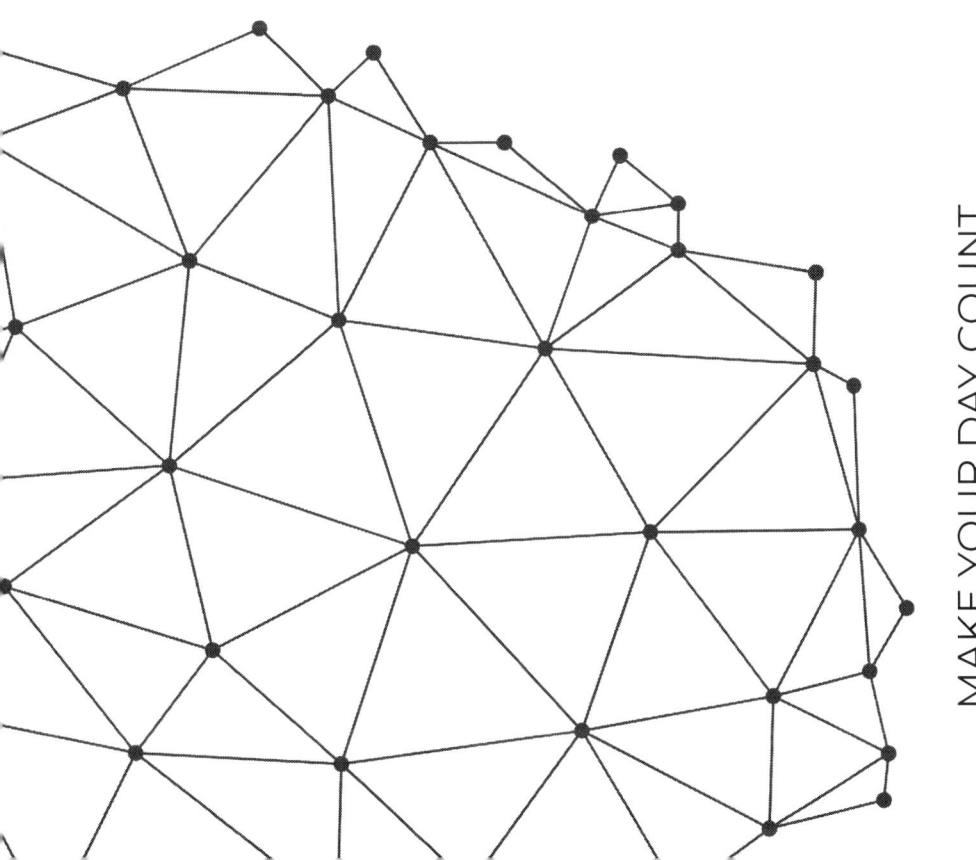

MAKE YOUR DAY COUNT

101 DEVOTIONALS — PART TWO

WHAT ARE YOU LOOKING FOR?

BIG THOUGHT

What you are looking for, depends on what you see!

Proverbs 19:21 – "Many are the plans in the mind of a man, but it is the purpose of the Lord that will stand."

Have you ever wondered, "what is the meaning of life," or "why am I here?" These are questions that have been asked for centuries. The truth is, we all have one life to live, and finding our purpose is one of the most important quests we can undertake. God has a purpose for every single person, and He desires for us to live with meaning and direction. The only way to truly find that purpose is through a relationship with Jesus Christ.

When we seek God, we discover why we are here and what we are meant to do. Without this relationship, our search for meaning can feel like chasing after things that ultimately don't matter. We may search for success, possessions, relationships, or status, but these things alone will never fill the deep longing within us. True purpose comes from knowing God and living according to His plan.

THE RICH YOUNG RULER

In the book of Mark, we find the story of a rich young ruler who came to Jesus with a question about eternal life.

> *"And as he was setting out on his journey, a man ran up and knelt before him and asked him, 'Good Teacher, what must I do to inherit eternal life?'"* — Mark 10:17

Jesus tells him to follow the commandments. The young man responds that he has kept all of them, but Jesus sees that there is still something missing in his life.

> *"You lack one thing: go, sell all that you have and give to the poor, and you will have treasure in heaven; and come, follow me."* — Mark 10:21

The rich young ruler walked away sorrowful because he had great possessions. He thought he could have purpose without Christ, but Jesus shows him that Christ equals purpose. No Christ equals no true purpose.

STALLED WITHOUT CHRIST

Imagine starting your car in the morning, only to find out that the battery is dead. No matter how many times you turn the key, the engine won't start. The car is stalled. But then, if you connect the dead battery to a live one using jumper cables, within moments, the car starts up, and the engine is running again.

In life, without Jesus, we are like a car with a dead battery—unable to move, stuck, and going nowhere. But when we connect to Jesus, He recharges us. He gives us life and meaning, helping us to live with purpose.

Just as a car cannot run without a working battery, we cannot live with true purpose without Christ. He is the source of our strength, our energy, and our direction.

THE BALLOON ILLUSTRATION

Once, a seminar speaker gave each participant a balloon and asked them to write their name on it. After all the balloons were collected, everyone was asked to find their own balloon within five minutes. As they frantically searched, pushing and colliding with others, no one found their own balloon. The speaker then asked everyone to pick a random balloon and give it to the person whose name was on it. Within minutes, everyone had their own balloon.

The speaker pointed out that this chaotic search for our balloon is a lot like how we search for happiness or purpose in life. We often look for meaning in the wrong places—possessions, achievements, or relationships—but our true happiness and purpose are found in Jesus Christ. When we stop frantically searching and allow God to lead us, we will find our purpose.

> *"I cry out to God Most High, to God who fulfills His purpose for me."*
> — Psalm 57:2

> *"And we know that for those who love God all things work together for good, for those who are called according to His purpose."*
> — Romans 8:28

GOD HAS A PURPOSE FOR YOU

God has a unique and specific purpose for each one of us. The greatest thing we can do in life is to surrender our will to God's. When we choose to seek His purpose, we find true fulfillment. Our plans may seem good, but God's purpose will always stand:

> *"Many are the plans in the mind of a man, but it is the purpose of the Lord that will stand."* — Proverbs 19:21

We must choose to seek God's will for our lives. It's not about chasing after our own desires, but surrendering to God and trusting that He has a greater plan for us.

THINK ON IT

What you are looking for will shape what you see. True purpose and meaning are only found in Jesus Christ. Without Him, life can feel like a chaotic search for fulfillment, but when you connect to Christ, you discover the reason you were created.

> *"I cry out to God Most High, to God who fulfills His purpose for me."*
> — Psalm 57:2

God has a unique purpose for you. Surrender your plans to Him and trust that He will lead you to true fulfillment. Stop chasing what doesn't satisfy and allow God to guide you into His perfect plan. Through Christ, your search for meaning ends, and your journey of purpose begins.

DAY 60
TRAPPED IN THE DRAPES

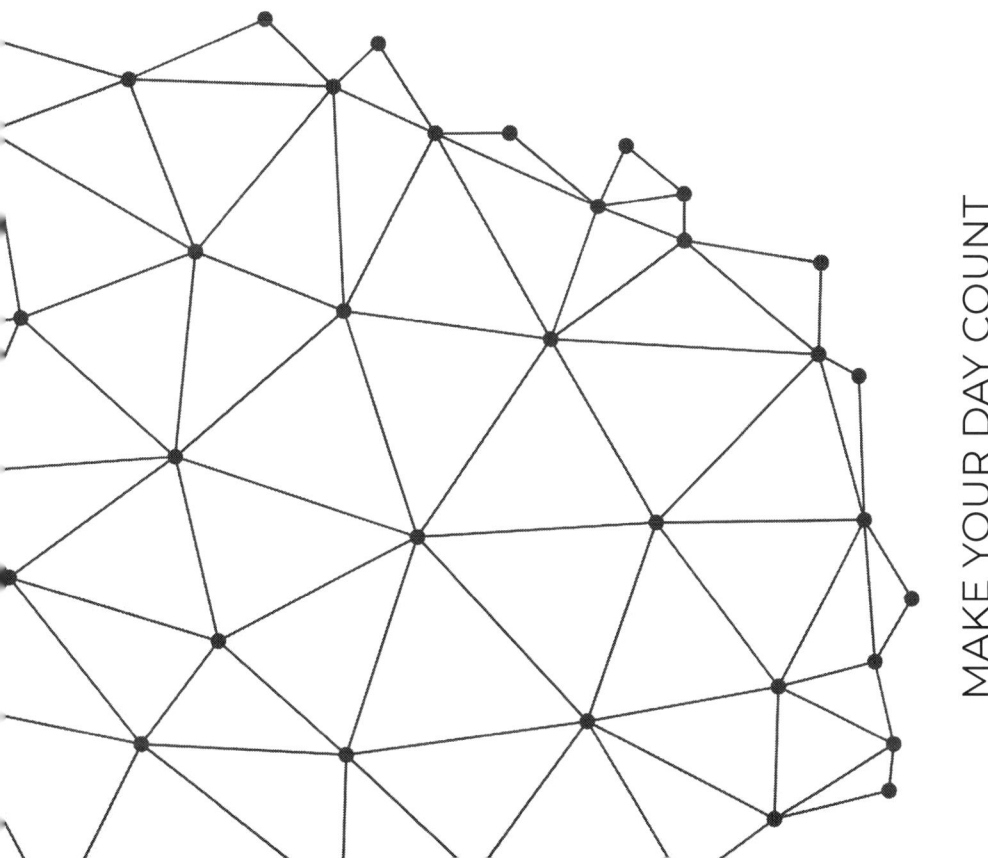

MAKE YOUR DAY COUNT

101 DEVOTIONALS — PART TWO

TRAPPED IN THE DRAPES

BIG THOUGHT
You are never trapped, unless you want to be trapped.

> **1 Corinthians 10:13** – "No temptation has overtaken you that is not common to man. God is faithful, and He will not let you be tempted beyond your ability, but with the temptation He will also provide the way of escape, that you may be able to endure it."

Have you ever seen a child run into a room, excited to hide behind the drapes, hoping to be found? But after a while, the child begins to feel stuck—trapped behind the fabric—and starts crying for help, unable to free themselves. This image is a lot like how we can feel in life sometimes. We find ourselves in situations that seem overwhelming, and we begin to feel trapped. But the good news is, you are never truly trapped—not unless you choose to stay there. Jesus Christ has already made a way for you to escape, to find freedom and deliverance from life's traps.

THE WAY OF ESCAPE

Life can sometimes feel like we're stuck, unable to move forward. Whether it's unforgiveness, fear, worry, temptation, or stress, many of us feel like we're trapped in situations with no way out. But God always provides a way of escape. Jesus paid a high price so that we could live in freedom, and when we trust in Him, we are never without hope.

Think of it like this: If you were trapped in a burning building, the only way out might be to jump out of the window. It would be painful, but it's better than staying trapped and facing a worse fate. Similarly, God provides us with the way of escape, but sometimes it requires faith and courage to take that step.

The Bible promises that with God, there is always a way out. He will never allow you to be tempted beyond your ability, and He will provide a way to endure it.

> *"No temptation has overtaken you that is not common to man. God is faithful, and He will not let you be tempted beyond your ability, but with the temptation He will also provide the way of escape, that you may be able to endure it."* — 1 Corinthians 10:13

SCRIPTURAL PROMISES OF ESCAPE

God will deliver you from the snare:

> *"For He will deliver you from the snare of the fowler and from the deadly pestilence."* — Psalm 91:3

God is our refuge:

> *"You take me out of the net they have hidden for me, for you are my refuge."* — Psalm 31:4

God will preserve your life in the midst of trouble:

> *"Though I walk in the midst of trouble, you preserve my life; you stretch out your hand against the wrath of my enemies, and your right hand delivers me."* — Psalm 138:7

When you feel trapped in life, whether it's by tough and difficult circumstances or emotional struggles, remember that God is your refuge. He will make a way for you, even when it feels like there's no way out.

THE TESTIMONY OF WALLACE JOHNSON

There's a story of Wallace Johnson, the builder of Holiday Inn hotels, who experienced a major life setback at the age of 40. One morning, he was told he was fired from his job at a sawmill. Feeling hopeless and discouraged, he didn't know what to do next. But his wife asked him a crucial question: "What are you going to do now?"

Wallace decided to mortgage their home and start a building business, which eventually made him a multi-millionaire. In hindsight, he realized that getting fired was part of God's greater plan. If he hadn't lost that job, he would never have started his successful business. Wallace said, "If I could find the man who fired me, I would sincerely thank him for what he did."

Sometimes, we don't understand why things happen in the moment, but we should trust that God has a bigger plan for our lives. What may feel like a setback can actually be God's way of guiding us to something greater.

PAUL AND SILAS

In Acts 16, we see another powerful example of God providing a way of escape. Paul and Silas were in prison for preaching the gospel, wrongly accused and beaten. While in their prison cells, instead of being discouraged, they prayed and sang praises to God. Suddenly, there was a great earthquake, and the prison doors flew open. The chains fell off, and they were free. But rather than running away, they stayed in the prison to protect the jailer, who thought everyone had escaped and was ready to take his own life.

Paul and Silas's actions led the jailer and his family to faith in Christ. In that moment, God made a way out of an impossible situation, and the jailer's life was transformed.

GOD MAKES A WAY

No matter how trapped or impossible your situation may feel, know that God always makes a way. He is faithful to deliver you. There is no situation too difficult, no pit too deep, no storm too powerful for God to handle. If He could deliver Paul and Silas from a prison, He can deliver you from whatever you are facing.

In the darkest times, God will make a way where there seems to be no way. Trust in Him, and know that He is already working behind the scenes, even when you can't see it.

THINK ON IT

You are never truly trapped unless you choose to stay where you are. Just as God provided a way of escape for Paul and Silas, He will do the same for you. No matter how overwhelming life may feel, God is faithful to deliver you from every trap and storm.

> "No temptation has overtaken you that is not common to man. God is faithful, and He will not let you be tempted beyond your ability, but with the temptation He will also provide the way of escape, that you may be able to endure it." — 1 Corinthians 10:13

When you feel stuck, remember that God has already made a way. Trust Him, take the step of faith, and watch Him turn what feels like a setback into your breakthrough.

DAY 61
DO YOU SEE ANYTHING?

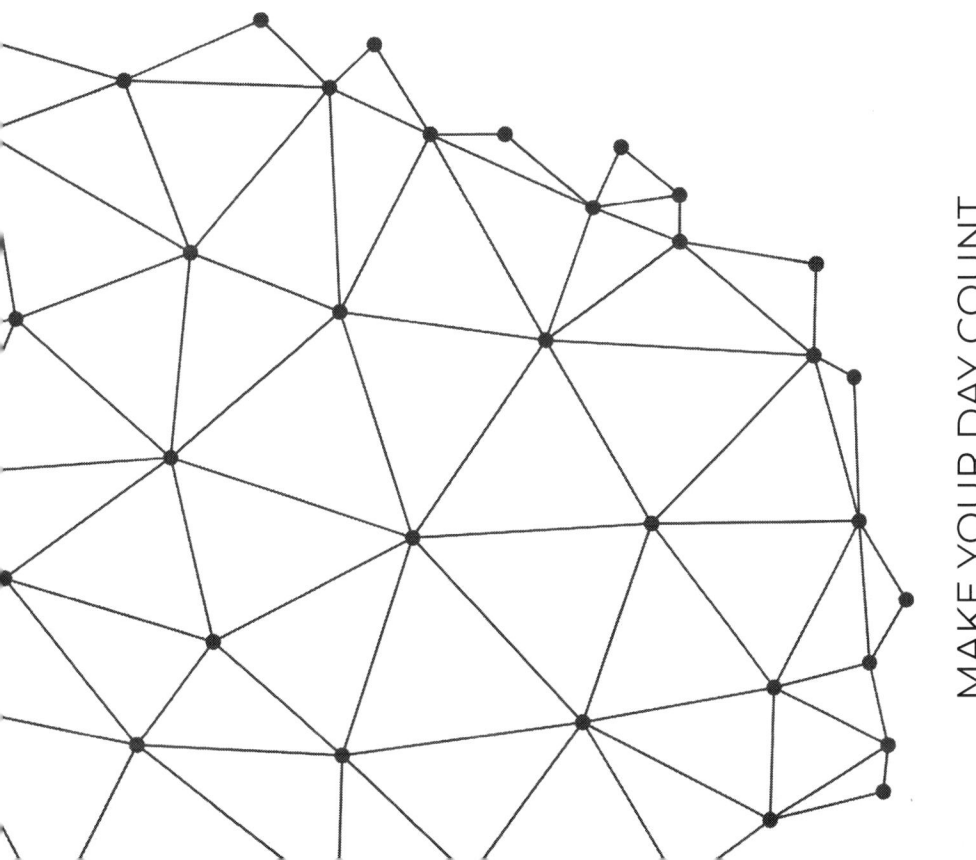

MAKE YOUR DAY COUNT

101 DEVOTIONALS — PART TWO

DO YOU SEE ANYTHING?

BIG THOUGHT
You see what you WANT to see, based on HOW you see.

> **Matthew 6:22** – "The eye is the lamp of the body. So, if your eye is healthy, your whole body will be full of light."

Imagine living for 50 years with blindness, only to discover later that surgery could have restored your sight. Rose Crawford, a woman in Ontario, lived in this very reality. For 20 years, she remained blind, unaware that a simple operation could have restored her vision at the age of 30. Why did she live in darkness for so long? Why did no one tell her about the advances in eye surgery? The wasted years of her life—years when she could have been seeing the world around her—were a result of her limited perspective and the lack of knowledge.

It's easy to get used to a limited way of living. We can get comfortable in our blindness, both physically and spiritually. This blindness can make us content with a life that's less than what God wants for us. Don't let blindness—whether it's spiritual, emotional, or mental—rob you of the vibrant, fulfilling life you were meant to live in Christ.

THE POWER OF PERSPECTIVE

The way we see life shapes everything about our existence. How we see the world—and our place in it—affects how we act, how we invest our time, how we make decisions, and how we build relationships. Your perspective defines your life. The way you view life, your circumstances, and your purpose will guide your path and impact your destiny.

The human eye is one of the most complex and essential organs in the body. But even more important than physical eyesight is spiritual vision—the ability to see clearly in the spiritual realm. In the Bible, Jesus teaches us how critical it is to have proper eyesight for our spiritual lives. Just as healthy eyes allow us to see the world around us clearly, spiritual vision allows us to see God's truth clearly and to live according to that truth.

> *"The eye is the lamp of the body. So, if your eye is healthy, your whole body will be full of light, but if your eye is bad, your whole body will be full of darkness…"* — Matthew 6:22-23

Jesus is saying that if our spiritual eyes are healthy, our whole life will be filled with light, clarity, and purpose. But if we're spiritually blind, we live in darkness, unable to see the truth, and unable to walk in God's will.

FAITH AND VISION

The Bible teaches that faith is the assurance of things hoped for, the conviction of things not seen. Faith is what gives us the ability to see beyond our current circumstances—to see things from God's perspective, even when we don't understand what's happening.

> *"Now faith is the assurance of things hoped for, the conviction of things not seen."* — Hebrews 11:1

Faith allows us to see what's invisible to the natural eye: God's promises, His plan for our lives, His provision, and His faithfulness. When we trust in God, we are not walking by what we see in the natural; we are walking by what we see in the spirit—the truth of God's Word.

THE "I WON'T QUIT" MINDSET

When life gets tough, it's easy to give up. We may feel like we're stuck in darkness, or that we can't see the way forward. But just like a child who refuses to stop searching for the light switch in a dark room, we must adopt an "I won't quit" mindset. No matter how hard things get, we must decide that we are going to trust God, keep our eyes fixed on Him, and never let go of His promises.

> "And let us not grow weary of doing good, for in due season we will reap, if we do not give up." — Galatians 6:9

> "And I am sure of this, that he who began a good work in you will bring it to completion at the day of Jesus Christ." — Philippians 1:6

Perseverance in faith leads to victory. No matter how dark it may seem, we can hold on to God's promises, knowing that He will bring us through.

JESUS: THE LIGHT IN THE DARKNESS

Have you ever stepped into a dark room and couldn't see anything, but when you flipped on the light, everything became visible? The light reveals what was previously hidden in the dark. It allows us to see things as they really are.

In a similar way, Jesus is the light in the darkness. When we allow Him into our lives, He illuminates our path and shows us the truth. His Word is a lamp to our feet and a light to our path. With Jesus, we no longer have to walk in darkness.

> "Your word is a lamp to my feet and a light to my path." — Psalm 119:105

When we face uncertain or dark times, Jesus is the one who guides us through the darkness, helping us see what we cannot see with our own eyes. Trust Him to illuminate your way.

THE MAN ON THE OCEAN LINER

A story is told of a man who booked a passage on an ocean liner. He could only afford the cost of his ticket and had no money for meals. Each day, he would look through the dining room window, watching the other passengers enjoy lavish meals. He ate nothing but cheese and crackers in his cabin, day after day. It wasn't until the last day of the journey that he discovered his ticket included all meals—he could have been eating the same meals as the others the whole time!

This story is a great illustration of how many of us live in spiritual ignorance. We have all the blessings of God available to us, but because we don't realize what's available or how to access it, we live in spiritual poverty. Jesus has already paid the price for us to live in abundance, and we need to claim the blessings He offers by aligning our lives with His truth.

YOU ARE MADE TO WIN

You are not meant to live in spiritual blindness. You are not meant to live in darkness. You are made to win! Don't let the enemy deceive you into thinking that you're stuck, or that you're not worthy of God's blessings. With God on your side, nothing is impossible.

> *"If God is for us, who can be against us?"* — Romans 8:31

God has made a way for you to walk in victory, to walk in light, and to see things from His perspective. Don't give up—keep your eyes on the Lord, and trust Him to guide you every step of the way.

THINK ON IT

What you see in life depends on how you see it. Don't let spiritual blindness or a limited perspective keep you in the dark. Jesus is the light that reveals truth, purpose, and the way forward. Trust Him to illuminate your path and guide you to the abundant life He has prepared for you.

> *"The eye is the lamp of the body. So, if your eye is healthy, your whole body will be full of light."* — Matthew 6:22

You were made to see clearly—not just with your physical eyes, but with your heart and spirit. Open your eyes to the truth of God's Word, claim the blessings He has for you, and step into the light of His promises. With Jesus, you are never in the dark!

DAY 62
WHAT IS YOUR LIFE BUILT ON?

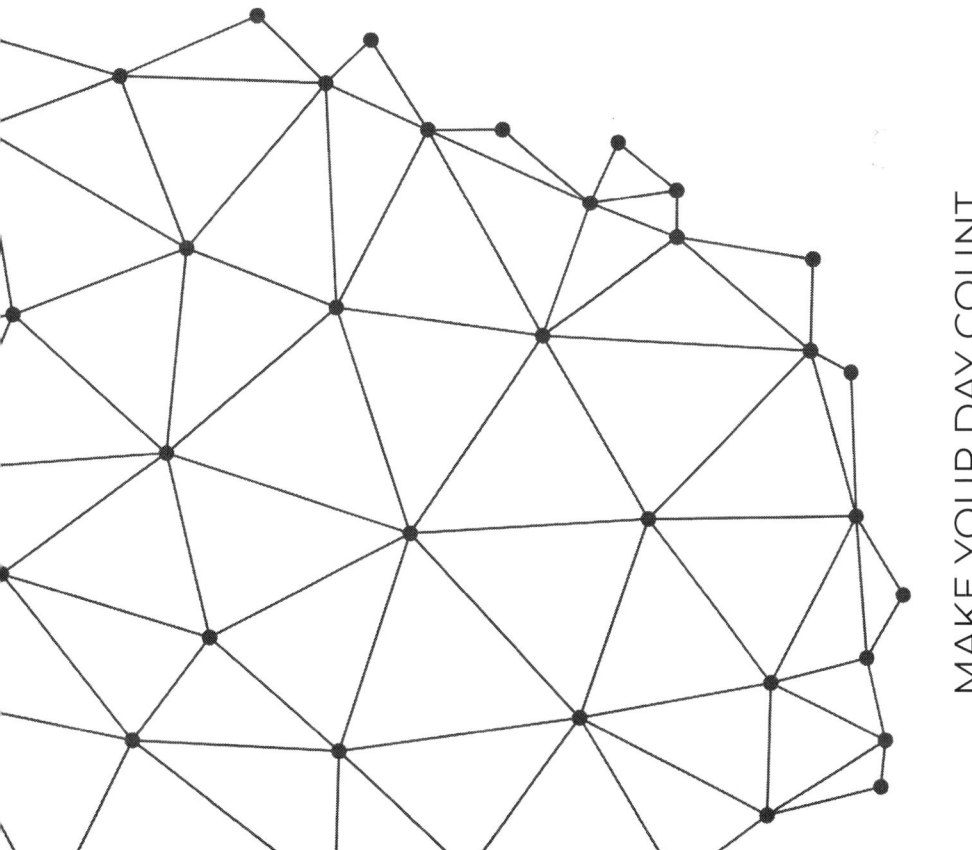

MAKE YOUR DAY COUNT

101 DEVOTIONALS — PART TWO

WHAT IS YOUR LIFE BUILT ON?

BIG THOUGHT
There is hope for your life.

> **Hebrew 6:19** – "We have this as a sure and steadfast anchor of the soul, a hope that enters into the inner place behind the curtain…"

Allow your life to be built on an anchor of hope and faith in God! Hope is one of the most powerful forces in the world. It is a feeling of expectation and trust—a belief that, no matter what is going on in your life, God has a plan for you. Hope is more than just wishful thinking; it is the assurance that God is in control and that He will work all things for good for those who love Him and are called according to His purpose (Romans 8:28). No matter the trials or struggles you face, hope in God is the anchor that keeps you steady through life's storms.

> *"I will not leave you or forsake you."* — Joshua 1:5
>
> *"It is the Lord who goes before you. He will be with you; He will not leave you or forsake you. "Do not fear or be dismayed."*
> — Deuteronomy 31:8

101 DEVOTIONALS — PART TWO

> *"The Lord is on my side; I will not fear. What can man do to me?"*
> *— Psalm 118:6*

HOPE NEVER QUITS

Hope is unshakable. It does not quit. Whatever challenges you face—whether it's low self-esteem, depression, bullying, peer pressure, addiction, stress, or even suicidal thoughts—there is hope. And that hope is Jesus Christ. God is not the god of doubt, fear, anxiety, or hopelessness; He is the God of Hope. When you place your trust in Him, your hope is unbreakable.

As Christopher Reeve once said, "Once you choose hope, anything is possible." When you choose to trust God, no matter how bleak your situation may seem, you are choosing to believe that something better is ahead. Hope allows you to rise above the circumstances and see the possibilities that God has prepared for you.

> *"May the God of hope fill you with all joy and peace in believing, so that the power of the Holy Spirit may abound in hope."*
> *— Romans 15:13*

BUILDING ON THE ROCK

In Matthew 7:24-27, Jesus tells the parable of the wise man and the foolish man. The wise man built his house on the rock, and when the storms came, his house stood strong. The foolish man, however, built his house on the sand, and when the storms came, his house was destroyed.

In this story, Jesus is telling us that He is the Rock—the foundation upon which we should build our lives. When we place our trust in Him and build our lives on His Word, we will be able to withstand any storm that comes our way. Jesus is our firm foundation, and with Him, we will remain strong, no matter how fierce the storm.

THE STORM OF THE CENTURY

In October 1991, a storm stronger than any in recorded history hit the coast of Gloucester, Massachusetts. This storm, which became known as "The Perfect Storm", produced waves that reached 100 feet (about the height of a ten-story building) and winds of 120 mph. The storm was deadly for the fishermen at sea, many of whom lost their lives. Though the storm didn't impact the land directly, it revealed the true power of nature and the importance of being prepared for the unexpected.

While most of us will never face a storm of that magnitude, we all face storms of life. Whether it's a financial crisis, relational struggles, health challenges, or emotional battles, the question remains: How will you handle the storms of life?

The key is to build your life on a solid foundation—Jesus Christ, the unshakable rock. When you trust in Him, you are anchored in hope. And no storm, no matter how fierce, can destroy the peace and security that come from building your life on Him.

> *"We have this as a sure and steadfast anchor of the soul, a hope that enters into the inner place behind the curtain..."*
> *— Hebrews 6:19*

An anchor steadies a boat, keeping it secure in the midst of surging waves and shifting tides. Similarly, hope is our anchor. It keeps us steady in life's storms. The storm may be violent, but the anchor holds firm. When you place your hope in Jesus, you are anchored in His love, His faithfulness, and His ability to carry you through.

GOD'S PROMISE TO NEVER LEAVE

When the storms of life come, you may feel overwhelmed. You may feel as though you're sinking or about to be washed away. But God's promise is clear: He will never leave you or forsake you. He is your constant, your refuge, your anchor.

> *"...for He has said, 'I will never leave you nor forsake you.' So we can confidently say, 'The Lord is my helper; I will not fear; what can man do to me?'"* — *Hebrews 13:5-6*

No matter the storm, you are not alone. God is with you, and He will see you through. Hope in Him is the source of your strength.

HOPE RESTORES AND ENCOURAGES

Hope is not just a passive feeling; it's an active force that restores, encourages, and gives you purpose. When you build your life on the hope of God, you can look beyond your current struggles and see a future filled with possibilities.

Hope helps you endure the trials of life, knowing that God is using them to shape you into the person He wants you to be. Jesus turns your storms into stories of His faithfulness. When your life is built on the God of Hope, you will not be shaken.

> *"For He has said, 'I will never leave you nor forsake you.'"*
> *— Hebrews 13:5*

THINK ON IT

Hope is the anchor that steadies your soul in life's storms. Build your life on the solid foundation of Jesus Christ, the Rock, and trust that He will never leave you nor forsake you. No matter how fierce the storm, hope in God will sustain you, restore you, and lead you to a future filled with His promises.

> *"We have this as a sure and steadfast anchor of the soul, a hope that enters into the inner place behind the curtain..."*
> *— Hebrews 6:19*

Don't let life's challenges shake your foundation. Trust in God's unchanging faithfulness, and let His hope carry you through every trial. With Jesus, you are secure, unshakable, and ready to weather any storm!

DAY 63
HOPE

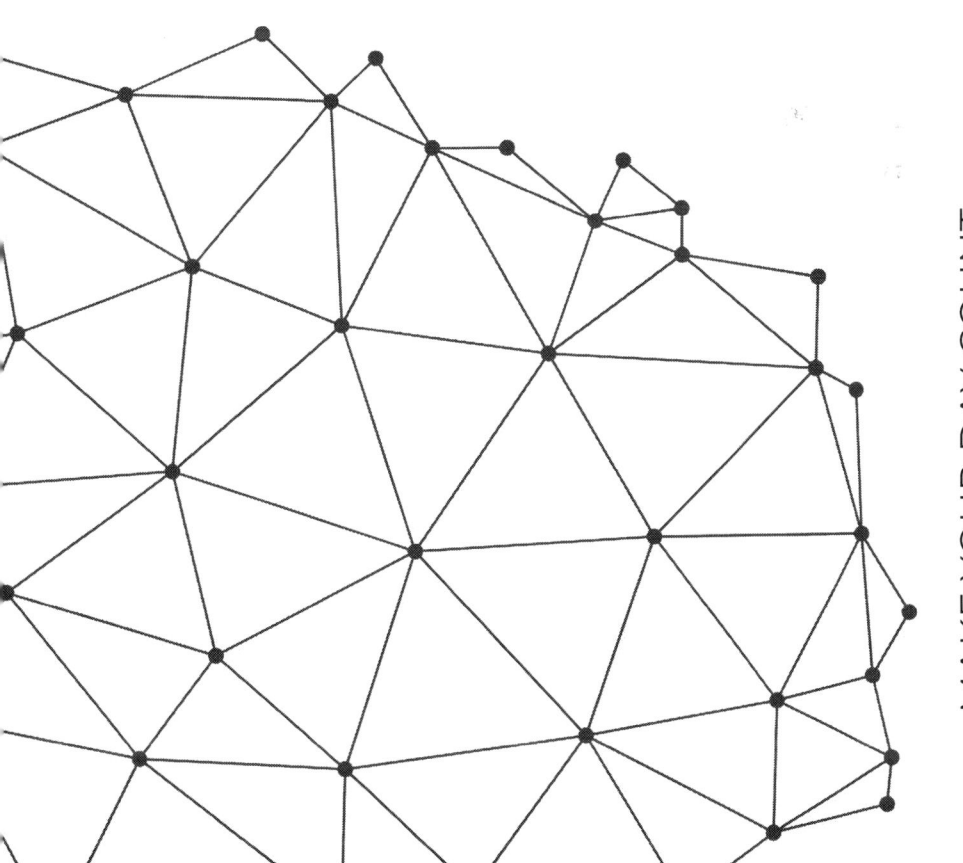

MAKE YOUR DAY COUNT

101 DEVOTIONALS — PART TWO

HOPE

BIG THOUGHT
Never lose hope—God is working even in the darkest of moments.

Hebrews 10:23 – "Let us hold fast the confession of our hope without wavering, for He who promised is faithful."

Have you ever felt like life's challenges have trapped you in a pit too deep to escape? It's in those moments when hope becomes your lifeline. Hope is trusting that no matter what you're going through, God is faithful. He knows you, loves you, and has a plan for your life. Hope reminds us that the impossible can become possible when God is involved.

"Let us hold fast the confession of our hope without wavering, for He who promised is faithful." — Hebrews 10:23

Hope isn't about wishful thinking—it's about knowing that God's promises never fail. It's standing firm in the belief that God is with you, even when the world feels overwhelming. When you hold onto hope, you hold onto the unshakable truth that God is in control.

101 DEVOTIONALS — PART TWO

THE POWER OF HOPE

Hope is what keeps us moving forward when life feels impossible. It gives us the strength to believe in God's promises and the courage to trust in His plan.

HOPE IN ACTION

In October 1987, the world watched as 18-month-old Jessica McClure fell into a narrow well in her aunt's backyard in Midland, Texas. Trapped 22 feet below the surface, she remained there for 58 hours while an entire nation prayed and worked tirelessly for her rescue. Engineers, firefighters, and strangers filled with hope joined forces to save her life. Against the odds, they pulled her out alive.

This story is a powerful example of hope in action. Despite the overwhelming odds, the rescuers believed in the possibility of saving her—and they didn't give up. Their hope turned a hopeless situation into a victory.

> *"May the God of hope fill you with all joy and peace in believing, so that by the power of the Holy Spirit you may abound in hope."*
> — Romans 15:13

JESUS, OUR SOURCE OF HOPE

In Mark 2:1-12, we read about a paralyzed man whose friends refused to let obstacles stand in their way. The house where Jesus was teaching was so crowded that there was no way to get their friend through the door. But hope doesn't quit. They climbed onto the roof, tore through the ceiling, and lowered the man down to Jesus.

Jesus, seeing their faith, healed the paralyzed man, saying, "Son, your sins are forgiven." Their hope and determination led to a miraculous healing. What seemed impossible became a powerful testimony of God's love and power.

Hope changes everything. It moves mountains, overcomes obstacles, and brings life to what seems lost.

UNSHAKEABLE HOPE

Let your hope be grounded in Jesus, the God of Hope. Life's circumstances may try to shake you, but God's promises are solid ground.

HOPE

> *"Rejoice in hope, be patient in tribulation, be constant in prayer."*
> *— Romans 12:12*

Rejoice in hope—always! When you hold onto hope, it has the power to lift you out of even the deepest wells of despair. Remember, hope isn't just an emotion; it's a confident expectation in God's goodness.

> *"For God alone, O my soul, wait in silence, for my hope is from Him."*
> *— Psalm 62:5*

Hope is a gift from God. It's not something you have to manufacture—it's something you receive when you trust in Him. No matter how dark the season or how deep the challenge, the God of Hope is working on your behalf.

THINK ON IT

Hope isn't passive—it's an active, unshakable trust in the goodness of God. When life feels overwhelming, choose to place your hope in the One who never fails.

> *"Let us hold fast the confession of our hope without wavering, for He who promised is faithful." — Hebrews 10:23*

No matter the situation, let hope be your anchor. Trust that God is working in ways you can't yet see. Rejoice in the assurance that He is the God of Hope, bringing light to the darkest places and transforming your challenges into victories. With God, there's always a reason to hope—and with hope, miracles happen every day.

101 DEVOTIONALS — PART TWO

DAY 64
COMMITMENT

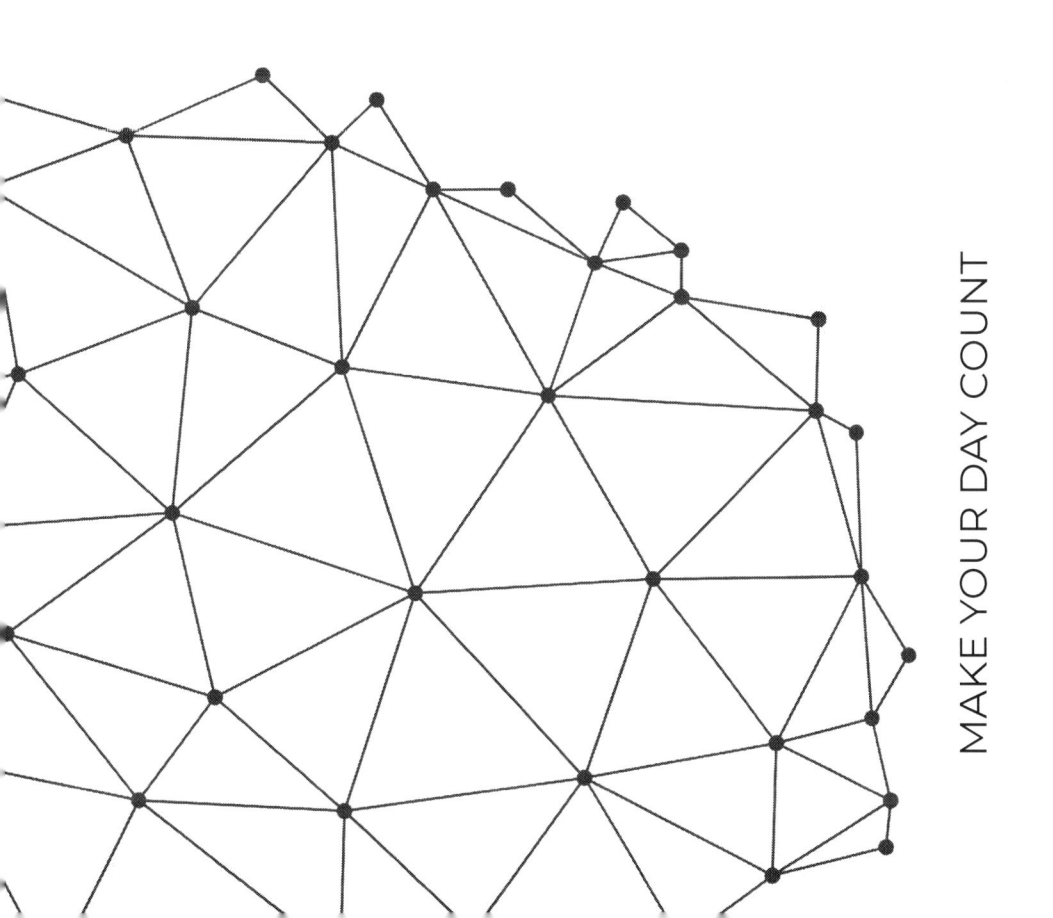

MAKE YOUR DAY COUNT

101 DEVOTIONALS — PART TWO

COMMITMENT

BIG THOUGHT
In order to go to your next level in life, it's going to take commitment.

> "Most people fail, not because of lack of desire, but, because of lack of commitment." — Vince Lombardi

Romans 12:1 – "I appeal to you therefore, brothers, by the mercies of God, to present your bodies as a living sacrifice, holy and acceptable to God, which is your spiritual worship."

Unless a commitment is made, there are only promises and hopes; but no plans. I've always heard that a dream without a goal is a wish. The Bible says in Proverbs 16:3, "Commit your work to the Lord, and your plans will be established."

Have you ever played the game called "Hokey Pokey"? It's the little kid's game where you sing, dance, and follow the instructions. You know, you put your left hand in and your left hand out, your right hand in and your right hand out, and you shake it all about. But my favorite part is when you put your whole self in.

> "I appeal to you therefore, brothers, by the mercies of God, to present your bodies as a living sacrifice, holy and acceptable to God, which is your spiritual worship." — Romans 12:1

To be a "living sacrifice" means to commit your whole self in—just like the "Hokey Pokey". This is what Paul is talking about in this passage of scripture. He's saying to be totally committed. If you have this kind of commitment, you will go to the next level, guaranteed.

TYPES OF PEOPLE WHEN IT COMES TO COMMITMENT

There are 4 different types of people:

- ◊ Cop-out: An individual who avoids doing what they know they have to do (procrastination).
- ◊ Hold-out: An individual who wants to accomplish something but just keeps making excuses.
- ◊ Drop-out: An individual who begins something but quits before it is finished.
- ◊ All-out: An individual who is committed and willing to do whatever it takes to go all the way.

A person who desires to be all-out has a mindset that says to themselves:

- ◊ "I'm committed…"
- ◊ To my family.
- ◊ To my church.
- ◊ To my friends.
- ◊ To my work.
- ◊ To my calling.
- ◊ To my dreams.
- ◊ To see God move in my life.

> *"For the eyes of the Lord range throughout the earth to strengthen those whose hearts are fully committed to Him."*
> *— 2 Chronicles 16:9*

This verse makes me think of this story about Julius Caesar. When Julius Caesar landed on the shores of Britain with his Roman legions, he took a bold and decisive step to ensure the success of his military venture. He ordered his men to march to the edge of the Cliffs of Dover and commanded them to look down at the water below. To their amazement, they saw every ship in which they had crossed the channel engulfed in flames. Caesar had deliberately cut off any possibility of retreat. Now that his soldiers were unable to return to the continent, there was nothing left for them to do but to advance and conquer! And that is exactly what they did.

Talk about commitment! Once he did that, there was no going back. That is the kind of attitude of the heart that you must have in order to fulfill your destiny. Some people want everything to be perfect before they're willing to commit, but commitment always precedes achievement. When you make a commitment, you create hope. When you keep a commitment, you create trust!

> *"No one can serve two masters, for either he will hate the one and love the other, or he will be devoted to the one and despise the other. You cannot serve God and money." — Matthew 6:24*

> *"Keep your heart with all vigilance, for from it flow the springs of life." — Proverbs 4:23*

> *"For what does it profit a man to gain the whole world and forfeit his soul?" — Mark 8:36*

COMMITMENT: WHAT IT REVEALS AND SHAPES

- ◊ My commitment reveals my value. (Matthew 6:24)
- ◊ My commitment shapes my life. (Proverbs 4:23)
- ◊ My commitment determines my destiny. (Mark 8:36)

ONE FINAL THOUGHT

If you choose to leave the chair of commitment, you will always have to compromise, which leads to conflict.

THINK ON IT

Commitment is the key that unlocks the door to the next level of your life. It's not just about desire or intention—it's about putting your whole self in, just like Paul's call to be a living sacrifice. To live fully committed means going all-out for God, your dreams, and your purpose.

> *"For the eyes of the Lord range throughout the earth to strengthen those whose hearts are fully committed to Him."*
> *— 2 Chronicles 16:9*

Be the person who burns the ships like Julius Caesar—someone with no retreat, no excuses, and no turning back. Let your commitment reveal your values, shape your life, and determine your destiny. Stay all-in, and you'll see God move powerfully in your life!

DAY 65
DREAM BIG

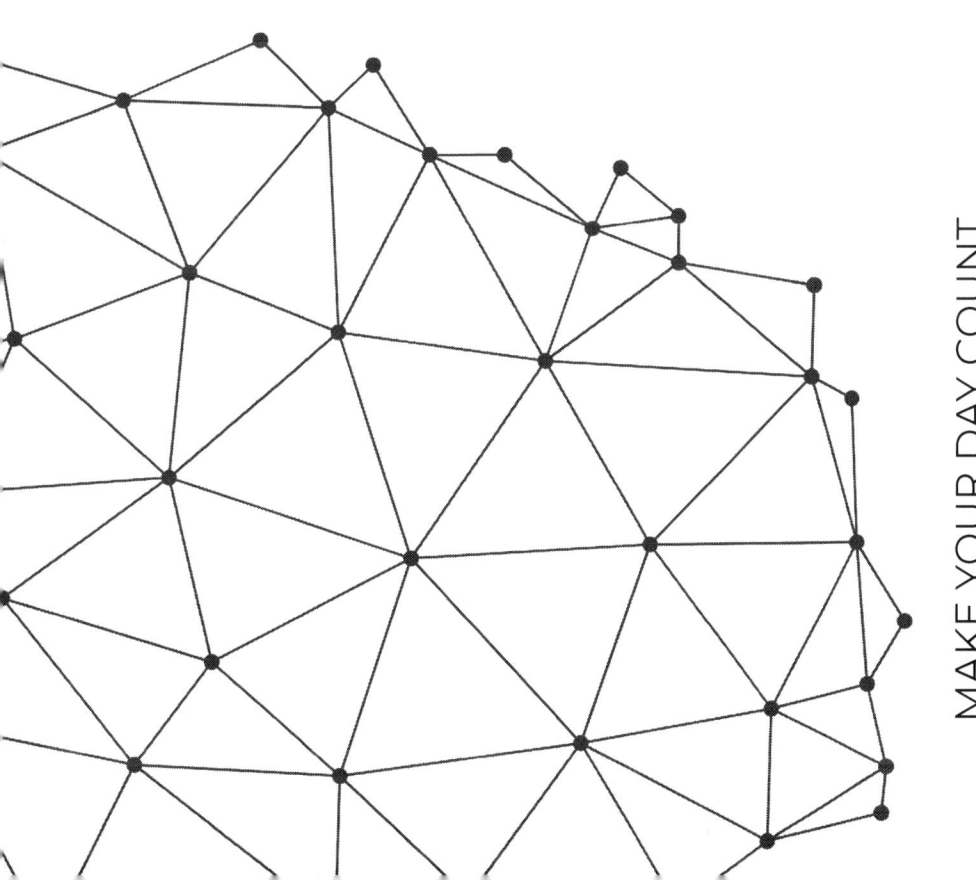

MAKE YOUR DAY COUNT

101 DEVOTIONALS — PART TWO

DREAM BIG

BIG THOUGHT
Your destiny is determined by how many times you rise, dust yourself off, and pursue your dreams.

> **Proverbs 16:3** – "Commit your work to the Lord, and your plans will be established."

Life is full of challenges, and sometimes the path to your dreams can feel like a long and difficult road. But every step forward brings you closer to the plans and purpose God has for you. Your dreams are not random—they are a gift from God, planted in your heart to give you vision and direction.

> *"Commit your work to the Lord, and your plans will be established."*
> *— Proverbs 16:3*

Dreams are not just a spark of imagination; they are a glimpse into what God wants to do in and through your life. When you commit your dreams to Him, He equips you with the strength, guidance, and opportunities to see them come to life.

DREAMS IN ACTION
In the early 1980s, an aspiring young actor named Jim Carrey was struggling to make his dreams a reality. He was broke, living in a beat-up car, and facing rejection after rejection. His family had been so

poor that at one point they lived in a Volkswagen van by the ocean.

One day, Jim drove to the top of a hill overlooking Los Angeles. There, he wrote himself a check for $10 million for "acting services rendered" and dated it five years into the future. He kept that check in his wallet, pulling it out whenever discouragement threatened to take over.

Through hard work and relentless commitment, Jim Carrey eventually made $16-$25 million per movie. What started as a distant dream became a reality because he never stopped believing and working toward it.

His story reminds us to keep our dreams in front of us. Whether it's a picture of your dream house, career, or ministry, keep it where you'll see it every day. Pray over it, speak life into it, and take steps toward making it happen.

GOD'S DREAM FOR YOU

Before you were born, God dreamed big dreams for your life. He crafted a plan filled with purpose, hope, and joy. Those dreams are not just for your benefit—they are meant to glorify Him and impact the world around you.

> *"For I know the plans I have for you, declares the Lord, plans for welfare and not for evil, to give you a future and a hope."* — Jeremiah 29:11

The poorest person isn't the one without money—it's the one without a dream. A God-sized dream fuels your purpose, pushing you toward greatness and reminding you that nothing is impossible with Him. "I am not going to let others:

- ◊ Shut me up
- ◊ Shut me down
- ◊ Shut me out
- ◊ Shut me in

> *"Delight yourself in the Lord, and He will give you the desires of your heart."* — Psalm 37:4

OVERCOMING OBSTACLES

The journey to your dreams will not be free of challenges:

- ◊ Friends might tell you "No."
- ◊ Family might tell you "No."
- ◊ Banks might tell you "No."
- ◊ Bosses might tell you "No."
- ◊ The industry might tell you "No."

But God's "Yes" is greater than every "No" you'll ever hear. His promises are unshakable, and His plans for your life will not be stopped by rejection or discouragement.

Decide today that quitting is not an option. Excuses will always be easy to find, but so are opportunities when you're determined to keep moving forward. Let God's faithfulness be the foundation of your perseverance.

DREAM BOLDLY, BELIEVE DEEPLY

God has called you to dream big. Don't settle for small dreams when you serve a BIG God. Allow His plans to fuel your faith and inspire you to move forward with boldness.

> *"And Jesus said to him, 'If you can'! All things are possible for one who believes.'"—Mark 9:23*

Dreaming big isn't about striving in your own strength; it's about partnering with God. Trust Him to provide the wisdom, resources, and timing to fulfill the dreams He's placed in your heart.

THINK ON IT

Your dreams are not just fleeting thoughts—they are God-given glimpses of what He wants to accomplish through you. Life's challenges may try to hold you back, but every step forward in faith brings you closer to the destiny He has prepared for you.

101 DEVOTIONALS — PART TWO

> *"Commit your work to the Lord, and your plans will be established."*
> *— Proverbs 16:3*

Keep your dreams alive by committing them to God. Let His "Yes" overshadow every "No" you face, and trust that His plans are greater than your imagination. Dream boldly, trust deeply, and never stop believing that with God, all things are possible!

DAY 66
FORWARD

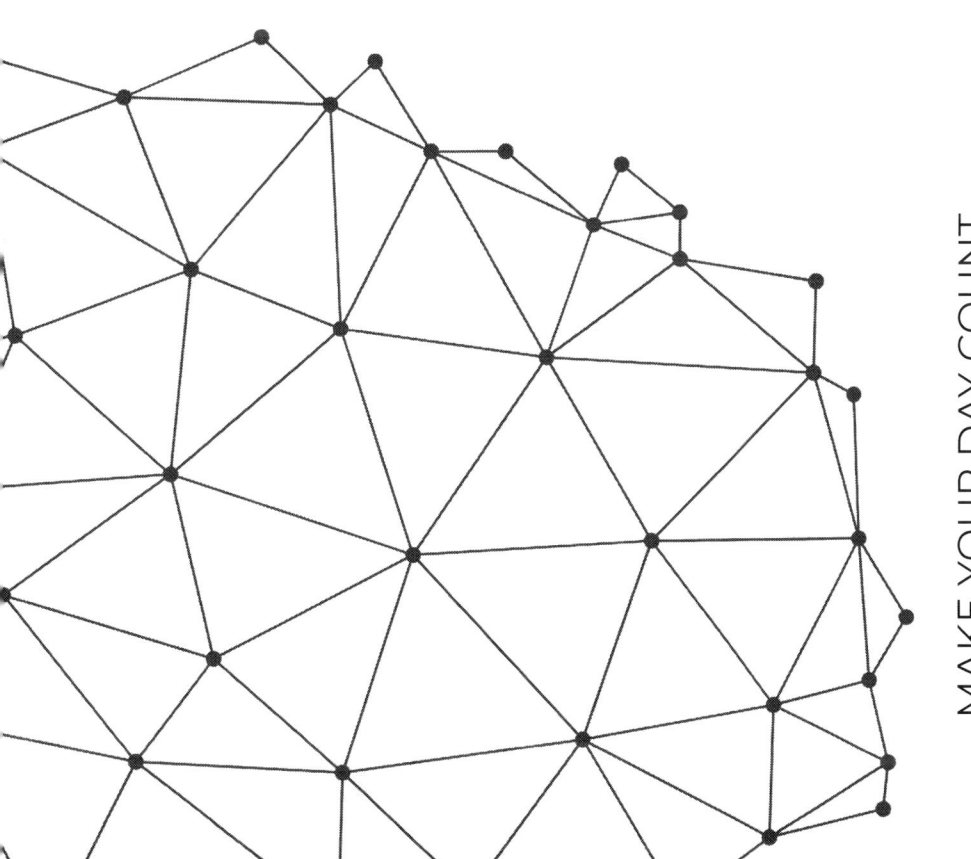

MAKE YOUR DAY COUNT

101 DEVOTIONALS — PART TWO

FORWARD

BIG THOUGHT
God hasn't created you to go backward—He's called you to move forward!

> **Philippians 3:12-14** – "Not that I have already obtained this or am already perfect, but I press on to make it my own, because Christ Jesus has made me his own. Brothers, I do not consider that I have made it my own. But one thing I do: forgetting what lies behind and straining forward to what lies ahead, I press on toward the goal for the prize of the upward call of God in Christ Jesus."

Life is meant to be lived moving ahead, growing, and stepping into the future God has prepared for you. Even the smallest step in the right direction can lead to the biggest transformation of your life.

God hasn't called us to stay still or retreat. He's called us to take ground, to grow, and to flourish. While the enemy's goal is to steal, kill, and destroy (John 10:10), Jesus came to bring life—life that is always moving forward and becoming more abundant.

STRETCH FORWARD

When Jesus told the man to stretch his hand forward, the moment of action brought instant healing. That simple act of stepping forward in faith changed everything.

This reminds us that the moment we're ready to give up is often the moment right before a breakthrough. Moving backward or staying still keeps us powerless. But stepping forward, even in faith as small as a mustard seed, invites God to work miracles in our lives.

> "Again, he entered the synagogue, and a man was there with a withered hand. And they watched Jesus, to see whether he would heal him on the Sabbath, so that they might accuse him. And He said to the man with the withered hand, 'Come here.' And He said to them, 'Is it lawful on the Sabbath to do good or to do harm, to save life or to kill?' But they were silent. And He looked around at them with anger, grieved at their hardness of heart, and said to the man, 'Stretch out your hand.' He stretched it out, and his hand was restored." — Mark 3:1-5

FORWARD BY DESIGN

Australia's coat of arms features two unique creatures—the emu, a flightless bird, and the kangaroo. Both animals were chosen because they cannot move backward. The emu's three-toed foot causes it to fall if it tries to step backward, and the kangaroo's large tail prevents it from moving in reverse.

These animals are a powerful symbol of forward movement. Just like them, we are designed to keep moving ahead. In life's battles, imagine yourself as part of an army. Your orders are to march forward, taking ground and following the path laid out by your Commander.

> "Let your eyes look directly forward, and your gaze be straight before you." — Proverbs 4:25

Distraction is one of the enemy's greatest weapons. If you begin to look from side to side, you lose focus. Whatever you choose to focus on will direct your attention, and whatever has your attention has your focus. Stay locked on the goal ahead.

STEP FORWARD WITH PURPOSE

God has called you to grow, flourish, and move forward. Don't let the past hold you back, and don't allow distractions to derail you. Stay focused on God's plan and take steps of faith, no matter how small.

> "If you don't grow forward, you will always be in the same place."

Forward movement requires intentionality. Like the man with the withered hand, you have to stretch forward. Like the emu and kangaroo, you have to refuse to look back. Growth comes when we choose to move in God's direction.

THINK ON IT

God has designed you to move forward, not backward. Just as the man with the withered hand experienced healing when he stretched forward, your breakthrough lies ahead of you—not behind. When you take even the smallest step of faith, God meets you there and begins to transform your life.

> *"Let your eyes look directly forward, and your gaze be straight before you."* — *Proverbs 4:25*

Stay focused on the plans God has for you. Don't let the past hold you back or distractions take your eyes off the goal. With faith and determination, press on toward the abundant life God has called you to. The best days of your life are still ahead—move forward with confidence and purpose!

101 DEVOTIONALS — PART TWO

DAY 67
MINDSET

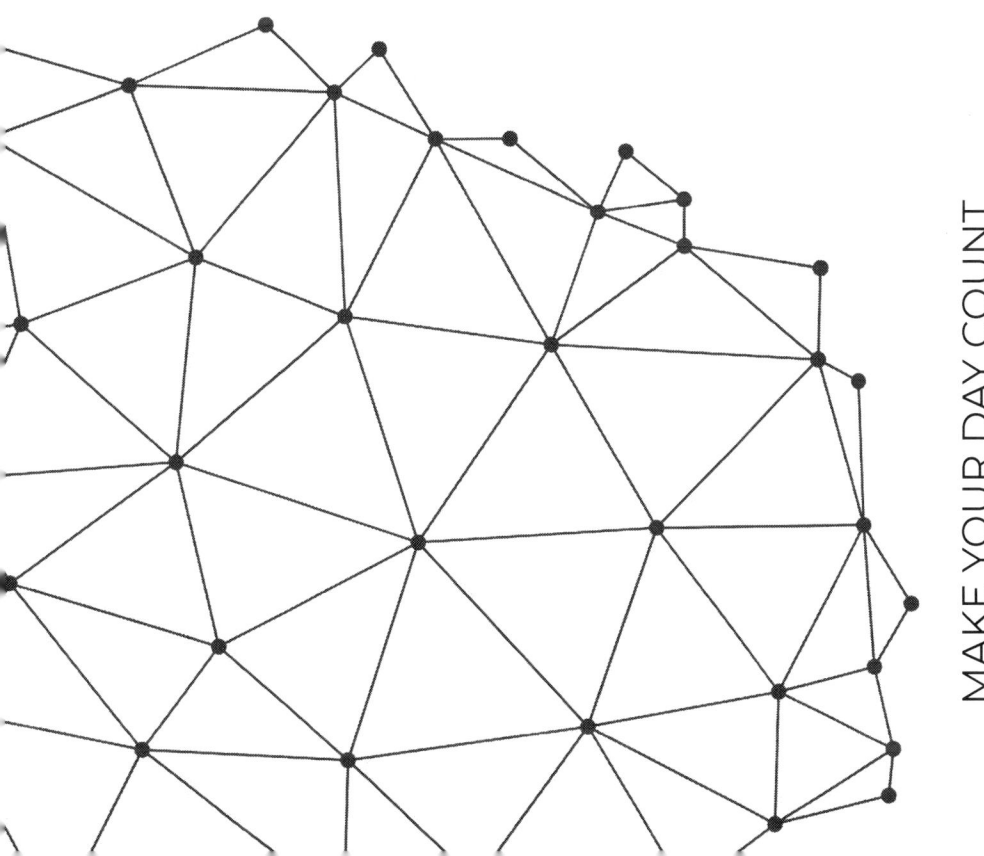

MAKE YOUR DAY COUNT

101 DEVOTIONALS — PART TWO

MINDSET

BIG THOUGHT

Your mindset matters—it shapes your reality and affects every area of your life.

> "Thinking is the hardest work in the world, which is probably why so few people engage in it." — Henry Ford

It is estimated that the average brain has anywhere from 60,000 to 80,000 thoughts a day, and 70% of them are believed to be negative. Imagine the impact this can have on your life! The good news is that you have the power to take control of your thought process. You serve a BIG God—the God of the impossible, the miracle-working God. It's time to start thinking big because He is able, not just sometimes, but ALL the time.

The mindset you have about yourself, your circumstances, and your life becomes your reality. That's why it's so important to align your mindset with the truth of God's Word.

THE ELEPHANT MINDSET

One day, a man was walking past a group of elephants when he noticed something strange. These massive creatures were being held by nothing more than a small rope tied around one leg. There were no chains, no cages—just a simple rope.

The man asked a nearby trainer why these powerful animals didn't break free. The trainer explained, "When they are very young, we use the same size rope to tie them, and it's enough to hold them. As they grow, they are conditioned to believe the rope is still strong enough to hold them, so they never try to break free."

These majestic creatures were stuck because of their mindset. They had the strength to break free but didn't even try because they were trapped by the belief that they couldn't.

This story reminds us of the power of our mindset. Many people live their lives feeling stuck, not because they lack the ability, but because they've been conditioned by negative experiences or self-doubt. But God never intended for His children to live in defeat. He has called you to live in freedom and abundance.

> *"We destroy arguments and every lofty opinion raised against the knowledge of God, and take every thought captive to obey Christ."*
> *— 2 Corinthians 10:5*

> *"Set your minds on things that are above, not on things that are on earth." — Colossians 3:2*

Your thoughts are powerful, and the Bible is clear that we are to take every thought captive and align it with the truth of God's Word. Negative thoughts will come, but they don't have to stay.

REPLACING WRONG THOUGHTS

If we let negative thoughts control our minds, they will dominate our lives. Some common thoughts might sound like this:

- ◊ "I will never be good enough."
- ◊ "I have too many weaknesses."
- ◊ "Have you seen all my secrets?"
- ◊ "I come from a dysfunctional family."
- ◊ "I'm never going to grow."

These lies are shaped by past experiences, self-doubt, and fear. But when we replace them with the truth of God's Word, we begin to transform our mindset.

MINDSET

Whatever has your thoughts, has your focus. Whatever has your focus, has your destiny. That's why having the right mindset is so critical to your success in life.

> *"Finally, brothers, whatever is true, whatever is honorable, whatever is just, whatever is pure, whatever is lovely, whatever is commendable, if there is any excellence, if there is anything worthy of praise, think about these things."* — Philippians 4:8

When your mindset is focused on problems instead of God's promises, it's easy to lose sight of who He is and who you are because of Him. You can't have a mindset of defeat and expect victory. Your thoughts have enormous power—they influence your actions, your habits, and ultimately, your destiny.

GUARD YOUR MIND

Be intentional about what you allow into your mind. Consider the things that feed your thoughts:

- The music you listen to.
- The movies you watch.
- The books you read.
- The shows you watch.
- The places you go.

What you think about plays a big part in who you are. If you allow negative, toxic input into your mind, it will produce negative, toxic output in your life. But when you fill your mind with God's truth, you will begin to see transformation.

GARBAGE IN, GARBAGE OUT

There's a computer term called GIGO—Garbage In, Garbage Out. What you put into your mind determines what you get out of your life.

- If you feed your mind with negativity, doubt, and fear, that's what you'll produce.
- If you feed your mind with God's Word, His promises,

and His truth, you will produce faith, confidence, and abundance.

You are not here to be average; you are here to be extraordinary! Your thoughts have the power to shape your life, so guard them carefully.

CONFESSION OF FAITH
- I take every thought captive to the obedience of Christ.
- My mind is set on things above, not on earthly problems.
- I will focus on God's promises, not my problems.
- My thoughts are aligned with God's truth.
- I am free from the chains of negative thinking.

THINK ON IT

Your mindset is the gateway to your destiny. What you think shapes how you live. Just like the elephant that didn't realize its strength, you have the power, through Christ, to break free from the limiting beliefs and negativity that hold you back.

> *"We destroy arguments and every lofty opinion raised against the knowledge of God, and take every thought captive to obey Christ."*
> *— 2 Corinthians 10:5*

Guard your mind and intentionally focus on God's promises, not your problems. Replace wrong thoughts with the truth of His Word. When you align your thoughts with God's truth, you'll begin to walk in freedom, confidence, and victory. Live boldly, knowing that your mindset matters, and through Christ, all things are possible!

DAY 68
THANKFULNESS

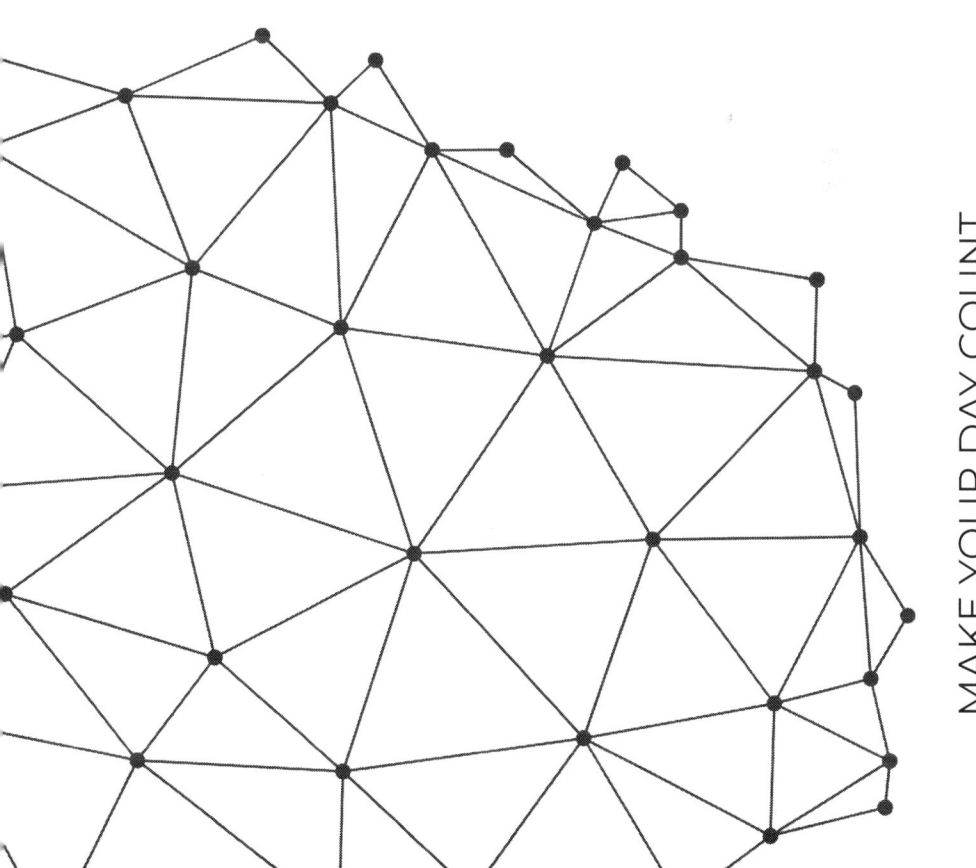

MAKE YOUR DAY COUNT

101 DEVOTIONALS — PART TWO

THANKFULNESS

BIG THOUGHT
Gratitude is one of the healthiest emotions we can cultivate, and it has the power to transform our lives.

> "Gratitude is the healthiest of all human emotions. The more you express gratitude for what you have, the more likely you will have even more to express gratitude for."
> — Zig Ziglar

Have you ever stopped to thank God for something as simple as the breath in your lungs? Every day, you take approximately 23,000 breaths—yet how often do you express gratitude for them? Many people spend more time complaining about what they lack than thanking God for what they have. But thankfulness is powerful—it has the ability to shift your focus from what's missing to the incredible blessings you already have.

Living a life of gratitude doesn't mean life won't be hard, but it equips you with the strength to face challenges. A thankful heart allows you to see the goodness of God in every situation. You woke up today, you're alive, and that alone is enough reason to be thankful!

A CHANGED LIFE THROUGH CHRIST

If you've asked Jesus to be your Lord and Savior, then you've already received the greatest gift of all—salvation through Christ. In Him, you are made new, and the old way of thinking is gone (1

Corinthians 5:17). Your life is now rooted in the hope and promises of God.

> *"Therefore, as you received Christ Jesus the Lord, so walk in him, rooted and built up in him and established in the faith, just as you were taught, abounding in thanksgiving." — Colossians 2:6-7*

This verse encourages us to live in Christ, strengthened in faith, and overflowing with thankfulness. When you are truly thankful, negativity cannot take root in your heart. Thankful people don't complain, because gratitude shifts their focus to God's blessings.

THE POWER OF GRATITUDE: THE 10 LEPERS

In Luke 17:12-19, Jesus healed ten lepers, but only one returned to thank Him. The other nine walked away, forgetting the miracle they had just experienced. Jesus called out the ungratefulness of the nine to show us the importance of gratitude.

This story is a powerful reminder that God deserves our thankfulness. It also highlights how easy it is to take blessings for granted. Gratitude keeps us humble, reminding us that every good thing comes from God.

> *"Giving thanks always and for everything to God the Father in the name of our Lord Jesus Christ." — Ephesians 5:20*

Whatever you think about most is what will flow out of you. If your thoughts are filled with gratitude, your heart will overflow with thankfulness. But if your thoughts are focused on lack, negativity will dominate your life. Start your day by thanking God for His goodness, and you'll find that gratitude has the power to reframe your perspective.

> *"Oh give thanks to the Lord, for He is good, for His steadfast love endures forever!" — Psalm 107:1*

THANKFULNESS IN ACTION

Gratitude isn't just an emotion—it's an action. Take a moment right now to thank God for His blessings. Whether it's the breath in your lungs, the roof over your head, or the gift of salvation, there is always something to be thankful for.

THANKFULNESS

> *"Make a joyful noise to the Lord, all the earth! Serve the Lord with gladness! Come into His presence with singing! Know that the Lord, He is God! It is He who made us, and we are His; we are His people, and the sheep of His pasture. Enter His gates with thanksgiving, and His courts with praise! Give thanks to Him; bless His name! For the Lord is good; His steadfast love endures forever, and His faithfulness to all generations." — Psalm 100:1-5*

This passage reminds us that thankfulness is an act of worship. When we express gratitude, we acknowledge God's goodness and faithfulness in our lives.

GUARDING A THANKFUL HEART

Thankfulness is a choice, and it's a habit you can cultivate in your daily life. Here are some practical ways to grow in gratitude:

- Start your morning by listing three things you're thankful for.
- End your day by thanking God for His blessings.
- Speak words of gratitude to others—express your appreciation to the people in your life.

Gratitude shifts your focus from what you don't have to what you do have. It turns lack into abundance and complaining into praise.

THINK ON IT

Gratitude is not just a feeling; it's a lifestyle. When you live with a thankful heart, you align your life with God's goodness.

> *"Enter His gates with thanksgiving, and His courts with praise! Give thanks to Him; bless His name!" — Psalm 100:4*

Start each day by giving thanks to God, and watch how gratitude transforms your heart and your life. Thankfulness turns what you don't have into enough, and it opens the door to joy, peace, and abundance in every area of your life.

101 DEVOTIONALS — PART TWO

DAY 69
FAITH

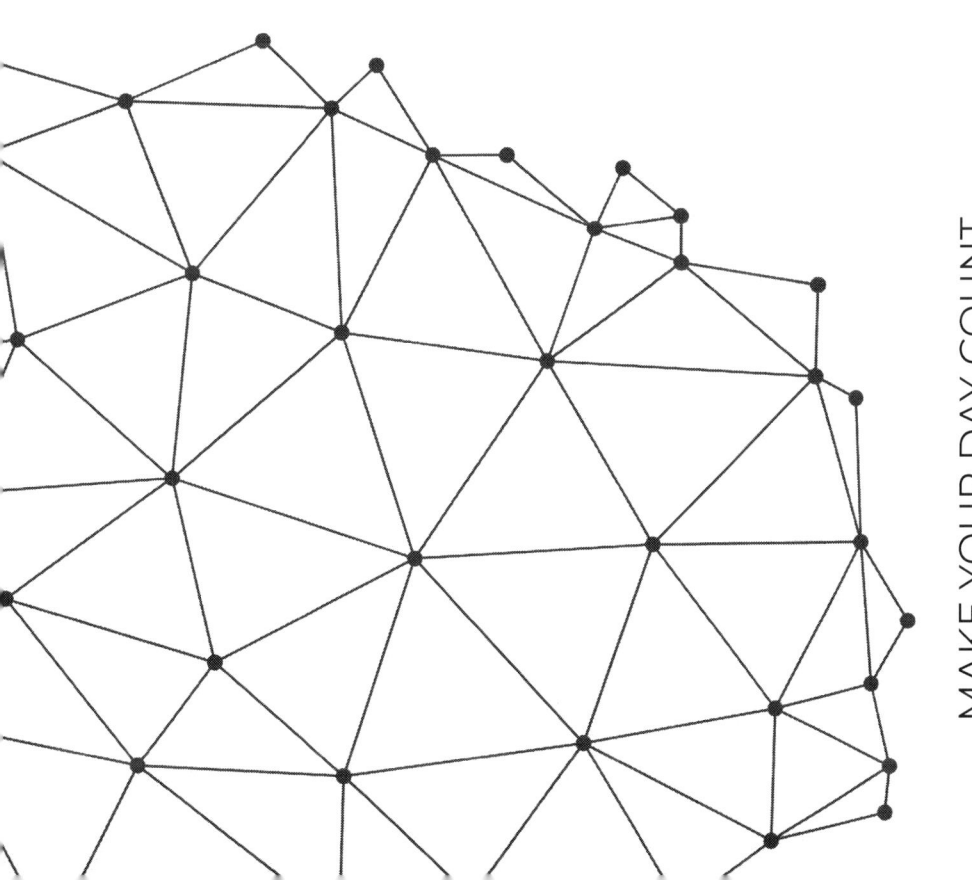

MAKE YOUR DAY COUNT

101 DEVOTIONALS — PART TWO

FAITH

BIG THOUGHT
Faith does not make things easy; it makes them possible.

> **Hebrews 11:1** – "Now faith is the assurance of things hoped for, the conviction of things not seen."

Faith is belief, trust, and loyalty to God—a firm conviction in something unseen but deeply known. It's more than just believing; it's trusting with all your heart that God is who He says He is and will do what He has promised.

Faith pleases God. The Bible says, "And without faith, it is impossible to please Him..." — Hebrews 11:6. When you trust God through every trial and circumstance, it brings Him joy. Your faith not only impacts your relationship with God but also plays a critical role in how you navigate life.

FAITH IN ACTION: THE MAJESTIC GAZELLE

Have you ever seen a gazelle in its natural habitat? These magnificent creatures can run up to 60 miles per hour, leap 15 feet into the air, and cover 30 feet in a single bound. But in captivity, their incredible abilities are rarely displayed. Confined by a small ditch and a fence, they live far below their potential.

However, in the wild, gazelles are free to reach their full design. They thrive on the vast, open plains, leaping and running as God intended.

Faith is like this. When you have faith in God, you are free to reach your full potential. Don't let fear, doubt, or circumstances keep you trapped. Faith is the key that unlocks the limitless potential God has placed within you. Step out in faith, and you'll experience the fullness of His plan for your life.

LET'S READ: WALKING ON WATER

> "Immediately, He made the disciples get into the boat and go before Him to the other side, while He dismissed the crowds. And after He had dismissed the crowds, He went up on the mountain by Himself to pray. When evening came, He was there alone, but the boat by this time was a long way from the land, beaten by the waves, for the wind was against them. In the fourth watch of the night, He came to them, walking on the sea. But when the disciples saw Him walking on the sea, they were terrified, and said, 'It is a ghost!' and they cried out in fear. But immediately Jesus spoke to them, saying, 'Take heart; it is I. Do not be afraid.' And Peter answered Him, 'Lord, if it is you, command me to come to you on the water.' He said, 'Come.' So Peter got out of the boat and walked on the water and came to Jesus. But when he saw the wind, he was afraid, and beginning to sink, he cried out, 'Lord, save me.' Jesus immediately reached out His hand and took hold of him, saying to him, 'O you of little faith, why did you doubt?' And when they got into the boat, the wind ceased. And those in the boat worshiped Him, saying, 'Truly, you are the Son of God.'"
> — Matthew 14:22-33

Peter's step of faith allowed him to walk on water toward Jesus. But when he shifted his focus from Jesus to the storm around him, he began to sink. The same is true in our own lives: when we take our eyes off Jesus and focus on our fears, doubts, and circumstances, we begin to sink. But faith keeps us walking above the storms of life.

Faith Is...

F- orsaking

A- ll

I

T- ake

H- im

Faith is believing in what God says, even when you don't see or feel it. It's stepping out in trust and confidence, knowing that He is with you and His promises are true.

> *"For in it the righteousness of God is revealed from faith for faith, as it is written, 'The righteous shall live by faith.'"* — Romans 1:17

LIVING BY FAITH

Faith is not a one-time decision—it's a daily walk. To grow from faith to faith, you must exercise your faith regularly. Faith grows when you intentionally lean into God and trust Him in every area of your life.

Here are a few ways to grow your faith:

- ◊ Praying: Spend time in conversation with God, sharing your heart and listening for His voice.

- ◊ Reading God's Word: The Bible is filled with promises that build your faith and remind you of God's goodness.

- ◊ Being part of a church community: Surround yourself with believers who encourage you to grow in your faith.

- ◊ Listening to worship music: Worship shifts your focus to God and strengthens your spirit.

- ◊ Spending time with the right people: Choose friends who build you up and inspire you to trust God more.

- ◊ Focusing on the positive: Guard your thoughts and choose to dwell on God's goodness instead of life's challenges.

- ◊ Dreaming big: Trust that God's plans for you are greater than you can imagine, and step out in faith to pursue them.

THINK ON IT

Faith doesn't make life easy—it makes the impossible possible.

> *"For we walk by faith, not by sight."* — 2 Corinthians 5:7

Faith is trusting in God's promises even when circumstances don't make sense. It's believing that He is working all things together for good and that He is faithful to fulfill His Word. As you grow in faith, you'll discover a life of freedom, purpose, and unshakable confidence in the One who holds your future.

Walk by faith, not by sight, and experience the incredible things God will do in and through your life!

DAY 70
GOD FIRST

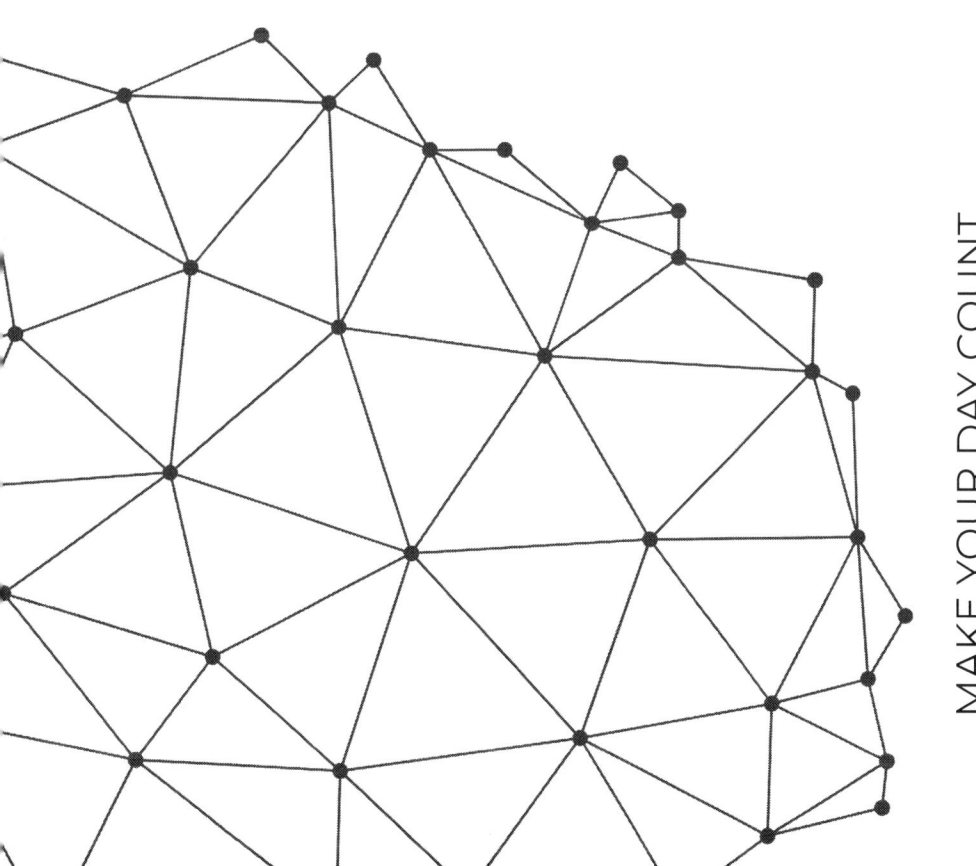

MAKE YOUR DAY COUNT

101 DEVOTIONALS — PART TWO

GOD FIRST

BIG THOUGHT
You will never be in second place by choosing to put God first every day.

> **Matthew 6:33** – "But seek first the kingdom of God and His righteousness, and all these things will be added to you."

Putting God first is not just a suggestion—it's the foundation of a life that stands strong through every season. God desires to be at the center of your life. As His beloved child, He longs to spend time with you and for you to know Him personally, just as He knows you.

When you prioritize God, you are laying the foundation for everything else in your life. That foundation is what holds you together when the storms of life come.

THE ROCK VS. THE SAND

> *"Everyone then who hears these words of mine and does them will be like a wise man who built his house on the rock. And the rain fell, and the floods came, and the winds blew and beat on that house, but it did not fall, because it had been founded on the rock. And everyone who hears these words of mine and does not do them will be like a foolish man who built his house on the sand. And the rain fell, and the floods came, and the winds blew and beat against that house, and it fell, and great was the fall of it."*
> *— Matthew 7:24-27*

When you put God first, you are building your life on the Rock—Jesus Christ. He is the cornerstone, the foundation upon which everything in your life should rest. Ephesians 2:20 reminds us that Jesus is the cornerstone, the essential piece that holds everything together.

Life will always throw distractions your way—jobs, friends, social media, sports—but God wants to be your priority. When He is the foundation, everything else aligns and strengthens.

> *"No one can serve two masters, for either he will hate the one and love the other, or he will be devoted to the one and despise the other. You cannot serve God and money." — Matthew 6:24*

> *"For where your treasure is, there your heart will be also." — Matthew 6:21*

God wants to be the treasure of your heart. When you put Him first, your heart naturally aligns with His will, and your life begins to reflect His goodness.

THE LEANING TOWER OF PISA

Every year, scientists visit the Leaning Tower of Pisa in Italy to monitor its slow descent. The 179-foot tower shifts about one-twentieth of an inch per year and is now 17 feet out of alignment. Renovations have stabilized it, but the issue remains—the tower's foundation is faulty, only 10 feet deep.

The tower began to lean before it was even completed because it wasn't built on a solid foundation.

In the same way, if God isn't your priority, your foundation in life will be unstable. Without God, your life will lean in the wrong direction, leaving you vulnerable to the storms of life. But when your life is built on the Word of God, you have a firm foundation that withstands anything.

THINK ON IT

When you put God first, you're building your life on a foundation that cannot be shaken. Like the wise man who built his house on the rock, your life will stand firm, no matter what storms come your way.

GOD FIRST

> *"But seek first the kingdom of God and His righteousness, and all these things will be added to you."* — *Matthew 6:33*

God desires to be the treasure of your heart, your anchor, and your cornerstone. Don't let distractions or worldly pursuits take priority over Him. Instead, align your life with His will and trust Him to guide your steps. When you choose to put God first, you'll find that everything else in your life falls into place. He is the Rock you can always depend on!

101 DEVOTIONALS — PART TWO

DAY 71
FEAR NOT

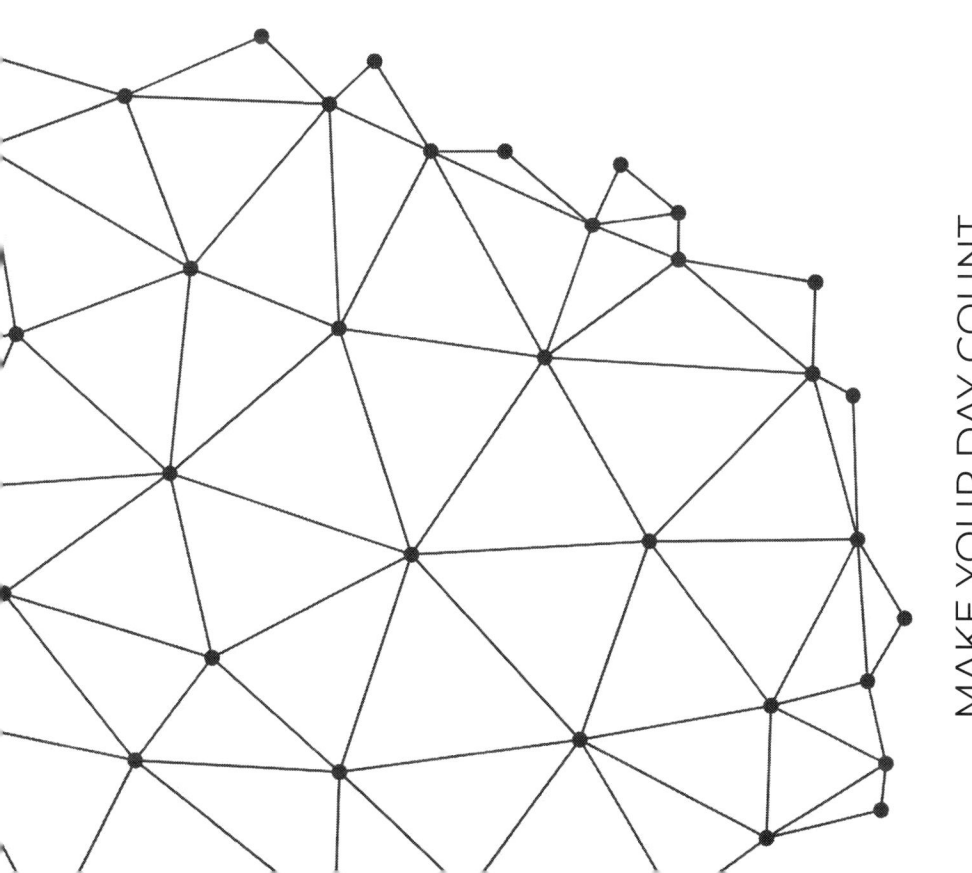

MAKE YOUR DAY COUNT

101 DEVOTIONALS — PART TWO

FEAR NOT

BIG THOUGHT
The fears we don't face become our limits.

> **2 Timothy 1:7** – "For God gave us a spirit not of fear but of power and love and self-control."

At some level, we all experience fear. It's a natural human emotion, but it's important to remember that fear doesn't come from God. Scripture reminds us:

> *"For God gave us a spirit not of fear but of power and love and self-control." — 2 Timothy 1:7*

God has equipped you with everything you need to face fear with courage. You don't have to fear when you know that God is on your side.

Fear has two meanings:

- ◊ Forget Everything And Run
- ◊ Face Everything And Rise

The choice is yours!

A LESSON FROM THE LOST GIRL

In 2006, a three-year-old girl wandered into a cornfield on her family's farm and became lost. For 12 hours, people from the community joined together in a search to find her. When they finally located her, she was scared but overjoyed to be found.

This story reminds us that fear can grip us in moments of uncertainty, but God is always with us. Just as people rallied to help the little girl, God is always by your side, walking with you through life's challenges.

TRUSTING IN GOD'S PRESENCE

The enemy wants to fill your heart with fear and doubt. But Jesus speaks peace to our hearts, encouraging us to trust Him fully.

King David also knew what it was like to face fear. In Psalm 56, he prayed to God while being captured by the Philistines. Instead of giving in to fear, he placed his trust in God.

> *"When I am afraid, I put my trust in you. In God, whose word I praise, in God I trust; I shall not be afraid. What can flesh do to me?" — Psalm 56:3-4*

When fear tries to take over, choose to fix your eyes on the One who is greater than anything you might face.

TAKE A DEEPER LOOK

Scripture is filled with promises of God's protection and presence in the face of fear:

> *"Fear not, for I am with you; be not dismayed, for I am your God; I will strengthen you, I will help you, I will uphold you with my righteous right hand." — Isaiah 41:10*

> *"There is no fear in love, but perfect love casts out fear. For fear has to do with punishment, and whoever fears has not been perfected in love." — 1 John 4:18*

> *"So we can confidently say, 'The Lord is my helper; I will not fear; what can man do to me?'" — Hebrews 13:6*

One of the most powerful examples of faith in the midst of fear is the story of Peter walking on water (Matthew 14:22-33). At first, Peter stepped out in faith, walking toward Jesus on the water. But when he shifted his focus to the storm around him, fear crept in, and he began to sink.

This story reminds us to keep our eyes on Jesus. Fear can only sink us when we let it distract us from the One who holds us up.

FROM FEAR TO FAITH

> "While He was still speaking, someone from the ruler's house came and said, 'Your daughter is dead; do not trouble the Teacher any more.' But Jesus, on hearing this, answered him, 'Do not fear; only believe, and she will be well.' ... But taking her by the hand, He called, saying, 'Child, arise.' And her spirit returned, and she got up at once." — Luke 8:49-56

Jairus faced an overwhelming situation, but Jesus urged him to replace fear with faith. The miracle that followed showed the power of trusting in Jesus even in the darkest moments.

THE WORDS OF JESUS

When fear tries to imprison you, remember Jesus' words:

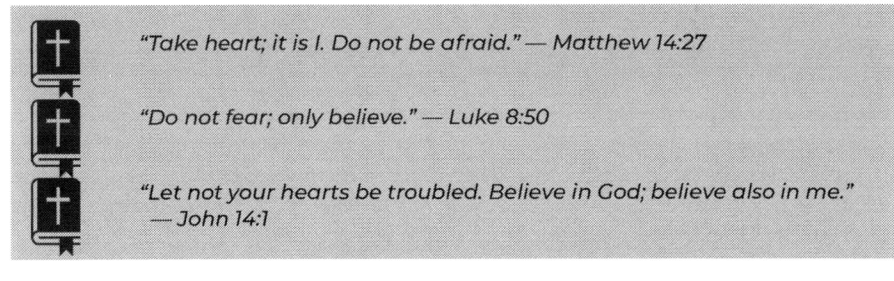

> "Take heart; it is I. Do not be afraid." — Matthew 14:27

> "Do not fear; only believe." — Luke 8:50

> "Let not your hearts be troubled. Believe in God; believe also in me." — John 14:1

These truths remind us that God is bigger than our fears. His perfect love casts out fear, and His presence gives us the courage to face whatever comes our way.

THINK ON IT

The fears we don't face become the limits in our lives. God calls you to step out in faith and trust Him completely. Remember, fear doesn't come from God—He has given you a spirit of power, love, and self-control (2 Timothy 1:7).

> *"Fear not, for I am with you; be not dismayed, for I am your God."*
> — Isaiah 41:10

Step out of the boat like Peter. Face your fears, and walk in faith. Trust in the Lord, and He will guide you through every storm. Fear does not define your destiny—God does. FEAR NOT!

DAY 72
WORDS

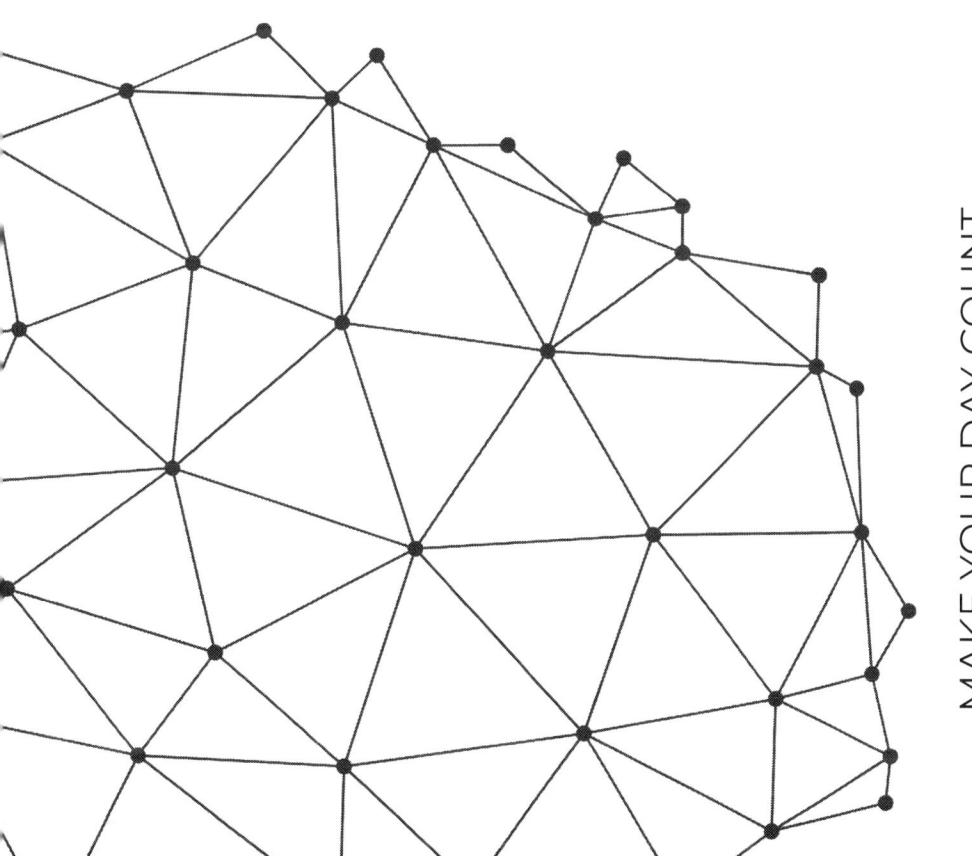

MAKE YOUR DAY COUNT

101 DEVOTIONALS — PART TWO

WORDS

BIG THOUGHT

Words are like an elevator; they can bring you up or bring you down. Words have power!

> **Proverbs 12:18** – "There is one whose rash words are like sword thrusts, but the tongue of the wise brings healing."

Sticks and stones may break my bones, but words will never hurt me...That saying is a BIG FAT LIE! Words carry immense power. They can heal or hurt, inspire or destroy. Words have started wars and mended broken hearts. Today, many people seek professional help because of the damaging words spoken over them.

Words have the power to bring health or hurt, life or death. That's why it's critical to choose your words wisely and to "taste" them before speaking.

> *"Death and life are in the power of the tongue, and those who love it will eat its fruits." — Proverbs 18:21*

> *"If you are snared in the words of your mouth, caught in the words of your mouth." — Proverbs 6:2*

101 DEVOTIONALS — PART TWO

Healthy Words

- ◊ You're Awesome
- ◊ You're Powerful
- ◊ You're Beautiful
- ◊ You're Wonderful
- ◊ You're Fantastic
- ◊ You're Amazing
- ◊ You're Incredible
- ◊ You're Strong
- ◊ You're Smart
- ◊ You're Lovely

Hurtful Words

- ◊ You're Ugly
- ◊ You're Stupid
- ◊ You're Crazy
- ◊ You're Gross
- ◊ You're Weak
- ◊ You're Disgusting
- ◊ You're Trash
- ◊ You're Broken
- ◊ You're Unwanted
- ◊ You're Worthless

THE POWER OF WORDS

Words can build up or tear down. God calls us to speak life and healing, to use our words to encourage, uplift, and inspire. Speak positivity, not negativity. Speak hope, not fear. Speak life, not death.

A father who traveled frequently for work made it a tradition to take his son to their favorite restaurant when he returned home. On one occasion, the father spent the meal telling his son how awesome, incredible, and fantastic he was. The boy's face lit up with joy. So overwhelmed by the encouragement, the son accidentally knocked over his father's food and exclaimed, "Tell me more! Tell me more!"

This story illustrates the immense power of words to nurture and build up.

THE POWER OF POSITIVE WORDS

Research supports what the Bible teaches about speaking life. Harvard Business Review conducted a study that found it takes about 6 positive phrases or affirmations to foster success and productivity.

> "So also the tongue is a small member, yet it boasts of great things. How great a forest is set ablaze by such a small fire! And the tongue is a fire, a world of unrighteousness. The tongue is set among our members, staining the whole body, setting on fire the entire course of life, and set on fire by hell." — James 3:5-6

The tongue may be small, but it holds tremendous power. It can cause damage like a wildfire or bring life and healing to those around you. Be intentional with your words, as they can never be taken back once spoken. Choose to be a life-giver.

THE CHICAGO FIRE

On October 8, 1871, a fire started in the barn of Patrick and Catherine O'Leary. The story goes that a cow kicked over a lantern, sparking a fire that would burn 3 1/3 square miles, destroy over $192 million in property, and leave 100,000 people homeless. More than 300 lives were lost—all from one small spark.

This story is a sobering reminder of the destructive power of even a small spark—just like the destructive potential of careless words.

> "For by your words you will be justified, and by your words you will be condemned." — Matthew 12:37

BUILDING A FIREWALL AROUND YOUR WORDS

- ◊ Choose words wisely. Speak life and encouragement,

not negativity with your words.

- ◊ Be intentional with your speech. Positive words create positive environments.
- ◊ Guard your self-talk. Speak uplifting words to yourself, not just to others.
- ◊ Let your words reflect God's love.

> *"Walk in wisdom toward outsiders, making the best use of the time. Let your speech always be gracious, seasoned with salt, so that you may know how you ought to answer each person."* — Colossians 4:5-6

💡 THINK ON IT

Words are like seeds—you can plant hope, joy, and love, or sow hurt, anger, and division. The power of your words lies in the choice you make before you speak them.

> *"Death and life are in the power of the tongue, and those who love it will eat its fruits."* — Proverbs 18:21

What you say has the ability to change someone's day, their mindset, or even their life. Speak life. Choose kindness. Use words to uplift, encourage, and inspire. Once spoken, words cannot be taken back, so let every word you speak be seasoned with grace and reflect the love of God.

Be intentional with your words today and always—speak life into those around you!

DAY 73
ATTITUDE

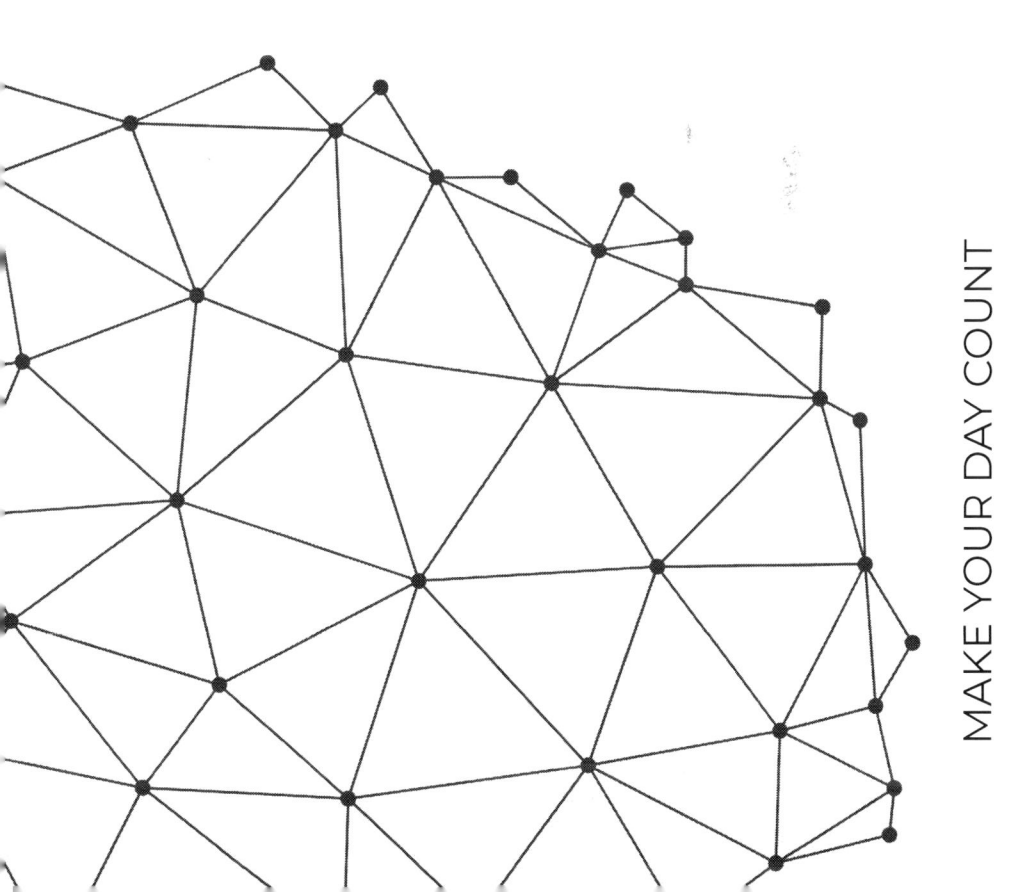

MAKE YOUR DAY COUNT

101 DEVOTIONALS — PART TWO

ATTITUDE

BIG THOUGHT
The only difference between a good day and a bad day is your attitude.

> **Ephesians 5:1** – Therefore, be imitators of God, as beloved children.

Two frogs, lost and thirsty, stumbled upon a large pot of cream. Thinking it was water, they jumped in, only to find themselves sinking in the thick liquid. Desperately trying to escape, they scrambled up the sides of the pot, but the slippery cream made escape impossible.

After some time, one frog said, "It's no use; we're going to die," and gave up, sinking to his fate. The other frog, however, refused to give up. "Don't quit; change your attitude!" he said to himself. He kept swimming and paddling, refusing to let the cream pull him under. Eventually, his perseverance churned the cream into butter, allowing him to hop out to safety.

Lesson: The attitude of the second frog was the difference between life and death. A positive attitude can change your perspective and your outcome, even in the toughest of situations.

101 DEVOTIONALS — PART TWO

Your Attitude Can...

- ◊ Make you or break you.
- ◊ Heal you or hurt you.
- ◊ Make you successful or a failure.
- ◊ Give you friends or enemies.
- ◊ Make you happy or miserable.

> *"Therefore, be imitators of God, as beloved children."*
> *— Ephesians 5:1*

Your attitude determines how you respond to life's challenges. The choice is always yours. Let's look at an example of how a negative attitude can affect your perspective.

GRANDPA AND THE MUSTACHE

One day, a cranky grandpa laid down for a nap. His mischievous grandson, wanting to play a prank, smeared some smelly cheese on grandpa's mustache. When grandpa woke up, he sniffed the air and growled, "This room stinks!"

Frustrated, he wandered through the house, shouting, "This whole house stinks!" Finally, he walked outside and yelled, "The whole world stinks!"

The truth? The problem wasn't the room, the house, or the world—the problem was right under grandpa's nose.

Lesson: Ninety-five percent of the time, when life feels like it "stinks," the problem isn't the world around us; it's our attitude. Change your attitude, and you'll change your world.

QUOTES ON ATTITUDE

> *"Your attitude, not your aptitude, will determine your altitude."*
> *— Zig Ziglar*

> *"Attitude is a little thing that makes a big difference."*
> *— Winston Churchill*

ATTITUDE

THE BLIND MEN AND THEIR POSITIVE ATTITUDE

> *"And as they went out of Jericho, a great crowd followed Him. And behold, there were two blind men sitting by the roadside, and when they heard that Jesus was passing by, they cried out, 'Lord, have mercy on us, Son of David!' The crowd rebuked them, telling them to be silent, but they cried out all the more, 'Lord, have mercy on us, Son of David!' And stopping, Jesus called them and said, 'What do you want me to do for you?' They said to Him, 'Lord, let our eyes be opened.' And Jesus, in pity, touched their eyes, and immediately they recovered their sight and followed Him."* — Matthew 20:29-34

Lesson: The blind men's positive attitude led them to cry out to Jesus, even when others tried to silence them. They didn't let the negativity of the crowd discourage them. Instead, they remained focused on Christ, believing in His power to heal them.

Your attitude shapes your outcomes. Even in difficult situations, you have the power to change a bad attitude into a positive one. Trust in God's power, and let your attitude reflect hope, faith, and perseverance.

THE POWER OF ATTITUDE

Your attitude has the ability to shape your life. It affects your perspective on challenges, your relationships, and the way you perceive the world. Remember, the outcome of your situation often depends on the attitude you choose to take—and the power of God working through you.

TAKE A DEEPER LOOK

> *"A joyful heart is good medicine, but a crushed spirit dries up the bones."* — Proverbs 17:22

> *"Do all things without grumbling or disputing,"* — Philippians 2:14

> *"Finally, brothers, whatever is true, whatever is honorable, whatever is just, whatever is pure, whatever is lovely, whatever is commendable, if there is any excellence, if there is anything worthy of praise, think about these things. What you have learned and received and heard and seen in me—practice these things, and the God of peace will be with you."* — Philippians 4:8-9

101 DEVOTIONALS — PART TWO

> *"Have this mind among yourselves, which is yours in Christ Jesus,"*
> *— Philippians 2:5*

💡 THINK ON IT

Your attitude is one of the most powerful tools you have. It can lift you up or pull you down. It can turn a bad day into a good one or make a small problem feel like a mountain. The choice is always yours—how will you respond?

> *"A joyful heart is good medicine, but a crushed spirit dries up the bones." — Proverbs 17:22*

Even in tough times, a positive attitude can bring healing, strength, and hope. Like the second frog who refused to give up, your perspective can change the outcome. Shift your focus from your problems to God's promises. Let your attitude reflect trust, joy, and perseverance, knowing that with God, all things are possible.

Choose today to guard your heart and your attitude—because the way you think and respond will shape your world!

DAY 74
CHOICES

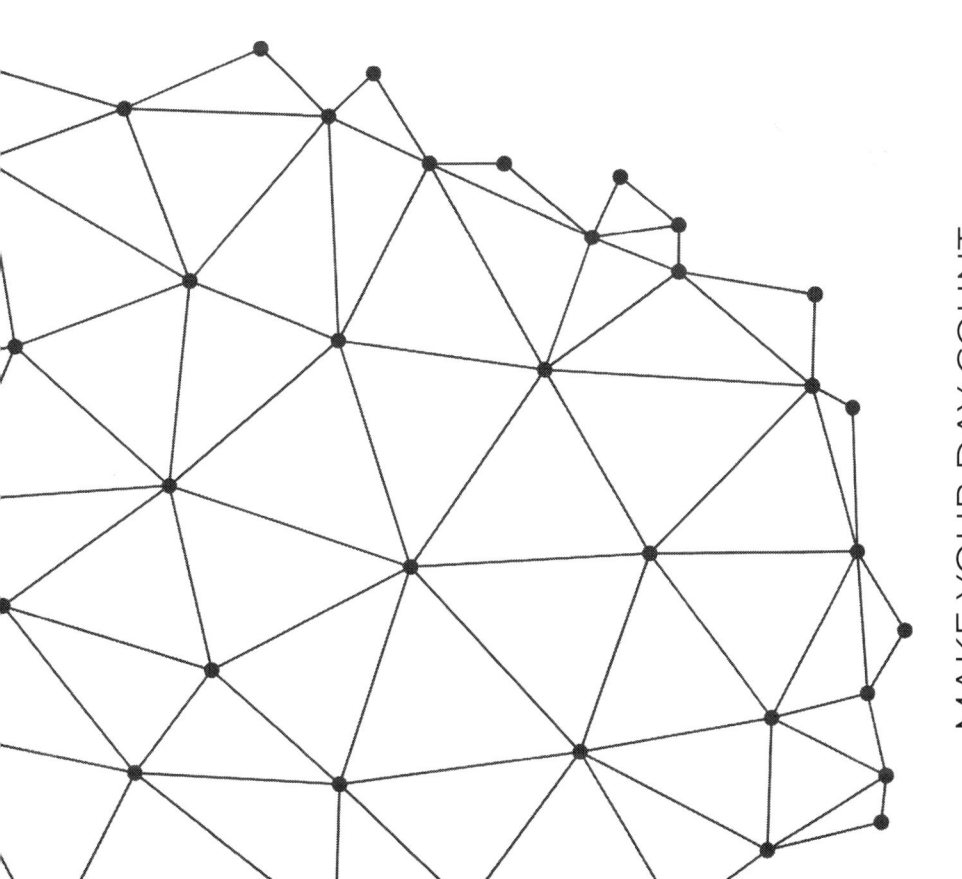

MAKE YOUR DAY COUNT

101 DEVOTIONALS — PART TWO

CHOICES

BIG THOUGHT
Choices have the power to determine your destiny

> "Life is a matter of choices, and every choice you make makes you." — John C. Maxwell

Every day is filled with decisions. Some may seem small, but every choice matters. Over time, the choices you make determine the direction of your life. Think about the decisions you face every day:

- ◊ To get up or sleep in
- ◊ To go to school or stay home
- ◊ To work hard or slack off
- ◊ To choose the right friends or the wrong ones
- ◊ To focus on positive or negative thoughts
- ◊ To have a good attitude or a bad one

Every choice matters, and every decision builds the foundation of your future. Remember, in the game of life, you are not born a winner or a loser—you are born a chooser.

> "See, I have set before you today life and good, death and evil. If you obey the commandments of the Lord your God that I command you today, by loving the Lord your God, by walking in His ways, and by keeping His commandments and His statutes and His rules, then you shall live and multiply, and the Lord your God will bless you in the land that you are entering to take possession of it."
> — Deuteronomy 30:15

STORY: THE CHOICES OF THE LOST SON

The parable of the Prodigal Son (Luke 15:11-27) teaches us about the consequences of our choices. The younger son chose to take his inheritance early and squander it in reckless living. His decisions led him to a place of desperation—lost, starving, and alone. But when he chose to return to his father, he was met with love, forgiveness, and restoration.

Lesson: The choices you make today shape your future. What choices are you making now to prepare for the life you want tomorrow?

THE POWER OF CHOICE

Did you know the average person makes about 70 decisions every day? That's 25,500 choices a year, and over 70 years, you'll make 1,788,500 decisions!

> "Do not be deceived: God is not mocked, for whatever one sows, that will he also reap. For the one who sows to his own flesh will from the flesh reap corruption, but the one who sows to the Spirit will from the Spirit reap eternal life." — Galatians 6:7-8

Your choices have consequences. If you sow good choices, you will reap blessings. If you sow bad choices, you will reap hardship. Every decision, big or small, matters.

STORY: THE FARMER AND THE HIRED MAN

A farmer hired a man to help with various tasks. The man was an excellent worker, completing jobs like painting the barn and cutting wood in record time. But when tasked with sorting a pile of potatoes into three categories—seed potatoes, food for hogs, and potatoes good enough to sell—the man barely got started. Frustrated, the farmer asked, "What's the matter here?" The hired man replied, "I can work hard, but I can't make decisions!"

Lesson: Making wise decisions is one of the most critical skills for success. Hard work is important, but without the ability to choose wisely, you will struggle to reach your goals.

QUOTES ON CHOICES

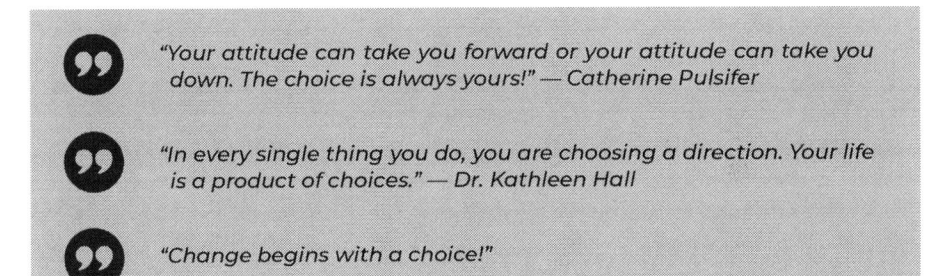

> "Your attitude can take you forward or your attitude can take you down. The choice is always yours!" — Catherine Pulsifer

> "In every single thing you do, you are choosing a direction. Your life is a product of choices." — Dr. Kathleen Hall

> "Change begins with a choice!"

THE LION AND THE GAZELLE

Every morning in Africa, a gazelle wakes up knowing it must run faster than the fastest lion to survive. Similarly, every morning, a lion wakes up knowing it must run faster than the slowest gazelle to avoid starvation.

It doesn't matter whether you are a lion or a gazelle—when the sun comes up, YOU HAVE A CHOICE!

TAKE A DEEPER LOOK

Scripture reminds us of the importance of choices:

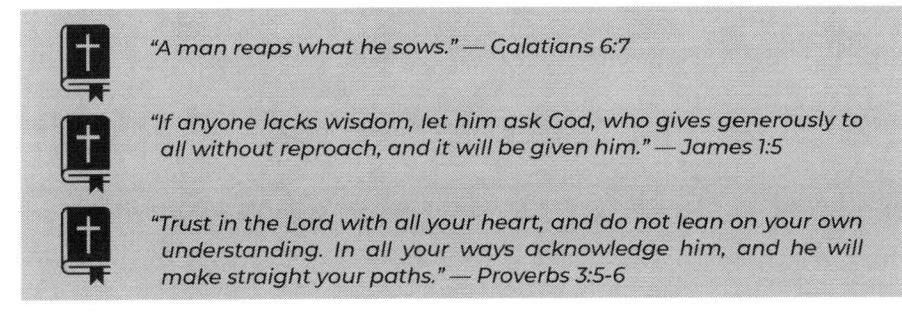

> "A man reaps what he sows." — Galatians 6:7

> "If anyone lacks wisdom, let him ask God, who gives generously to all without reproach, and it will be given him." — James 1:5

> "Trust in the Lord with all your heart, and do not lean on your own understanding. In all your ways acknowledge him, and he will make straight your paths." — Proverbs 3:5-6

THINK ON IT

Every day, you are faced with countless decisions, and each one shapes the person you are becoming and the life you are building. Choices are powerful—they have the ability to determine your direction, impact your future, and influence your relationships. The good news is, you get to choose!

> *"See, I have set before you today life and good, death and evil."*
> *— Deuteronomy 30:15*

God has given you the freedom to make decisions, but with that freedom comes responsibility. Are you sowing seeds of life, obedience, and trust in Him? Or are you allowing fear, complacency, or selfish desires to guide you?

Remember, even small choices matter. Every decision you make today lays the foundation for your tomorrow. Choose wisely, and trust God to guide your steps. Your future is shaped one choice at a time—so choose life, choose faith, and choose to honor Him.

DAY 75
PERSEVERANCE

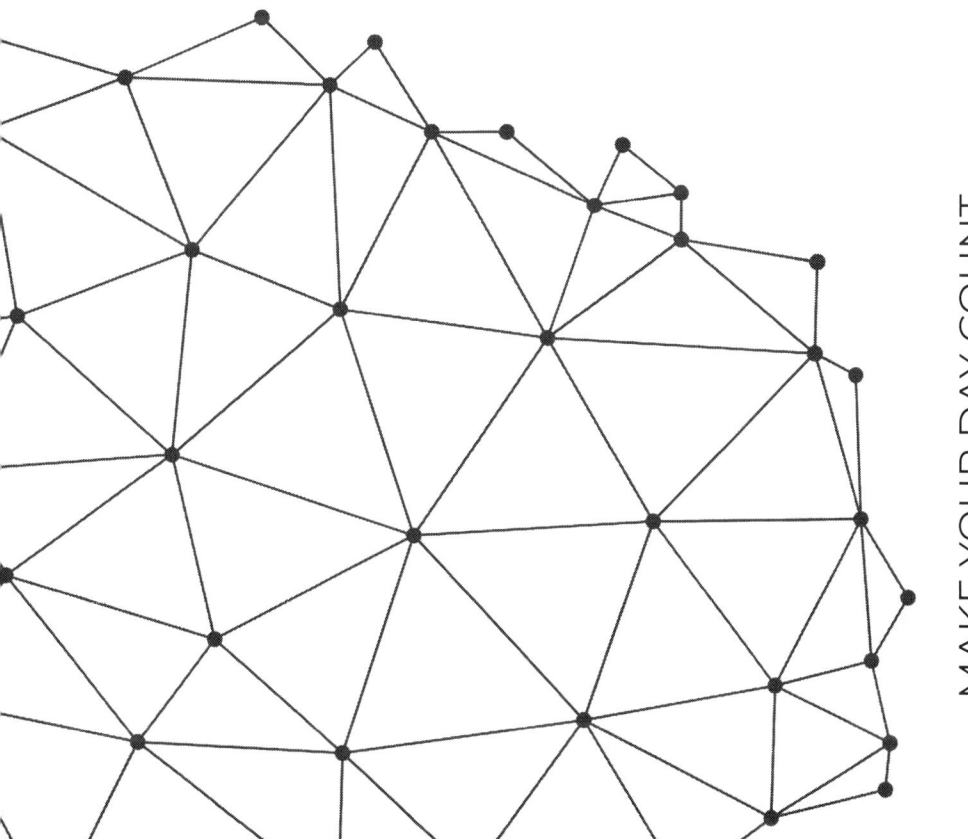

MAKE YOUR DAY COUNT

101 DEVOTIONALS — PART TWO

PERSEVERANCE

BIG THOUGHT
Do it anyway.

> "Perseverance is the hard work you do after you get tired of doing the hard work you already did." — Newt Gingrich

What is perseverance? Perseverance means doing something despite difficulties or delays in achieving success. Life is filled with challenges, but it's important to trust the process, stay committed, and work hard to finish the task, achieve the dream, or fulfill the calling God has placed on your life.

No matter what you're facing, you have the ability to win because God has made you more than a conqueror.

> "No, in all these things we are more than conquerors through Him who loved us." — Romans 8:37

> "And when He got into the boat, His disciples followed Him. And behold, there arose a great storm on the sea, so that the boat was being swamped by the waves; but He was asleep. And they went and woke Him, saying, 'Save us, Lord; we are perishing.' And He said to them, 'Why are you afraid, O you of little faith?' Then He rose and rebuked the winds and the sea, and there was a great calm. And the men marveled, saying, 'What sort of man is this, that even winds and sea obey Him?'" — Matthew 8:23-27

In life, storms will come. Perseverance is what allows you to press on and be victorious, even when the waves are crashing around you. Instead of being consumed by fear, trust in God's power and tell your storm how great He is.

PRODUCE IT ANYWAY

Henry Ford, the automobile pioneer, once envisioned a revolutionary new engine—the V-8. However, when Ford presented his idea to his engineers, they told him it was impossible. Ford's response? "Produce it anyway."

For a year, his team worked tirelessly, only to report failure after failure. Yet Ford never gave up. He told them to keep trying, and eventually, they succeeded in creating the V-8 engine.

> "And let us not grow weary of doing good, for in due season we will reap, if we do not give up." — Galatians 6:9

Perseverance is refusing to quit when others say it can't be done. Success often comes after the hardest work and the longest wait.

Perseverance is about continuing to work toward the goal, even when the process is hard and the results seem far away.

GET BACK UP

Life will knock you down—it's inevitable. Perseverance is the ability to get back up, again and again, and keep moving forward. The obstacles you face will test your character and your faith, but God promises that perseverance will lead to hope.

> "...and endurance produces character, and character produces hope." — Romans 5:4

> "Rejoice not over me, O my enemy; when I fall, I shall rise; when I sit in darkness, the Lord will be a light to me." — Micah 7:8

THE MAN LOST IN THE SNOWSTORM

A man lost in a snowstorm stumbled through the blizzard, too tired to go on. He fell into the snow, ready to give up. But as he lay there, he realized he had tripped over another body. Brushing away the snow, he discovered the person was still alive.

Summoning all his strength, the man lifted the body onto his shoulders and pushed through the storm. Eventually, he found a cabin and safety. In helping another, he saved himself.

Perseverance often involves putting others before yourself. The determination to keep going can lead to salvation—not just for you, but for those around you.

> *"Blessed is the man who remains steadfast under trial, for when he has stood the test, he will receive the crown of life, which God has promised to those who love Him." — James 1:12*

Perseverance leads to blessing. When you remain steadfast and faithful through life's challenges, God promises a reward greater than you can imagine—the crown of life.

THINK ON IT

Do you recall a time in your life where you had to have perseverance?

Life is full of storms, challenges, and setbacks, but perseverance is what allows you to rise above. It's about pressing forward, even when the path is difficult and the results seem far away. Remember, you are more than a conqueror through Christ who loves you. "Tough times don't last, but tough people do."

Perseverance means trusting in God's strength when your own runs out, getting back up after every fall, and believing that the best is yet to come. Don't give up—your endurance leads to blessings beyond what you can imagine.

> *"Blessed is the man who remains steadfast under trial, for when he has stood the test, he will receive the crown of life, which God has promised to those who love Him." — James 1:12*

101 DEVOTIONALS — PART TWO

DAY 76
I AM'S

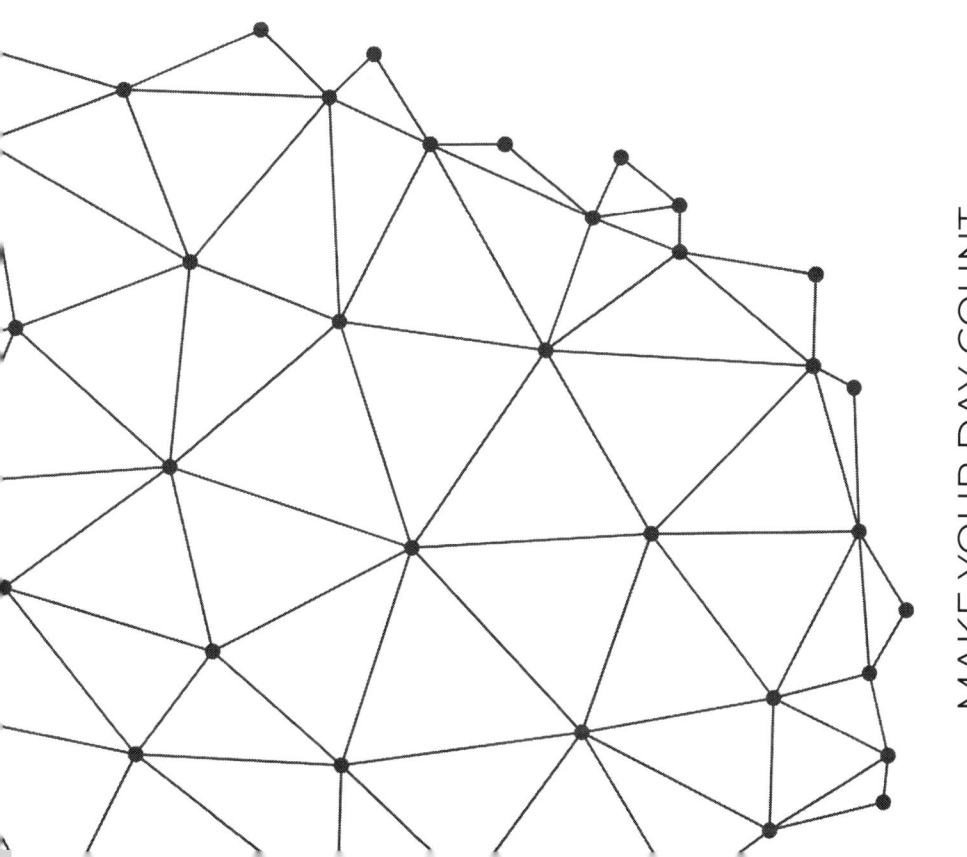

MAKE YOUR DAY COUNT

101 DEVOTIONALS — PART TWO

I AM'S

BIG THOUGHT

People's opinion of me doesn't define who I AM; who I AM comes from who HE is!

> **Exodus 3:14** – God said to Moses, "I am who I am." And he said, "Say this to the people of Israel: 'I am has sent me to you..

In Exodus 3:14-15, God reveals Himself to Moses as "I AM." This eternal name signifies His infinite and unchanging nature: "God said to Moses, 'I am who I am.' And he said, 'Say this to the people of Israel: I AM has sent me to you.'"

The same God who called Himself "I AM" in the Old Testament sent His Son, Jesus Christ, who declared seven "I AM's" in the Gospel of John, showing us who He is:

- ◊ I AM the bread of life. (John 6:35) – Jesus sustains you.
- ◊ I AM the light of the world. (John 8:12) – Jesus illuminates your path and provides truth.
- ◊ I AM the door. (John 10:9) – Jesus is the only way to salvation.
- ◊ I AM the true vine. (John 15:1) – Jesus nourishes your soul.
- ◊ I AM the good shepherd. (John 10:11) – Jesus takes care

of all your needs.

- ◇ I AM the resurrection and the life. (John 11:25) – Jesus brings life in the midst of death.
- ◇ I AM the way, the truth, and the life. (John 14:6) – Jesus is the source of everything.

No one can ever be truly fulfilled without Jesus. Knowing who HE is helps you understand who YOU are in Him.

WHO ARE YOU?

When you know who you are, you know where you are going. Your identity in Christ is unshakable. Here are some of your "I AM's" according to God's Word:

- ◇ I AM a child of God. (Romans 8:16)
- ◇ I AM redeemed from the hand of the enemy. (Psalm 107:2)
- ◇ I AM a new creature. (2 Corinthians 5:17)
- ◇ I AM an imitator of Jesus. (Ephesians 5:1)
- ◇ I AM justified. (Romans 5:1)
- ◇ I AM more than a conqueror. (Romans 8:37)
- ◇ I AM the light of the world. (Matthew 5:14)
- ◇ I AM not moved by what I see. (2 Corinthians 4:18)
- ◇ I AM above only and not beneath. (Deuteronomy 28:13)
- ◇ I AM an heir of eternal life. (1 John 5:11-12)

STORY: THE GIRL WHO KNEW WHO SHE WAS

During a motivational talk at school, a young girl stood up and boldly declared, "I know who I am!" Though her peers laughed, she stood confidently, fueled by her dream of becoming a professional singer. Her determination caught the attention of the speaker, who paused to say, "Knowing who you are is the most important thing in life."

I AM'S

This girl didn't let the opinions of others define her. She went on to fulfill her dream because she knew who she was and stayed true to her identity.

Lesson: Confidence in who you are shapes your future. When you know who you are in Christ, you can overcome the doubts and opinions of others.

AFFIRMATIONS FOR THE DAY

Speak these affirmations over yourself to align with who God has created you to be:

- ◊ I AM kingdom minded.
- ◊ I AM a servant leader.
- ◊ I AM a leader of leaders.
- ◊ I AM a world-changer.
- ◊ I AM a lifetime learner.
- ◊ I AM an energy producer.
- ◊ I AM a motivator.
- ◊ I AM a difference maker.
- ◊ I AM an odds defier.
- ◊ I AM a winner.

CONFESSION: YOUR "I AM'S"

Just as Jesus declared His "I AM's," you have the authority to declare yours. What are your "I AM's"?

- ◊ I AM faithful.
- ◊ I AM strong.
- ◊ I AM dependable.
- ◊ I AM honest.
- ◊ I AM alert.

- I AM unstoppable.
- I AM creative.
- I AM passionate.
- I AM honorable.

THINK ON IT

When you root your identity in Christ, no opinion, failure, or criticism can shake you. The great "I AM" has defined you, loved you, and called you His own.

> *"I AM who God says I am, not what the world says I should be."*

Your "I AM" statements are not just affirmations; they are declarations of the truth found in God's Word. Speak them boldly, knowing that your identity and worth come from the One who created you.

DAY 77
LEADERSHIP

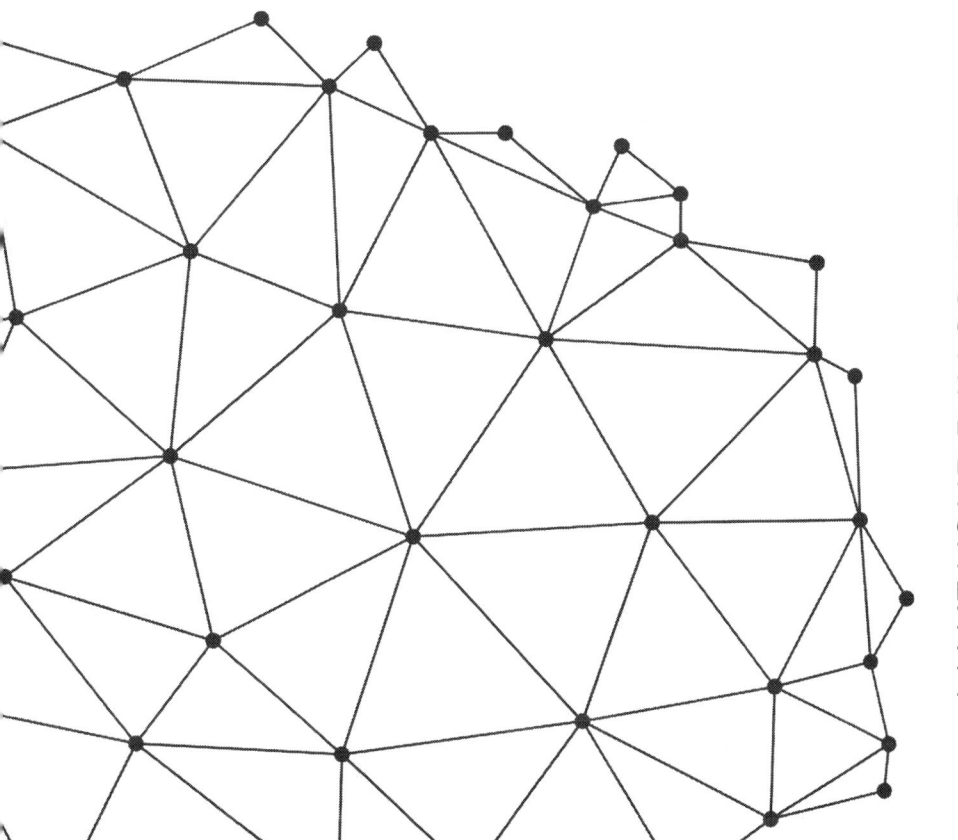

MAKE YOUR DAY COUNT

101 DEVOTIONALS — PART TWO

LEADERSHIP

BIG THOUGHT
Leaders find a way to win.

> "A leader is one who knows the way, goes the way, and shows the way." — John C. Maxwell

John 14:6 – Jesus said to him, "I am the way, and the truth, and the life. No one comes to the Father except through me."

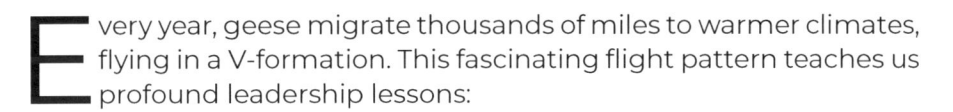

Every year, geese migrate thousands of miles to warmer climates, flying in a V-formation. This fascinating flight pattern teaches us profound leadership lessons:

- ◊ Rotation of Leadership: The lead goose rotates with others. When one goose gets tired, it moves to the wing, and another takes its place. This shows that leadership requires shared responsibility and teamwork.

- ◊ Uplift Through Unity: Each goose's wing flap creates an uplift for the one behind it, allowing them to conserve energy. This demonstrates the power of unity—when everyone works together, the team is stronger.

- ◊ Support in Times of Need: When a goose is sick or injured, two others leave the formation to stay with it until it recovers. This highlights the importance of caring for and supporting team members during challenging times.

- ◊ Encouragement: Geese in the back honk to encourage those at the front to keep going. This symbolizes how essential encouragement and motivation are in leadership.

The geese show us that leadership thrives on unity, shared responsibilities, mutual support, and encouragement. Together, great things can be accomplished.

WHAT MAKES A GREAT LEADER?

- ◊ Motivation & Encouragement: A great leader knows how to inspire and lift others, especially during uncertainty or hardship.
- ◊ Decision Making: Leaders make wise decisions, even in the face of challenges.
- ◊ Leading by Example: True leadership is not about words—it's about action. Great leaders model the behavior they want to see in others and lead by example.

> *"But seek first the kingdom of God and his righteousness, and all these things will be added to you." — Matthew 6:33*

To be a great leader, you must first seek God's will above all else. Leadership begins with putting God at the center of your life.

YOU ARE CALLED TO LEAD

Leadership isn't just about standing on a stage or commanding a team; it's about living a life that follows Jesus. When Jesus called His disciples, they were ordinary people with flaws and weaknesses, but He used them to change the world.

Jesus didn't just save you from something—He saved you for something.

You are called to lead in your home, your workplace, your community, and your daily life.

QUALITIES OF GREAT LEADERS

- ◊ Leaders believe there is always a way.
- ◊ Leaders are encouraging.
- ◊ Leaders operate with excellence.
- ◊ Leaders maintain a positive attitude.
- ◊ Leaders lead a healthy lifestyle.
- ◊ Leaders surround themselves with the right people.
- ◊ Leaders live by the Word of God.
- ◊ Leaders spend time with Jesus.
- ◊ Leaders find a way to win.

> *"He must increase, but I must decrease." — John 3:30*

True leadership is grounded in humility and the understanding that Jesus must come first in all things.

THE HEART OF A LEADER

A great leader knows that putting Jesus first is essential to fulfilling their God-given purpose. Leading yourself daily with discipline and seeking God's wisdom is key to becoming the leader He has called you to be.

> *"Trust in the Lord with all your heart, and do not lean on your own understanding. In all your ways acknowledge him, and he will make straight your paths." — Proverbs 3:5-6*

THE CAPTAIN'S LEADERSHIP DURING A CRISIS

When the Titanic struck an iceberg and began to sink, the ship's captain exemplified true leadership. Despite the chaos, he remained calm and ensured that passengers were safely evacuated. After spotting a young boy who had been left behind, the captain ordered the lifeboat to return and personally gave up his own seat to save the child.

Before the boy was rescued, the captain's final words to him were, "Son, never forget what has been done for you today."

Leadership often requires sacrifice, selflessness, and prioritizing the needs of others.

> *"Remember your leaders, those who spoke to you the word of God. Consider the outcome of their way of life, and imitate their faith."*
> *— Hebrews 13:7*

THINK ON IT

Leadership is not about commanding authority—it's about serving, influencing, and inspiring others. Great leaders model the way, encourage their teams, and prioritize the needs of others over their own.

True leadership begins with following Jesus. When He is at the center, you can lead with purpose, humility, and faith.

The geese's V-formation teaches us that unity, shared responsibilities, and mutual encouragement strengthen leadership. Great leaders lift others, sacrifice when needed, and seek God's wisdom in every decision.

"Lead with purpose. Lead with faith. Lead with Jesus at the center."

DAY 78
LIFE

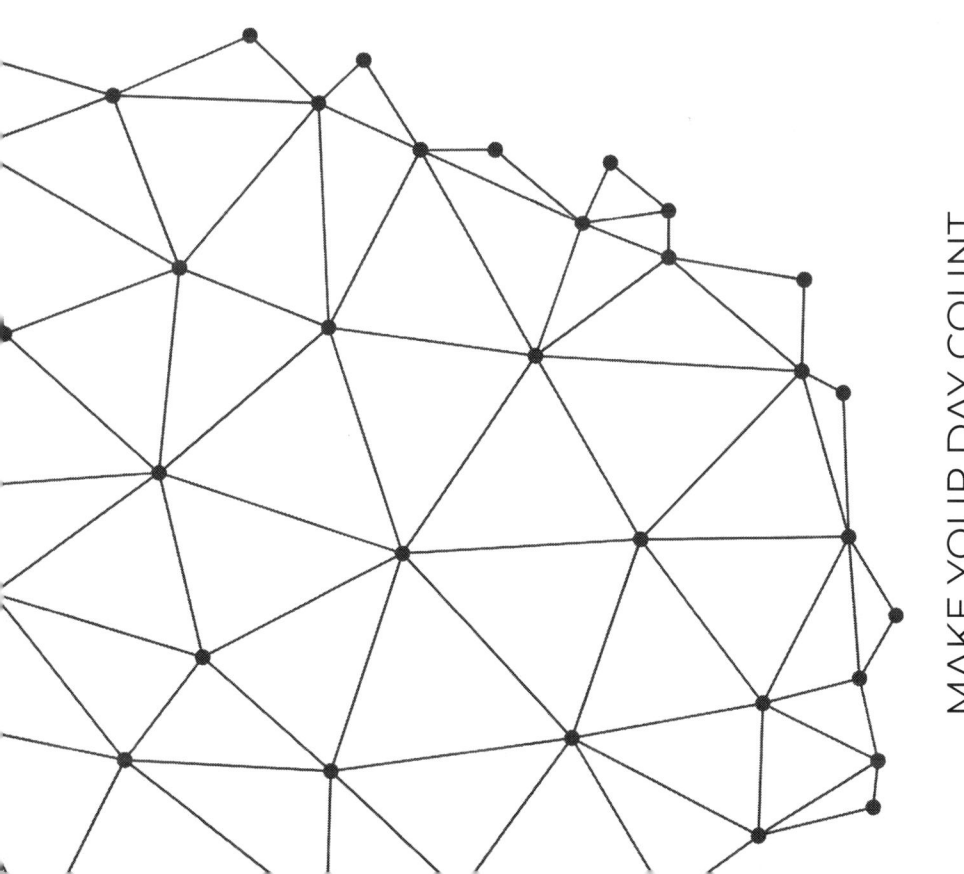

MAKE YOUR DAY COUNT

101 DEVOTIONALS — PART TWO

LIFE

BIG THOUGHT
If you don't do something with life, life will do something with you

> "The mission in life is not merely to survive, but to thrive; and to do so with some passion, some compassion, some humor, and some style." — Maya Angelou

John 10:10 I came that they may have life and have it abundantly.

Life is a gift from God—one that must always be honored and valued. If you don't take an active role in living with purpose, life will take control of you. We are not called to merely exist; we are called to live with passion, purpose, and a deep appreciation for the opportunities God has given us.

> *"Yet you do not know what tomorrow will bring. What is your life? For you are a mist that appears for a little time and then vanishes."* — James 4:14

> *"Do not boast about tomorrow, for you do not know what a day may bring."* — Proverbs 27:1

STORY OF TELEMACHUS

In 404 A.D., a monk named Telemachus felt a call from God that led him to Rome. There, he witnessed the brutal gladiator fights in the Coliseum, where men fought to the death for the crowd's entertainment. Horrified by the violence, Telemachus ran onto the battlefield and shouted, "Stop! In the name of Christ, stop!"

The crowd was enraged, and they called for his death. Despite the danger, Telemachus stood his ground and repeated his plea. One of the gladiators struck him down, killing him on the spot. However, after his death, a profound silence fell over the Coliseum. One by one, people left the arena, and the gladiator games eventually ended forever.

LESSON: Telemachus' life, though short, made a profound impact. His courage and passion changed history. He didn't just exist—he lived with purpose and took a stand for what was right.

CAN ONE PERSON MAKE A DIFFERENCE?

Yes! Telemachus showed that one person can make an incredible difference when they live with purpose and boldness. You, too, have been created with a unique purpose. God has a plan for your life, and your existence is not accidental.

"For I know the plans I have for you, declares the Lord, plans for welfare and not for evil, to give you a future and a hope." — Jeremiah 29:11

Your life is a gift, and you are called to make it count. Don't simply survive—thrive. Live with intention, courage, and passion to fulfill the destiny God has for you.

LIFE IS A GIFT

Every day is a gift from God. Each moment is an opportunity to glorify Him, make a difference, and grow into the person He has created you to be. Life isn't meant to be wasted or taken for granted—it's meant to be lived fully and abundantly.

> *"The thief comes only to steal and kill and destroy. I came that they may have life and have it abundantly." — John 10:10*

The enemy's plan is to steal your joy, kill your purpose, and destroy your potential. But Jesus came to give you abundant life—a life filled with hope, passion, and purpose.

Life is a gift—treat it with the honor and value it deserves. Live with passion, compassion, and an unwavering commitment to making a difference.

Your life is a masterpiece created by God, filled with potential

LIFE

and purpose. Like Telemachus, you can live in a way that impacts the world for good. Whether big or small, your actions, choices, and attitude matter.

> *"For I know the plans I have for you, declares the Lord, plans for welfare and not for evil, to give you a future and a hope."*
> *— Jeremiah 29:11*

CONFESSION

Speak these truths over your life daily:

- ◊ My life is full of unlimited possibilities.
- ◊ My life is blessed.
- ◊ My life is beautiful.
- ◊ My life is full of favor.
- ◊ My life is amazing.
- ◊ My life is important.
- ◊ My life is awesome.
- ◊ Life is a gift from God.
- ◊ I do not take life for granted.

THINK ON IT

Life is not just about existing; it's about living with purpose, passion, and intention. Every moment is a gift from God, and how you live reflects your gratitude for this precious gift.

Like Telemachus, you can make a difference when you live courageously and stand for what is right. Remember, your life matters—every choice, action, and attitude leaves an impact.

"Your life is a masterpiece created by God, meant to glorify Him and fulfill His divine purpose. Live abundantly, live boldly, and live for

Him."

DAY 79
GROWTH

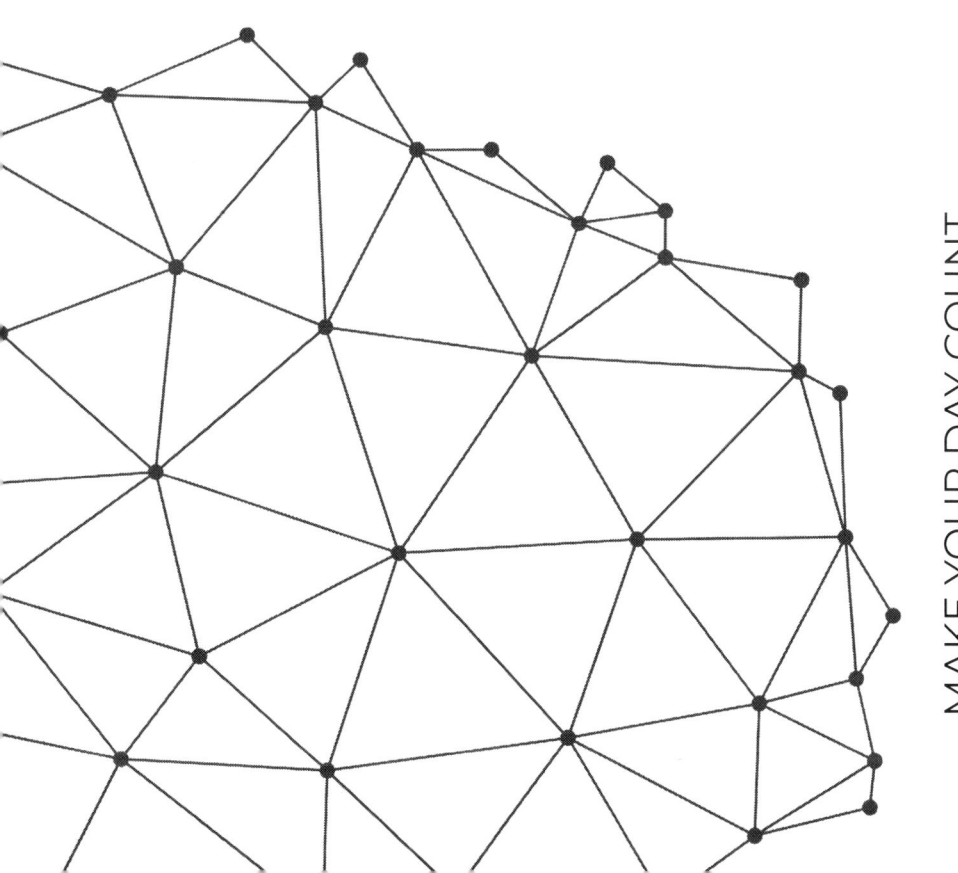

MAKE YOUR DAY COUNT

101 DEVOTIONALS — PART TWO

GROWTH

BIG THOUGHT

Growth isn't for everybody. Some people just want to stay the same forever.

> **Hebrews 6:1** – Therefore let us leave the elementary doctrine of Christ and go on to maturity.

Growth is a natural and essential part of existence. Plants grow, animals grow, and humans grow. Likewise, Jesus calls us to grow in faith, love, and understanding of God's Word. However, growth doesn't happen automatically—it requires intentional effort and a plan.

Many people don't grow simply because they don't plan to grow. Spiritual growth takes commitment through prayer, Bible reading, learning, and surrounding yourself with the right people.

Remember: An unteachable spirit is an unusable spirit. Commit to being a lifelong learner who pushes through challenges to reach the next level.

THE ELDERLY LADIES

A police officer stopped an elderly woman driving far too slow on the highway. She explained she thought the "20" sign indicated the speed limit. When the officer clarified that it was the highway number, he noticed her passengers—three elderly women clutching their seats, terrified. They had just exited Highway 101, explaining their current pace.

This humorous story reminds us that learning and growth are possible at any age. We all have the ability to adapt, grow, and gain new understanding, no matter our stage of life.

GROWTH IN GOD

Spiritual growth is a process that happens over time as we commit to drawing closer to God.

> *"Draw near to God, and He will draw near to you."* — James 4:8

The more time you spend with God, the more you grow in spiritual maturity and closeness to Him.

> *"But grow in the grace and knowledge of our Lord and Savior Jesus Christ."* — 2 Peter 3:18

This verse shows us that growth requires patience, effort, and commitment. It's a journey, not a one-time event.

THE FORMULA FOR GROWTH

Just as distance in algebra is calculated as Rate x Time = Distance, spiritual growth works the same way.

Some people have been following Christ for years but move very slowly in their spiritual growth—like someone traveling at 1 mile per hour.

Growth happens when you commit to actively pursuing God with consistent effort over time. Without effort, you might find yourself stuck, creating a "traffic jam" for others trying to grow around you.

Lesson: Growth requires effort, patience, and a plan—there's no shortcut.

GROWTH TAKES EFFORT

Growth doesn't happen overnight. It's a process that requires stretching, nourishment, and rest. Just as muscles grow through effort and persistence, so does your spirit.

True growth begins with self-awareness—being honest with yourself about where you are in life and your spiritual journey.

> *"Rather, speaking the truth in love, we are to grow up in every way into Him who is the head, into Christ."* — Ephesians 4:15

This verse reminds us that growth involves every area of life, not just selective parts. To grow, you need to take intentional action and seek maturity in all areas of your life.

HOW TO GROW SPIRITUALLY

Here are practical steps to grow closer to God:

- ◊ Reading God's Word: Immerse yourself in Scripture to learn more about His truth and promises.
- ◊ Praying: Build your relationship with God through honest and intentional communication.
- ◊ Worshipping the Lord: Worship draws your heart closer to God and reminds you of His greatness.
- ◊ Taking Bible Classes: Equip yourself with knowledge and understanding of God's Word.
- ◊ Studying Growth Resources: Seek out materials and tools that encourage personal and spiritual development.

These intentional actions will help you grow spiritually and strengthen your walk with God.

KEY TAKEAWAYS

- ◊ Growth Requires Intention: Spiritual growth doesn't happen by accident. You need to plan for it and remain consistent in your efforts.
- ◊ Growth is a Process: Just like physical growth, spiritual growth takes time. Embrace the process and don't rush it.
- ◊ Self-Awareness is Key: Be honest with yourself about where you are in your spiritual journey. This self-awareness will help you understand what steps to take next.

101 DEVOTIONALS — PART TWO

COMMIT TO GROWTH

Make a daily, lifelong commitment to grow spiritually, no matter the obstacles you face.

THINK ON IT

Growth isn't always easy, but it's always worth it. Whether in faith, knowledge, or character, every step forward brings you closer to fulfilling the purpose God has for your life.

> *"Draw near to God, and He will draw near to you." — James 4:8*

Make the decision today to prioritize your growth. Seek God intentionally, embrace the process, and trust that He is leading you to become all He created you to be. Growth is a journey—keep moving forward!

DAY 80
FRIENDS

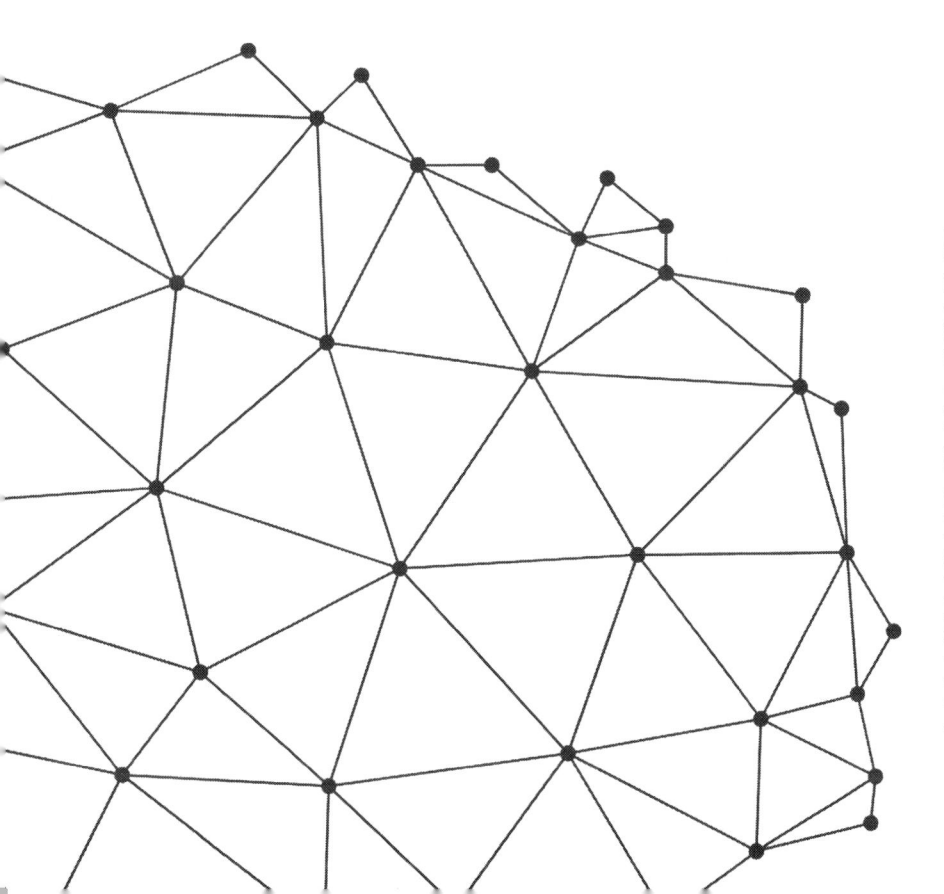

MAKE YOUR DAY COUNT

101 DEVOTIONALS — PART TWO

FRIENDS

BIG THOUGHT

The voices will determine your choices. Be careful who you're listening to.

Proverbs 13:20 – Whoever walks with the wise becomes wise, but the companion of fools will suffer harm.

The people you spend time with influence you more than you realize. Your friends shape your thoughts, actions, and ultimately your destiny. As Proverbs 27:17 reminds us: "Iron sharpens iron, and one man sharpens another."

Choose friends who uplift, inspire, and challenge you to grow. Surrounding yourself with the right people can elevate your life and help you fulfill your potential.

WHO YOU ASSOCIATE WITH SHAPES YOUR FUTURE

The saying, "Show me your friends, and I'll show you your future," holds profound truth. You rise or fall to the level of the people you surround yourself with. If your friends lack ambition or integrity, they'll pull you down. On the other hand, if they encourage, inspire, and challenge you, they'll lift you to new heights.

John C. Maxwell explains in The Law of the Inner Circle: "A leader's potential is determined by those closest to them."

Similarly, Jim Rohn said: "You are the average of the 5 people you spend the most time with."

These insights remind us of the importance of cultivating relationships with people who elevate and inspire us.

WHAT IS A TRUE FRIEND?

A true friend is someone who:

- ◊ Brags about your strengths and defends your weaknesses.
- ◊ Supports you through thick and thin, staying by your side in both good and bad times.
- ◊ Challenges you to grow and pushes you to be better.
- ◊ Encourages and motivates you, helping you believe in yourself.
- ◊ Believes the best in you, empowering you to reach your potential.
- ◊ Sacrifices for you, demonstrating unconditional love and loyalty.

STORY: THE PRAYING HANDS

In the 1500s, two brothers, Albrecht and Albert Dürer, grew up in poverty but shared a dream of pursuing art. They agreed that one would work to support the other's education, and Albrecht won the coin toss. Albert labored in the mines for four years, enabling Albrecht to attend art school.

Albrecht became a renowned artist and returned home to honor his brother's sacrifice. However, Albert's hands were damaged from years of hard labor, preventing him from pursuing his own artistic dreams. In gratitude, Albrecht sketched his brother's hands in prayer. This drawing became the famous piece known as "The Praying Hands"—a lasting symbol of selfless love and friendship.

THE IMPORTANCE OF FRIENDSHIPS

Friendships hold immense power. The Bible warns: "Do not be deceived: Evil communications corrupt good manners." — 1 Corinthians 15:33

Be mindful of the people you allow to influence you. Surround yourself with friends who uplift, challenge, and motivate you to be better. Jesus exemplified the ultimate friendship when He said:

> "Greater love has no one than this, that someone lay down his life for his friends." — John 15:13

True friendship is rooted in sacrificial love, the willingness to give of yourself for the benefit of another.

THE FOUR TYPES OF FRIENDS

- Lifters: These friends brighten your day, cheer you up, and help you feel better about yourself. They elevate your mood and inspire optimism.

- Thrusters: These friends push you forward and motivate you to grow. They challenge you to aim higher and improve.

- Weights: These friends bring you down. They focus on their own problems and leave you feeling drained.

- Drags: These friends are always negative, pessimistic, and stuck in their own struggles. They drag you into their negativity and discourage growth.

Choose Lifters and Thrusters who help you grow, and be cautious of Weights and Drags who hold you back.

THINK ON IT

Friendship is a powerful force that shapes your thoughts, actions, and destiny. The people you choose to spend time with either elevate or diminish your potential. Surround yourself with true friends who inspire, challenge, and motivate you to grow closer to your God-given purpose.

> "Greater love has no one than this, that someone lay down his life for his friends." — John 15:13

Evaluate your friendships today. Are they helping you move closer to your dreams, values, and calling? Be intentional about choosing relationships that bring out the best in you.

DAY 81
FOCUS

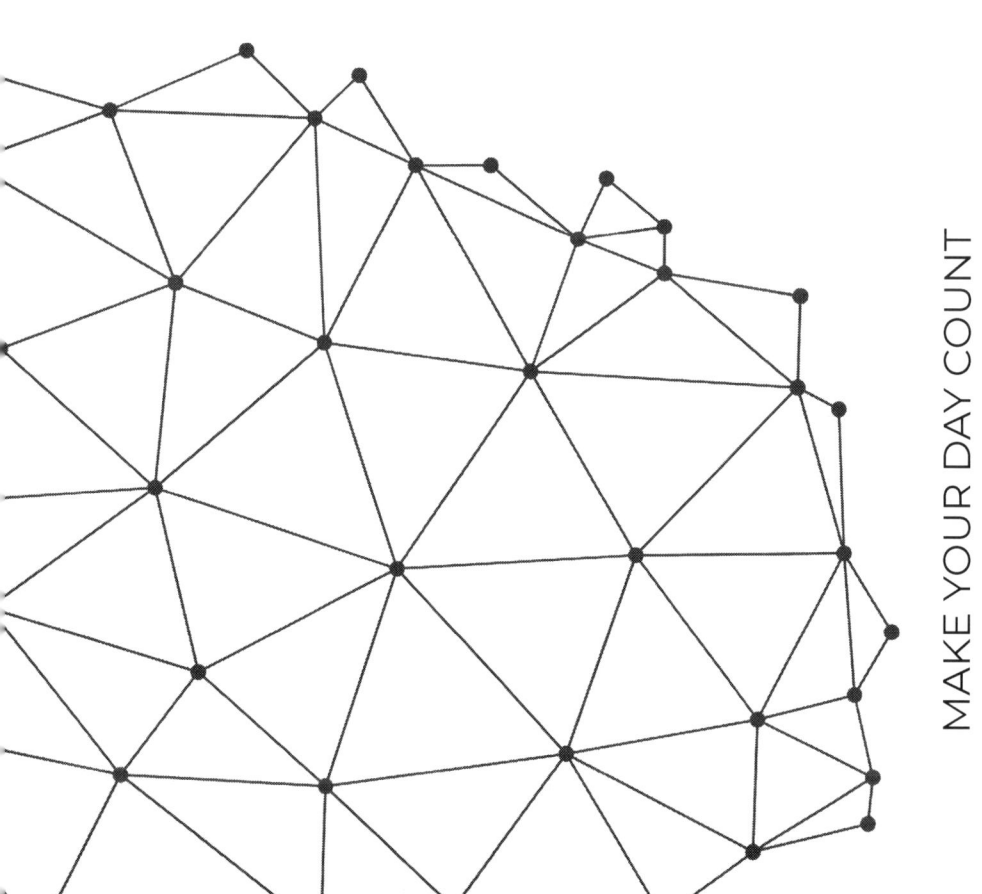

MAKE YOUR DAY COUNT

101 DEVOTIONALS — PART TWO

FOCUS

BIG THOUGHT

The more you focus on what you want, the more you will get what you want.

> **1 Peter 1:13** – Therefore, preparing your minds for action, and being sober-minded, set your hope fully on the grace that will be brought to you at the revelation of Jesus Christ.

Have you ever wondered why a lion tamer carries a stool when entering a lion's cage? The reason is quite interesting. The lion tamer holds the stool and directs its legs toward the lion's face. The lion, unsure of where to focus, tries to concentrate on all four legs at once. This confusion causes a kind of paralysis, rendering the lion helpless.

This situation mirrors how we often become distracted by life's challenges. We may feel inspired and focused during a church service, but once life hits, circumstances like relationships, work, or school distract us, just like the lion with the stool. This is exactly what the enemy wants—when you lose focus, you lose direction in life.

Hebrews 12:1-4 says, "Therefore, since we are surrounded by so great a cloud of witnesses, let us also lay aside every weight, and sin which clings so closely, and let us run with endurance the race that is set before us, looking to Jesus, the founder and perfecter of our faith."

Paul encourages believers to stay focused on Christ. Whatever you focus on gets your attention, and what you give your attention to will determine your direction. Just like the lion tamer distracts the lion, we can be distracted by the many things in life. But focus is key to success and progress.

HOW TO STAY FOCUSED ON JESUS

- ◊ Spend time with God daily. Pray and talk to Him.
- ◊ Read His Word daily. Let Scripture guide your thoughts and actions.
- ◊ Spend time in God's presence through worship.
- ◊ Surround yourself with like-minded people who are focused on Jesus.
- ◊ Follow only one course until you are successful. Stay focused on your journey and goal until you reach it.

> *"The successful warrior is the average man, with laser-like focus."*
> —Bruce Lee

Focus is crucial to success, and this is as true in our spiritual journey as it is in any other area of life.

STORY: THE DISTRACTED TIGER

In a fable, a hungry tiger starts tracking a deer. Along the way, he smells the scent of a rabbit and becomes distracted. He abandons the deer to follow the rabbit. Then, he picks up the scent of a mouse and loses even more focus. By the end of the day, he is hungrier than when he started, having accomplished nothing.

This fable illustrates how many people live their lives distracted by one thing after another, chasing fleeting pleasures or goals. At the end of the day, they've achieved little. Stay focused on your primary goal—nothing is more important than following Jesus.

STAYING FOCUSED ON YOUR JOURNEY

Les Brown says, "You must remain focused on your journey to greatness." Focus is essential to achieving greatness in any area of life, especially in our spiritual walk.

> *"Do you not know that in a race all the runners run, but only one receives the prize? So, run that you may obtain it. Every athlete exercises self-control in all things. They do it to receive a perishable wreath, but we an imperishable one." — 1 Corinthians 9:24-27*

Athletes focus on their race with discipline, self-control, and endurance. If they can train and focus for a temporary prize, how much more should we, as Christians, focus on the eternal prize awaiting us? Like athletes, we must be disciplined and stay focused on our spiritual goals.

SCRIPTURE TO GUIDE YOUR FOCUS

> *"Let your eyes look directly forward, and your gaze be straight before you." — Proverbs 4:25*

> *"Commit your work to the Lord, and your plans will be established." — Proverbs 16:3*

> *"Set your minds on things that are above, not on things that are on earth." — Colossians 3:2*

These verses remind us to keep our focus on God and His eternal purposes, not on temporary distractions.

THE POWER OF FOCUS

Focus is one of the most powerful things a person can control. It determines what you see and what you accomplish. Without focus, life can feel like a roller coaster, with constant ups and downs. The enemy wants to distract believers, but if you remain focused, you'll stay on track to accomplish your goals.

Think of your life as aiming a rifle. To hit your target, you must be:

- ◊ Ready — spiritually prepared and focused on where you're going.
- ◊ Aim — have a clear vision of your goal.
- ◊ Fire —take action with passion and determination to reach your goal.

THINK ON IT

Focus is the key to unlocking your potential and achieving your purpose. Without focus, you risk being distracted and losing sight of what truly matters. Just like the lion tamer uses the stool to confuse the lion, distractions in life can paralyze you and pull you away from your goals.

What you focus on gets your attention, and what gets your attention shapes your direction. Fix your eyes on Jesus, the author and perfecter of your faith. Commit your plans to Him, stay disciplined, and trust that He will guide you to victory.

> *"Let your eyes look directly forward, and your gaze be straight before you."* — Proverbs 4:25

Ask yourself: What am I focusing on today? Are my priorities aligned with God's purpose for my life? Eliminate distractions, set your mind on things above, and let God's Word direct your steps. Focus isn't just about achieving goals—it's about walking faithfully in the journey God has set before you.

DAY 82
PRAYER

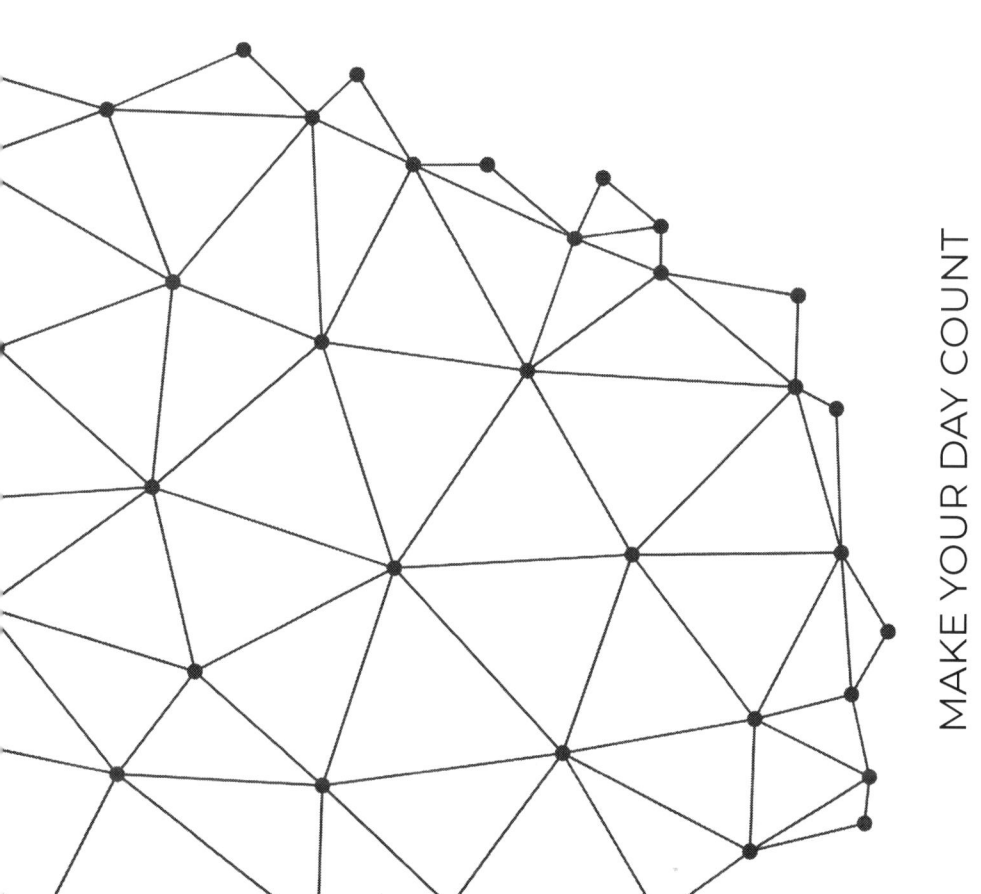

MAKE YOUR DAY COUNT

101 DEVOTIONALS — PART TWO

PRAYER

BIG THOUGHT
A life without prayer is a life without God

> "Prayer is simply a two-way conversation between you and God." — Billy Graham

Matthew 21:22 – And whatever you ask in prayer, you will receive, if you have faith."

P rayer is one of the most powerful ways to stay connected with God. It's not just about talking; it's about listening, too. Through prayer, we maintain a deep, personal relationship with our Heavenly Father. It's a sacred conversation where we share our hearts, seek His guidance, and tune in to His voice.

> *"The prayer of a righteous person has great power as it is working."* — James 5:16

Even when you feel like your prayers aren't being answered immediately, trust that God hears you. Prayer works, and it has the power to change circumstances and hearts.

GOD IS ALWAYS LISTENING

> *"The Lord is near to all who call on Him, to all who call on Him in truth."* — Psalm 145:18

God promises to be near to those who seek Him. When you feel like He isn't answering or doesn't hear you, don't lose heart—He is always listening and cares about every word you pray. Trust that He is working behind the scenes, even when you don't see immediate results.

> *"Ask, and it will be given to you; seek, and you will find; knock, and it will be opened to you."* — Matthew 7:7

God invites us to come to Him boldly, to ask for what we need, to seek His will, and to trust Him to open doors. He longs for us to spend time in His presence and build our faith through prayer.

THE POWER OF PERSISTENT PRAYER

A grandmother prayed for her rebellious grandsons for fourteen years, never giving up even when her faith wavered. One day, both grandsons gave their lives to Christ at a Christian concert while on leave in the Philippines. As it turned out, she had been financially supporting the missionary evangelist who led them to Christ, without knowing it.

This story shows the power of persistent prayer. God hears every prayer, and He answers them in His perfect time and way. Even when it seems like nothing is happening, don't give up—God is always at work.

THE LORD'S PRAYER: A MODEL FOR PRAYER

In Matthew 6:9-13, Jesus gives us a powerful guide for prayer:

> *"Pray then like this: Our Father in heaven, hallowed be Your name. Your kingdom come, Your will be done, on earth as it is in heaven. Give us this day our daily bread, and forgive us our debts, as we also have forgiven our debtors. And lead us not into temptation, but deliver us from evil."*

THE LORD'S PRAYER REMINDS US TO

- ◊ Acknowledge God's greatness: "Our Father in heaven, hallowed be Your name."

- ◊ Seek His will: "Your kingdom come, Your will be done."
- ◊ Ask for provision: "Give us this day our daily bread."
- ◊ Repent and forgive: "Forgive us our debts, as we also have forgiven our debtors."
- ◊ Ask for protection: "Lead us not into temptation, but deliver us from evil."

This prayer is not just words to recite but a guide to align our hearts with God's purposes.

HOW TO BUILD A LIFE OF PRAYER

The more you pray, the more natural and meaningful your conversations with God will become. You can pray anytime, anywhere, and about anything. Here are practical ways to grow in prayer:

- ◊ Start Your Day with Prayer: Dedicate the first moments of your day to connecting with God.
- ◊ Be Honest: Share your thoughts, fears, and dreams with God—He cares about every detail.
- ◊ Listen: Take time to be still and listen for His guidance.
- ◊ Pray Scripture: Use God's Word as a foundation for your prayers.
- ◊ Be Persistent: Don't give up when answers seem delayed—trust God's timing.

SCRIPTURE ON PRAYER

> "Rejoice always, pray without ceasing, give thanks in all circumstances; for this is the will of God in Christ Jesus for you." — 1 Thessalonians 5:16-18

> "Do not be anxious about anything, but in everything by prayer and supplication with thanksgiving let your requests be made known to God." — Philippians 4:6

101 DEVOTIONALS — PART TWO

> *"Call to Me, and I will answer you, and will tell you great and hidden things that you have not known." — Jeremiah 33:3*

THINK ON IT

Prayer is more than a ritual—it's a lifeline connecting you to the heart of God. It's your opportunity to share your deepest thoughts, ask for guidance, and align yourself with His will. The power of prayer is undeniable; it can transform situations, renew hope, and strengthen faith.

> *"Call to Me, and I will answer you, and will tell you great and hidden things that you have not known." — Jeremiah 33:3*

Take a moment today to reflect: Are you making prayer a priority in your life? Are you trusting God to answer in His perfect timing? Persistent, honest, and heartfelt prayer is your pathway to experiencing the fullness of God's presence and promises. Never stop praying, for God hears and answers every call.

DAY 83
EVANGELISM

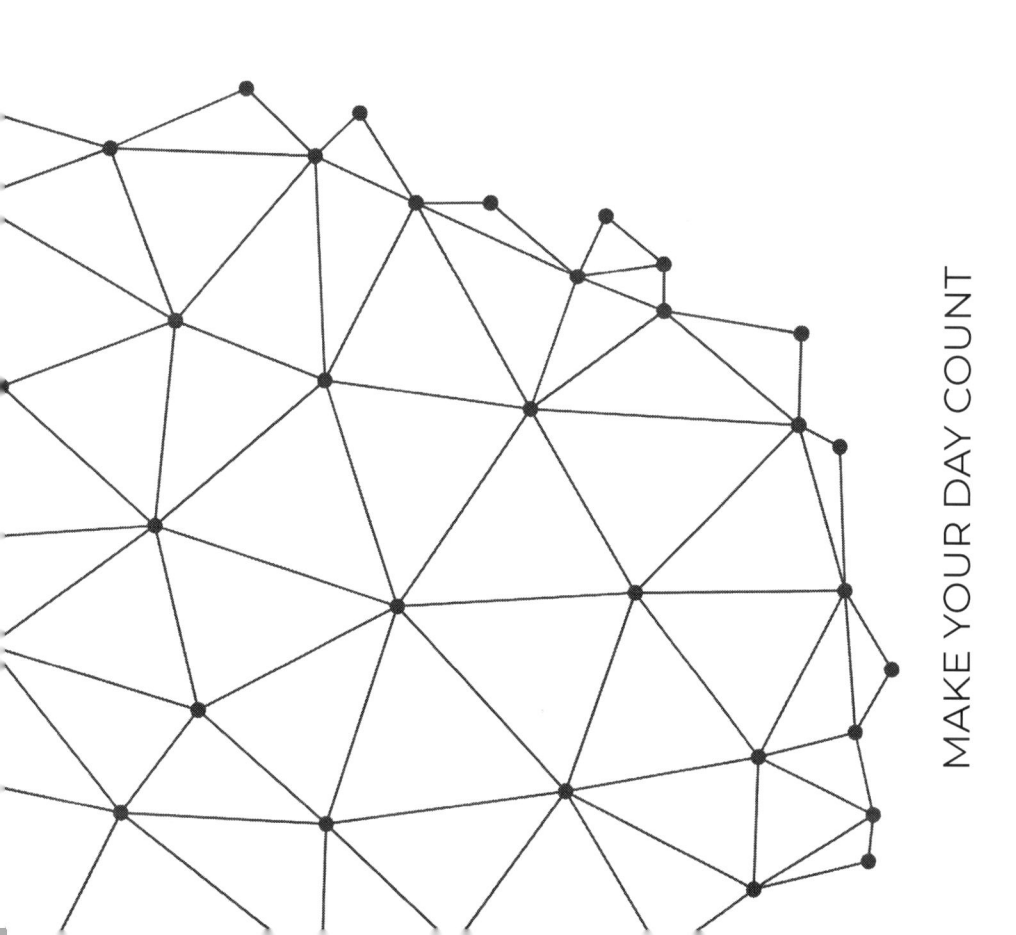

MAKE YOUR DAY COUNT

101 DEVOTIONALS — PART TWO

EVANGELISM

BIG THOUGHT
Evangelism is sharing the gospel with every person.

> "The Great Commission is not an option to be considered; it is a command to be obeyed."— Hudson Taylor

Matthew 28:16-20 —"Now the eleven disciples went to Galilee, to the mountain to which Jesus had directed them. And when they saw him they worshiped him, but some doubted. And Jesus came and said to them, 'All authority in heaven and on earth has been given to me. Go therefore and make disciples of all nations, baptizing them in the name of the Father and of the Son and of the Holy Spirit, teaching them to observe all that I have commanded you. And behold, I am with you always, to the end of the age.'"

Evangelism is spreading the gospel—the Good News of Jesus Christ. It's sharing the love of God so others can come to know Him. Jesus gave us a clear command in the Great Commission: "Go into all the world and proclaim the gospel to the whole creation." — Mark 16:15

In the Great Commission, Jesus calls us to share the gospel with the lost, the broken, and the hurting. The Good News is simple: God loves the world so much that He sent His Son, Jesus, to save us.

101 DEVOTIONALS — PART TWO

> *"For God so loved the world, that he gave his only Son, that whoever believes in him should not perish but have eternal life."* — John 3:16

THREE MAJOR POINTS FROM JOHN 3:16

- The Giver: God is the ultimate giver, offering the greatest gift of all—His Son, Jesus.
- The Gift: Jesus is the greatest gift humanity has ever received, bridging the gap between us and God.
- The Guarantee: Eternal Life

By believing in Jesus, we receive the assurance of eternal life with Him in heaven.

THE STORY OF THE PAINTING

A wealthy man and his son shared a love for art, collecting rare masterpieces together. The son went to war and gave his life saving another soldier. Afterward, a young man visited the father, presenting him with a portrait of the son he had painted in gratitude for his sacrifice. The father cherished the portrait, placing it in a place of honor.

When the father passed away, his art collection was auctioned. The first piece up for sale was the portrait of the son, but no one wanted it. A poor gardener bid $10, saying it was all he could afford. The auctioneer accepted the bid and then revealed the terms of the father's will: "Whoever buys the painting of the son gets everything."

This story mirrors the gospel. When we accept the Son—Jesus—we receive everything: salvation, peace, and eternal life. God calls us to share this incredible gift with the world.

THE ROMANS ROAD: A GUIDE FOR SHARING THE GOSPEL

The "Romans Road" is a step-by-step outline for sharing God's plan of salvation:

- Romans 3:10 —"None is righteous, no, not one."
  - → We all fall short of God's standard.

- ◊ Romans 3:23 —"For all have sinned and fall short of the glory of God."

  → Everyone has sinned and needs salvation.

- ◊ Romans 5:8 — "But God shows his love for us in that while we were still sinners, Christ died for us."

  → God's love was demonstrated through Jesus' sacrifice.

- ◊ Romans 6:23 —"For the wages of sin is death, but the free gift of God is eternal life in Christ Jesus our Lord."

  → Sin brings death, but Jesus offers eternal life.

- ◊ Romans 10:9-10 —"If you confess with your mouth that Jesus is Lord and believe in your heart that God raised him from the dead, you will be saved."

  → Salvation comes through confessing and believing in Jesus.

- ◊ Romans 10:13 —"For everyone who calls on the name of the Lord will be saved."

  → God's offer of salvation is available to all.

- ◊ Romans 12:1 — "I appeal to you therefore, brothers, by the mercies of God, to present your bodies as a living sacrifice, holy and acceptable to God, which is your spiritual worship."

  → In response to God's gift, we should dedicate our lives to Him.

THE STORY OF THE RICH YOUNG MAN

In Matthew 19:16-22, a rich young man asks Jesus how to obtain eternal life. Jesus tells him to keep the commandments, which the young man claims he has done. Then Jesus challenges him further: "Sell what you possess and give to the poor, and you will have treasure in heaven; and come, follow me."

The young man walks away sorrowful, unwilling to let go of his wealth.

Lesson: Many people hear the gospel but are unwilling to give up what the world offers to follow Jesus. Evangelism is about encouraging people to see that Jesus is worth more than anything else.

THINK ON IT

Evangelism is more than a task; it's a calling that aligns us with God's heart for the lost. Every believer has the privilege and responsibility to share the Good News. Take a moment to reflect: Are you intentional about sharing the hope and salvation found in Jesus?

> *"For God so loved the world, that he gave his only Son, that whoever believes in him should not perish but have eternal life." — John 3:16*

This week, ask God to give you opportunities to share His love with those around you. Remember, when you offer the gift of the Son, you are offering everything—eternal life, peace, and the assurance of His presence. Don't keep this treasure to yourself; share it boldly and lovingly.

DAY 84
WHAT IF?

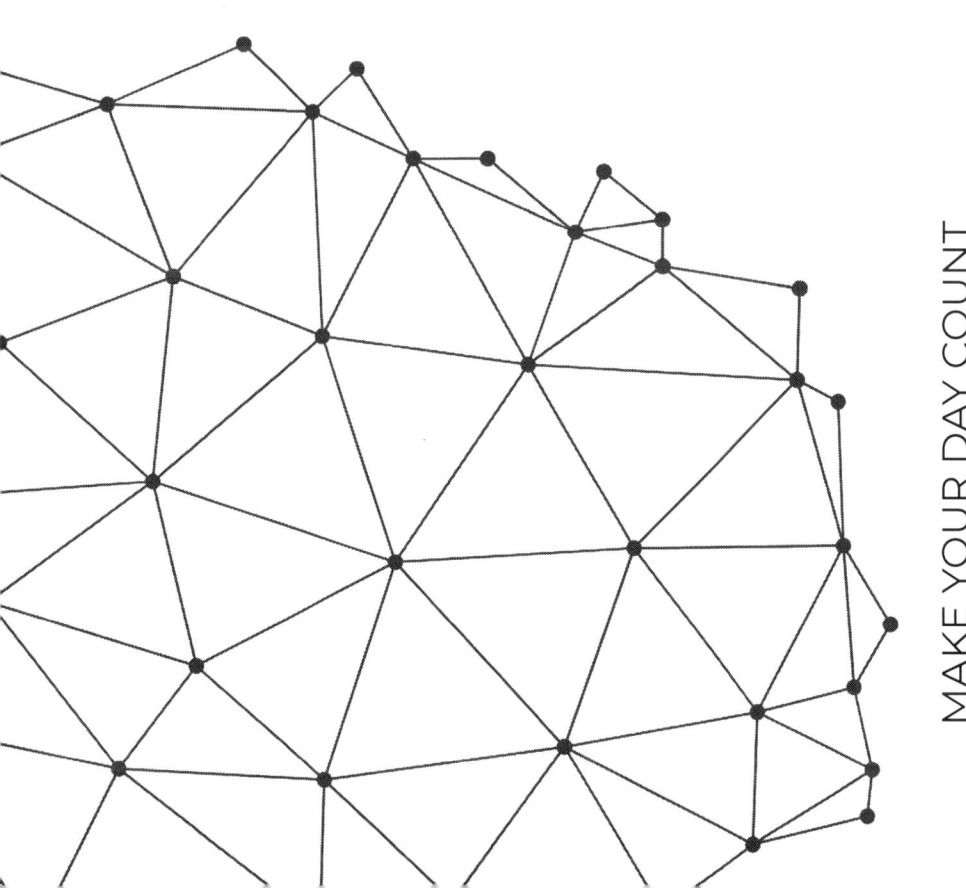

MAKE YOUR DAY COUNT

101 DEVOTIONALS — PART TWO

WHAT IF?

BIG THOUGHT

If success was guaranteed, and failure wasn't an option, what would you desire to do?

> "What if we knew what tomorrow would bring? Would we fix it? Could we?" — Cecelia Ahern

The phrase "what if" is a powerful tool. It sparks the imagination to dream of greater things, yet it can also stir up fear and doubt. It challenges us to think outside the box or, at times, tempts us to stay safely within it. "What if" implies possibility and wonder, inviting us to explore the unknown.

- What if you couldn't lose?
- What if no one could stop you?
- What if all you did was win?

Will the "what if" in your life break you or make you stronger? God created you to be victorious, but you must choose to see yourself that way.

THE WHAT IFS OF FAITH

- ◊ What if there was a movement that brought the world to Jesus?
- ◊ What if the impossible became possible?
- ◊ What if fear transformed into faith?
- ◊ What if your dreams came true?
- ◊ What if you gave God everything?
- ◊ What if God loves you more than you know?

Every day is a fresh start—an opportunity to move beyond "what might have been" and embrace "what can be." Ask yourself, "What if I can make a difference?" Many people live in fear, never expecting to make an impact. They give up before they even begin.

THE REALITY OF OPPORTUNITY

> "Opportunity is missed by most people because it comes dressed in overalls and looks like work." — Thomas Edison

Edison's words remind us that fulfilling our "what ifs" requires effort. There will be challenges, but God is always with you, guiding and strengthening you along the way.

GROWTH IN THE VALLEYS

Someone once said: "There is little growth on the mountaintop. Growth occurs in the valley."

Our most significant growth happens not in life's highs but in its lows. Just as the saying goes:

"No pain, no gain."

> "A successful person is one who gets up one more time than he is knocked down." — Paul Harvey

STORY OF PAUL AND SILAS

In Acts 16:16-34, Paul and Silas were imprisoned for casting out a spirit of divination. Beaten and chained, they chose to pray and sing hymns at midnight. Suddenly, an earthquake shook the prison, opening all the doors and unfastening the prisoners' chains.

Rather than escape, Paul and Silas stayed, sparing the jailer's life. This act of faith led the jailer and his entire household to salvation.

Lesson: Sometimes, God's plan for your "what if" is bigger than you realize. The earthquake wasn't about Paul's freedom—it was about the jailer's salvation. What if God wants to use your situation to bring freedom to others?

TURNING "WHAT IF" INTO REALITY

If you have faith in God, the impossible can become possible. In order for your "what if" to work, you must:

- ◊ Believe in Jesus: Trust that He can do the miraculous in your life.

- ◊ Believe in Yourself: Know that God has equipped you with everything you need to succeed.

- ◊ Be Sold Out to the Gospel: Dedicate your life to sharing the Good News and living for Christ.

- ◊ Be Sold Out to Your "What If": Pursue your dreams with faith, discipline, and determination.

YOUR DESTINY REQUIRES YOUR DISCIPLINE

To fulfill your "what if," you must be willing to do whatever it takes. The possibilities with God are limitless. Don't limit what He can do in your life!

KEY TAKEAWAYS

"What if" sparks possibilities: Use it to dream big and imagine what God can do in and through your life.

- ◊ Challenges lead to growth: Growth happens in the valleys, not the mountaintops. Embrace the process.

- ◊ Faith makes "what if" possible: Trust God, believe in yourself, and be fully committed to your dreams.

God's plans are bigger than ours: Be open to His purpose, even if it's not what you expected.

THINK ON IT

What if today was the day everything changed? What if the dream in your heart became a reality? What if the obstacles you face are the very stepping stones God will use to grow your faith and expand your influence?

Take a moment to reflect on the "what ifs" in your life. Ask God to give you the faith to step out boldly, the courage to persevere through challenges, and the wisdom to see His greater plan in every situation.

> *"Now to Him who is able to do far more abundantly than all that we ask or think, according to the power at work within us..."*
> *— Ephesians 3:20*

Your "what if" begins with God. Trust Him to make the impossible possible and take the next step in faith.

DAY 85
IDENTITY

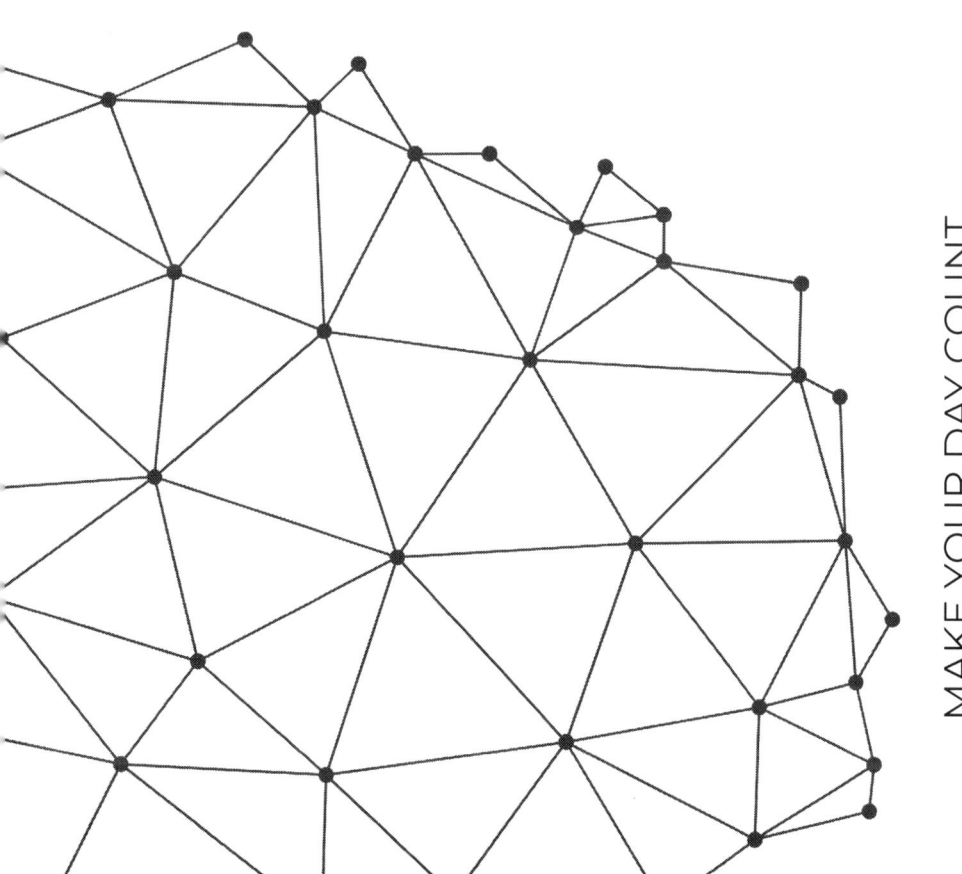

MAKE YOUR DAY COUNT

101 DEVOTIONALS — PART TWO

IDENTITY

BIG THOUGHT
If you know whose you are, you already know your worth.

> "God can't bless who you pretend to be." — Steven Furtick

> "Man was designed for accomplishment, engineered for success, and endowed with seeds of greatness." — Zig Ziglar

What is Identity? Identity is the essence of who you are—the qualities, beliefs, and traits that set you apart. It answers the question, "Who am I?"

The Bible provides the ultimate answer: You are a son or daughter of the Most High God. Genesis 1:27 tells us that we are made in God's image. Your true identity is found in Him.

YOU WERE CREATED IN GOD'S IMAGE

> "Then God said, 'Let us make man in our image, after our likeness. And let them have dominion over the fish of the sea and over the birds of the heavens and over the livestock and over all the earth and over every creeping thing that creeps on the earth.' So God created man in His own image, in the image of God He created him; male and female He created them." — Genesis 1:26-27

You were designed by God to reflect His image and to have dominion over the earth. You are destined for greatness and called to imitate Him—not anyone else.

YOU ARE UNIQUE

> *"When I look at Your heavens, the work of Your fingers, the moon and the stars, which You have set in place, what is man that You are mindful of him, and the son of man that You care for him? Yet You have made him a little lower than the heavenly beings and crowned him with glory and honor. You have given him dominion over the works of Your hands; You have put all things under his feet." — Psalm 8:3-6*

YOU HAVE BEEN FEARFULLY AND WONDERFULLY MADE BY GOD

> *"I praise You, for I am fearfully and wonderfully made."*
> *— Psalm 139:14*

God's Word reminds us of who we are in His eyes:

- ◊ You are His handiwork. (Ephesians 2:10)
- ◊ You are complete in Christ. (Colossians 2:10)
- ◊ You are forgiven and redeemed. (Ephesians 1:7)
- ◊ You are the salt and light of the world. (Matthew 5:13-14)

> *"You have a fingerprint that no one else has, to leave an imprint in this world that no one else can leave." — Pastor Keith Craft*

God made you one-of-a-kind, with a purpose only you can fulfill.

THE STORY OF SHADRACH, MESHACH, AND ABEDNEGO

In Daniel 3:24-30, three young men—Shadrach, Meshach, and Abednego—refused to bow to a golden statue, even under threat of death in a fiery furnace. They trusted God completely and stood firm in their identity as His servants.

When the king had them thrown into the furnace, God delivered them. Instead of burning, they walked unharmed, and a fourth figure, "like a son of the gods," appeared with them. Their faith led the king to declare:

IDENTITY

> 📖 *"Blessed be the God of Shadrach, Meshach, and Abednego, who sent his angel and delivered his servants, who trusted in him." — Daniel 3:28*

Their courage came from knowing who they were in God. Like them, when you understand your identity in Christ, you can face any challenge with faith and confidence.

💡 THINK ON IT

Who are you, really? Is your identity shaped by the opinions of others, your achievements, or your failures? Or is it rooted in the unchanging truth of who God says you are?

Take time to reflect on the following questions:

Am I living as the person God created me to be?

Do I let external circumstances define my worth, or do I anchor my identity in Christ?

How can I remind myself daily of the truth that I am fearfully and wonderfully made?

> 📖 *"Therefore, if anyone is in Christ, he is a new creation. The old has passed away; behold, the new has come." — 2 Corinthians 5:17*

Your identity is not in what you do or what others say—it's in who God made you to be. Live confidently, knowing you are His masterpiece, created for greatness.

101 DEVOTIONALS — PART TWO

DAY 86
TRUST

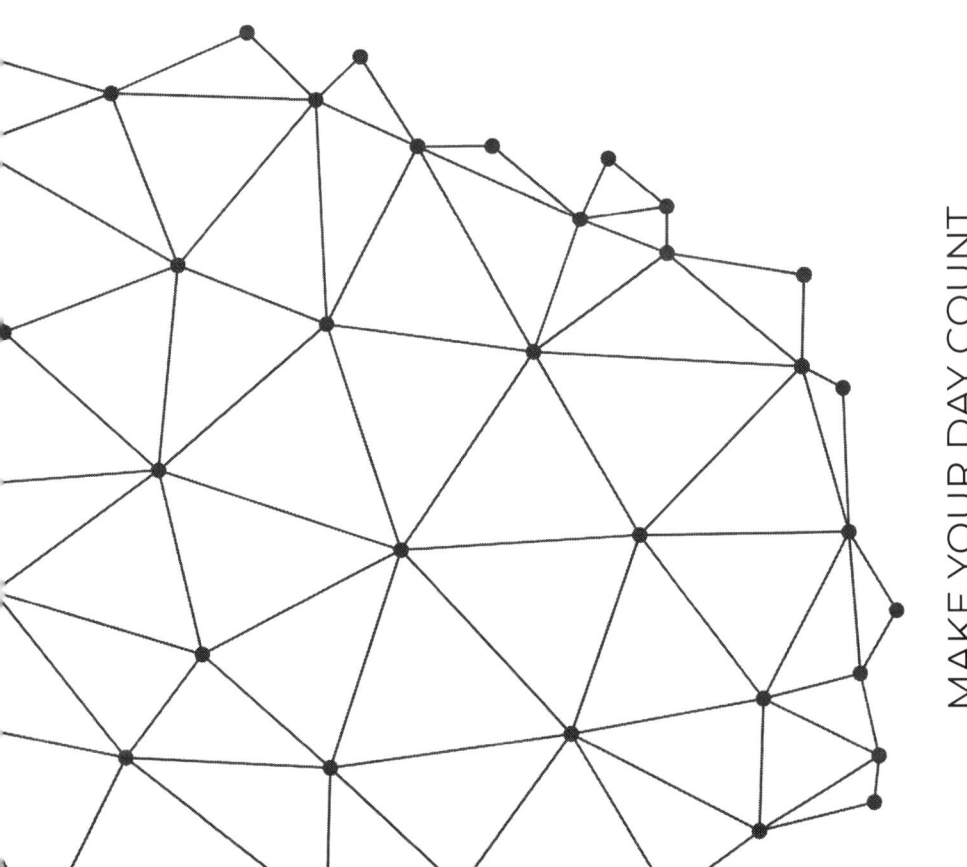

MAKE YOUR DAY COUNT

101 DEVOTIONALS — PART TWO

TRUST

BIG THOUGHT

A relationship without trust is like a car without gas; you can stay in it all you want, but it won't go anywhere.

> **"Never be afraid to trust an unknown future to a known God."** — Corrie Ten Boom

Trust means depending on the strength or ability of a person or thing.

Many people place their trust in temporary things—people, money, fame, or possessions. But the only true and unshakable foundation for trust is God. He is always faithful, never failing, and His love for us is unfathomable.

Think about it: every day, we unconsciously place trust in something, whether it's the people we interact with, the cars we drive, or the systems we rely on. The question is, are we putting that same trust in God?

> *"Trust in the Lord with all your heart, and do not lean on your own understanding. In all your ways acknowledge Him, and He will make straight your paths."* — Proverbs 3:5-6

This verse reminds us that trusting God is the key to navigating life's challenges. When we lean on Him instead of our limited understanding, He will guide and steady us.

BETHANY HAMILTON'S STORY: A TESTIMONY OF TRUST

Bethany Hamilton, a professional surfer, has an inspiring story of trust. At 13 years old, while surfing in Hawaii, a shark attacked her, taking her left arm. Despite this life-altering event, Bethany remained calm, clinging to her faith.

On her way to the hospital, a paramedic comforted her with the words: "God will never leave you or forsake you."

Those words became her anchor. Though her physical recovery was grueling, Bethany chose to trust in God's plan for her life. She returned to surfing and became a symbol of resilience and faith.

Her story reminds us that trust is a personal decision. Even when life throws unimaginable challenges at us, choosing to trust in God provides strength and hope.

"The most expensive thing in the world is trust. For every setback, God has a major comeback. Trust Him!"

DANIEL IN THE LION'S DEN

Daniel's story in Daniel 6 is one of unwavering trust. Daniel was a man of integrity and deep faith. Even when the law prohibited praying to anyone but the king, Daniel stayed faithful to God, praying three times a day. His enemies used this against him, convincing the king to throw Daniel into a lion's den as punishment.

But God honored Daniel's trust. He sent angels to shut the mouths of the lions, sparing Daniel's life.

> *"Blessed is the man who trusts in the Lord, whose trust is the Lord."*
> *— Jeremiah 17:7*

Daniel's story teaches us that God is faithful to those who trust Him. No matter how dire the situation, God's power is greater than any threat we face.

THINK ON IT

What—or who—do you trust most in your life? Is it your own abilities, the approval of others, or material possessions? Or do you fully rely on God, the only unshakable foundation?

TRUST

> *"Blessed is the man who trusts in the Lord, whose trust is the Lord."*
> *— Jeremiah 17:7*

Trusting God doesn't mean life will always be easy, but it does mean you'll never face it alone. Let His faithfulness be your anchor, and trust Him to guide you through every situation.

101 DEVOTIONALS — PART TWO

DAY 87
PASSION

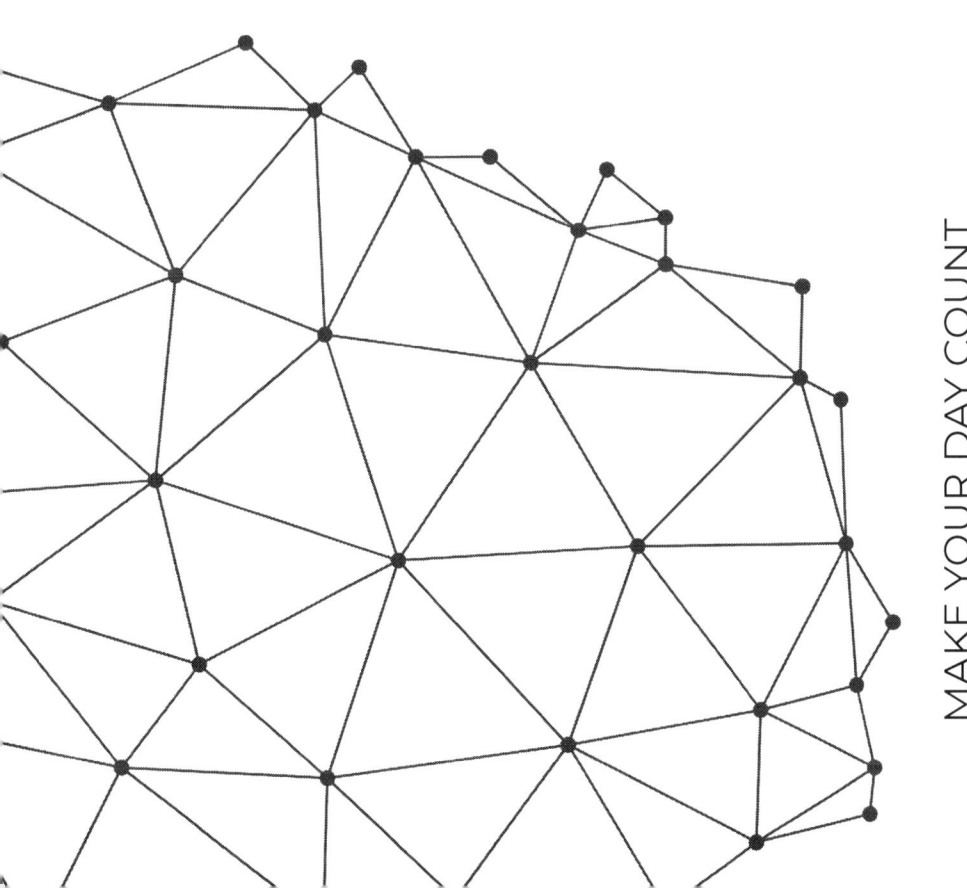

MAKE YOUR DAY COUNT

101 DEVOTIONALS — PART TWO

PASSION

BIG THOUGHT

People with great passion can make the impossible happen.

> "The most powerful weapon on earth is the human soul on fire." —Ferdinand Foch

Passion is the force that separates success from failure. It ignites purpose and transforms ordinary lives into extraordinary ones. Helen Keller observed, "Life is either a daring adventure or it's nothing." Passion fuels every aspect of life, turning dreams into reality and struggles into victories.

> *"Nothing great in the world has been accomplished without passion." —George Wilhelm Friedrich Hegel*

Passion isn't just about enthusiasm—it's the persistence to keep going when the odds are stacked against you. As William Ward noted:

"Enthusiasm and persistence can make an average person superior; indifference and lethargy can make a superior person average."

BIBLICAL ZEAL

The Bible emphasizes the importance of passion. Zeal, a synonym for passion, is vital in serving God and pursuing His purpose for your life. A passionate life is like a river flowing with purpose and energy. Without passion, life becomes stagnant.

> *"And let us consider how to stir up one another to love and good works, not neglecting to meet together, as is the habit of some, but encouraging one another, and all the more as you see the Day drawing near." — Hebrews 10:24-25*

> *"Do not be slothful in zeal, be fervent in spirit, serve the Lord." — Romans 12:11*

Surrounding yourself with passionate people is essential. Their energy will inspire and encourage you to pursue your purpose with renewed fervor.

MACREADY AND THE PREACHER

The famous English actor Macready once responded to a preacher's question about their differing impacts:

"The difference is simple. I present fiction as though it were truth, and you present truth as though it were fiction."

This story underscores the power of passion. When you approach truth with enthusiasm and conviction, it transforms into something extraordinary.

CIRCUS LION VS. JUNGLE LION

The lion tamer doesn't defeat the lion through strength but by convincing the lion that he is stronger. The once-mighty jungle lion is subdued, not by force, but by losing the knowledge of its greatness.

This mirrors how challenges can overpower us—not because they are insurmountable, but because we believe they are.

Don't let the enemy strip you of your God-given greatness. Passion, fueled by faith, gives you the power to overcome.

PASSION IN ACTION: PETER HEALS THE LAME MAN

In Acts 3:1-16, Peter and John encounter a lame beggar at the Beautiful Gate. When the beggar asked for money, Peter responded:

"I have no silver or gold, but what I do have I give to you. In the name of Jesus Christ of Nazareth, rise up and walk."

Peter took the man's hand, helped him up, and immediately he was healed. The man walked, jumped, and praised God.

Peter's passion for God moved him to act, and his faith brought healing. The crowd was amazed, and Peter explained that it was faith in Jesus' name that made the miracle possible.

LIVING WITH PASSION

Passionate people do amazing things because they are driven by purpose and fueled by love for God.

Key Lessons on Passion

- ◊ Passion ignites action: It transforms ordinary efforts into extraordinary outcomes.

- ◊ Passion requires persistence: Enthusiasm alone isn't enough; persistence keeps the fire burning.

- ◊ Passion inspires others: Surround yourself with people who challenge and encourage you to live with purpose.

- ◊ Passion glorifies God: When fueled by a love for God, passion leads to actions that honor Him and fulfill His plan for your life.

THINK ON IT

Passion is more than enthusiasm; it's the persistence to keep going when things get tough. As William Ward said, "Enthusiasm and persistence can make an average person superior."

Romans 12:11 urges us to be "fervent in spirit, serve the Lord." Passion fuels our purpose and keeps us moving forward.

Surround yourself with passionate people who will inspire you, as Hebrews 10:24-25 reminds us. Their zeal will ignite your own.

101 DEVOTIONALS — PART TWO

DAY 88
COURAGE

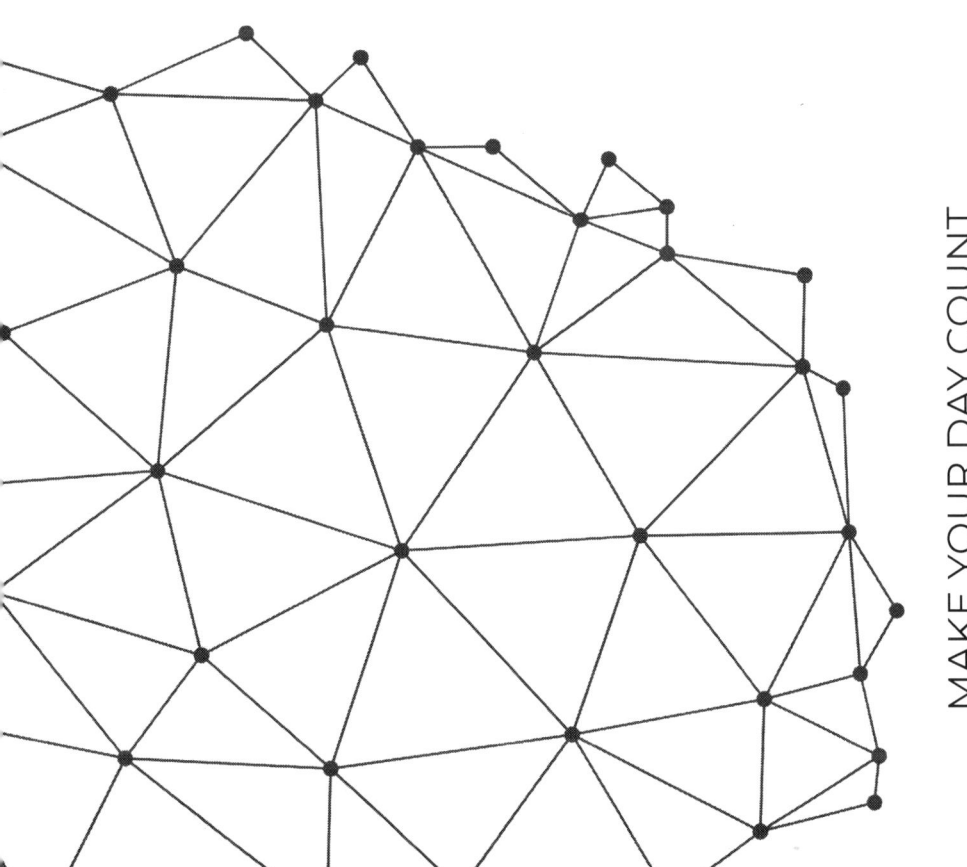

MAKE YOUR DAY COUNT

101 DEVOTIONALS — PART TWO

COURAGE

BIG THOUGHT

Courage is not not having the strength to go on. It is going on when you don't have the strength.

> "Only those who will risk going too far can possibly find out how far one can go." —T. S. Eliot

Courage is doing what you're afraid to do. It's stepping up when no one else does. Courage is making the hard decisions. With courage, you will win!

In the face of fear, courage is not having all the answers, but trusting that God has them. With God's protection and guidance, you can overcome fears and live a courageous life. God commands us to be courageous, as having courage means having faith and confidence in Him.

> *"Finally, be strong in the Lord and in the strength of His might."*
> *— Ephesians 6:10*

> *"Be strong and courageous. Do not fear or be in dread of them, for it is the Lord your God who goes with you. He will not leave you or forsake you."* *— Deuteronomy 31:6*

> *"The Lord is my light and my salvation; whom shall I fear? The Lord is the stronghold of my life; of whom shall I be afraid?"*
> *— Psalm 27:1*

101 DEVOTIONALS — PART TWO

> "For God gave us a spirit not of fear but of power and love and self-control." — 2 Timothy 1:7

> "Have I not commanded you? Be strong and courageous. Do not be frightened, and do not be dismayed, for the Lord your God is with you wherever you go." — Joshua 1:9

> "Be strong, and let your heart take courage, all you who wait for the Lord!" — Psalm 31:24

There are so many verses in the Bible that remind us to have courage and not be afraid. God is for you—He is on your side. Be confident in what His Word says. God will never leave you or forsake you!

STORY: THE LAST STAND OF LEONIDAS

In 480 B.C., King Leonidas of Sparta was preparing to make a stand against the Persian army. A Persian envoy came and mocked their efforts, saying their archers were so numerous that their arrows darkened the sky. Leonidas, with unshakable courage, responded, "So much the better, for we shall fight them in the shade."

Leonidas didn't back down from the battle, knowing that he was fighting for something far greater than just survival. He showed courage in the face of impossible odds, knowing that he wasn't alone.

STORY: DAVID AND GOLIATH (1 SAMUEL 17:1-54)

David, a young shepherd, was sent to deliver food to his brothers at the battlefield. When he arrived, he heard the giant Goliath mocking God and the Israelites. While others cowered in fear, David stepped forward and said, "Who is this uncircumcised Philistine that he should defy the armies of the living God?"

David's courage didn't come from his own strength, but from his confidence that God would fight for him. He boldly faced Goliath, knowing that God was with him. Through faith and courage, David defeated the giant.

COURAGE WILL FOLLOW WHEN FAITH TAKES THE LEAD!

> "A ship is always safe at shore, but that is not what it's built for."
> – Albert Einstein

COURAGE

Were you ever afraid of the dark? You lie in bed, eyes wide open, staring at shadows, hearing the faintest noise. In that moment, fear grips you. But when you finally gather the courage to turn on the light, you realize the danger was just a harmless object.

Courage doesn't mean you're never afraid—it means you act despite the fear. God has big plans for your life, so don't stop moving forward. With God, you have the victory!

> *"No, in all these things we are more than conquerors through Him who loved us."* — *Romans 8:37*

With God, you have the victory. Be courageous! Don't let anything stop you from what God has placed on your heart.

3 Reasons to Take Courage in Your Life:

- ◊ God made you! (Psalm 139:14)
- ◊ God is for you! (Romans 8:31)
- ◊ God is with you! (Isaiah 41:10)

THINK ON IT

Courage isn't the absence of fear—it's moving forward despite it. It's doing what scares you, trusting that God is with you every step of the way.

> *"Be strong and courageous. Do not fear or be in dread... for it is the Lord your God who goes with you."* — *Deuteronomy 31:6*

Courage comes when we rely not on our own strength but on God's. Like David facing Goliath, we can stand firm, knowing that God fights for us. Courage doesn't mean you're fearless—it means you act in faith, trusting God's protection and power.

With God on your side, you have the victory. Step forward with courage, no matter what lies ahead.

101 DEVOTIONALS — PART TWO

DAY 89
LOVE

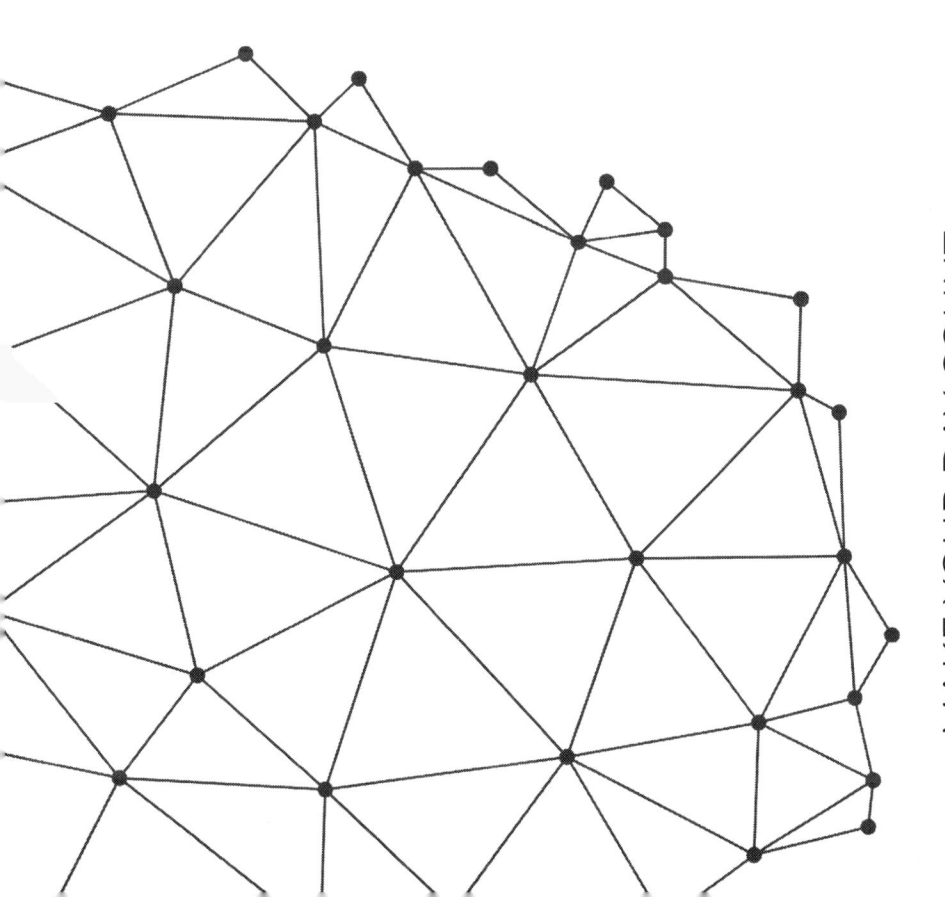

MAKE YOUR DAY COUNT

101 DEVOTIONALS — PART TWO

LOVE

BIG THOUGHT
Love is more than a feeling—it's an action

> "It is not how much you do, but how much love you put into what you do that counts." — Mother Teresa

Matthew 22:37 —"And He said to him, 'You shall love the Lord your God with all your heart and with all your soul and with all your mind.'"

Loving God with your whole heart enables you to love others better. If you struggle to love God, you will find it difficult to love others with unconditional love. However, when God's love fills your heart, it empowers you to love deeply and selflessly.

Love is a powerful four-letter word! We love others best when we love God most. Love is central to being a follower of Jesus.

Definition of Love: Unselfish, loyal, and benevolent concern for the good of another; the object of devotion or admiration.

THE WOMAN AT THE WELL (JOHN 4:7-10)

A Samaritan woman came to draw water. Jesus said, "Give me a drink." She was surprised, as Jews didn't interact with Samaritans. Jesus responded, "If you knew the gift of God and who it is that is saying to you, 'Give me a drink,' you would have asked Him, and He would have given you living water."

Unconditional love comes only from God. His love cannot be earned, bought, or won—it is freely given, unconditional, and unending. God's love fills the void in our hearts, offering wholeness and peace. You don't have to be someone you're not to be loved by God. His love is beyond anything else in life!

> "Greater love has no one than this, that someone lay down his life for his friends." — John 15:13

STORY: JOHN GRIFFITH, THE BRIDGE OPERATOR

In the 1920s, John Griffith was living the American dream, but the Great Depression shattered it. He and his family moved, and he took a small job as a bridge operator over the Mississippi River. Despite the loss of his earlier dreams, John found a new purpose as he worked alongside his son, Greg, tending to the massive bridge.

One day, disaster struck when a train was approaching the bridge while John and Greg were at the observation deck. As John hurried to lower the bridge, he saw that his son had fallen into the gears. With no time to save him, John made the agonizing decision to lower the bridge, sacrificing his son's life to save 400 passengers aboard the train.

John watched as the train passed, and no one even noticed his sacrifice. He cried out in desperation, "What's the matter with you people? Don't you know? Don't you care? Don't you know I've sacrificed my son for you?" But no one seemed to care.

This story is a glimpse of what God did for us. He sacrificed His own Son, Jesus, for the salvation of the world. Unlike John Griffith's shock, God knew exactly what He was doing when He gave His Son to die for us.

> "For God so loved the world that He gave His only Son, that whoever believes in Him should not perish but have eternal life." — John 3:16 NKJV

God's love is so passionate that He gave His only Son so we could experience His love. The best way to find love is to find God. God's Love for You:

◊ God designed you.

◊ God created you.

◊ God blessed you.

LOVE

- ◊ God heals you.
- ◊ God cares for you.
- ◊ God defends you.
- ◊ God forgives you.
- ◊ God loves you.
- ◊ Nothing can separate you from God's love.

THINK ON IT

Love is more than a feeling—it's an action. When we love God with our whole heart, His love empowers us to love others deeply and selflessly.

> *"You shall love the Lord your God with all your heart and with all your soul and with all your mind." — Matthew 22:37*

God's love fills the emptiness in our hearts, enabling us to love unconditionally. Just as Jesus showed love to the woman at the well (John 4:7-10), we are called to reflect that same love. When God's love is the foundation of our hearts, we can love beyond what's easy or convenient.

101 DEVOTIONALS — PART TWO

DAY 90
OBEDIENCE

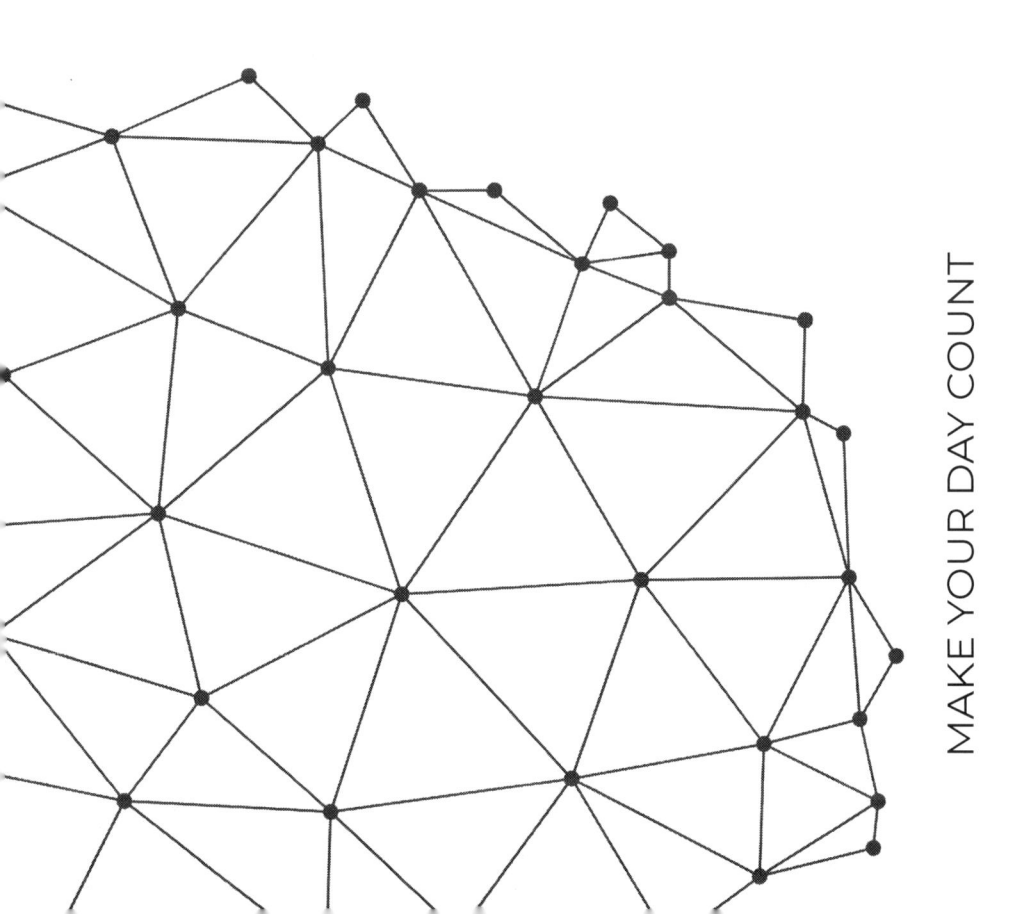

MAKE YOUR DAY COUNT

101 DEVOTIONALS — PART TWO

OBEDIENCE

BIG THOUGHT

Obedience to God is a powerful expression of faith.

> **"Obedience is the act of faith; disobedience is the result of unbelief."** — Edwin Lewis Cole

Obedience to God is a powerful expression of faith. When we obey, we not only align ourselves with God's will but also position ourselves to receive His blessings.

> "On one occasion, while the crowd pressed in on Jesus to hear the word of God, he stood by the lake of Gennesaret. He saw two boats by the lake, but the fishermen had gone out of them and were washing their nets. Getting into one of the boats, which was Simon's, he asked him to put out a little from the land. Jesus sat down and taught the people from the boat. After he finished speaking, he said to Simon, 'Put out into the deep and let down your nets for a catch.' Simon answered, 'Master, we toiled all night and took nothing! But at Your word, I will let down the nets.' When they did, they enclosed a large number of fish, and their nets began to break. They signaled to their partners in the other boat to come and help them. They filled both boats so that they began to sink. When Simon Peter saw it, he fell down at Jesus' knees, saying, 'Depart from me, for I am a sinful man, O Lord.' Jesus replied, 'Do not be afraid; from now on, you will be catching men.' And when they brought their boats to land, they left everything and followed Him.'" — Luke 5:1-11

In this passage, we see a remarkable example of obedience. The disciples had been fishing all night with no success. But when Jesus told them to cast their nets again, they obeyed—even though it didn't make sense. As a result, they experienced a miraculous catch of fish. Their obedience led to blessings, and they were able to bless others.

KEY TAKEAWAYS ON OBEDIENCE

- ◊ Obedience Lights the Way: Obedience leads to greater understanding and blessings. The disciples' obedience to Jesus' command turned their empty boat into a boat full of fish. When we obey God, He shows us His plan and blesses us in ways we couldn't have imagined.

- ◊ Small Obedience Leads to Bigger Things: When you obey God in the small things, He will entrust you with bigger tasks. Like the disciples, who started by obeying Jesus in a simple task, you can grow in faith and responsibility as you follow God's direction.

- ◊ Obedience Blesses Others: When you obey God, not only do you benefit, but others do too. In the story, Simon's obedience brought a blessing not only to him but also to his partners in the other boat.

> *"But whoever keeps His word, in him truly the love of God is perfected. By this we may know that we are in Him." — 1 John 2:5*

Obedience is a reflection of God's love in us. When we choose to obey, we are honoring God's will for our lives. Obeying Him leads to peace, blessings, and deeper fellowship with Him.

PERSONAL REFLECTION

When I was a little boy, I would always play outside, and when my mom told me to come in, I never wanted to. It was a decision: would I obey or not? I often chose disobedience, which would lead to punishment. However, when I obeyed, it pleased my mom and strengthened our relationship. This is true with God, too—when we obey, it blesses us and brings us closer to Him.

> "Obedience to God is the pathway to the life you really want to live." – Joyce Meyer

Obedience is often difficult because it goes against our natural desire to do things our way. But God's way is always the best way. In Romans 5:19, we read, "For as by the one man's disobedience the many were made sinners, so by the one man's obedience the many will be made righteous." Jesus' obedience led to our salvation, and now, as we choose to obey God, we open ourselves to the blessings He has in store for us.

> "There is no peace in any soul until it is willing to obey the voice of God." – D. L. Moody

THINK ON IT

Obedience to God is a powerful expression of faith. It's when we trust Him enough to follow His commands, even when we don't fully understand the outcome.

> "But whoever keeps His word, in him truly the love of God is perfected." — 1 John 2:5

When we obey God, we align ourselves with His plan and open the door to unexpected blessings. Obeying God, even in the small things, prepares us for bigger tasks and deeper relationships with Him. Obedience leads to peace, trust, and deeper understanding of His will. Trust God's way—it always leads to greater things.

101 DEVOTIONALS — PART TWO

DAY 91
WINNING

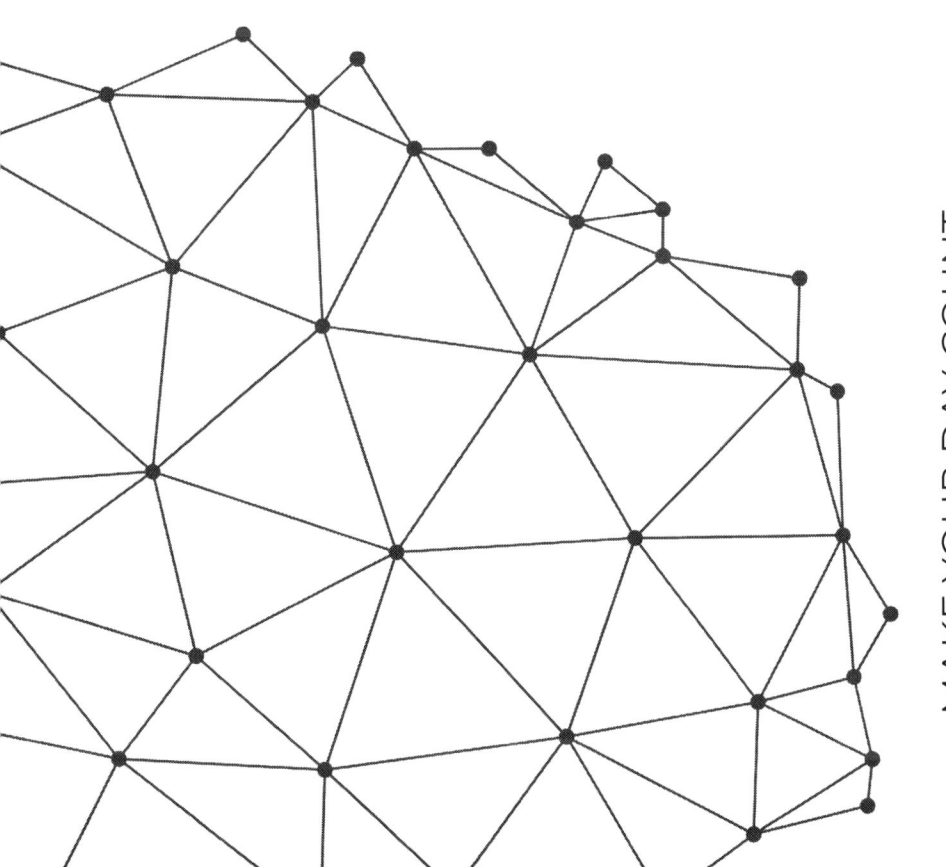

MAKE YOUR DAY COUNT

101 DEVOTIONALS — PART TWO

WINNING

BIG THOUGHT
Winners are not people who never fail, but people who never quit.

> **2 Corinthians 2:14** – "But thanks be to God, who in Christ always leads us in triumphal procession…"

In September of 1995, the world-famous Harlem Globetrotters were defeated on the basketball court during their tour of Europe. The score was 91-85, marking the end of their impressive winning streak that had lasted for 8,829 straight games since their last defeat in January of 1971.

Some people believe they are destined to lose, but as followers of Christ, we see things differently. We are born to win!

> *"Now to him who is able to do far more abundantly than all that we ask or think, according to the power at work within us."*
> *— Ephesians 3:20*

To be a winner, you have to see it, believe it, and do it. God believes in you, and He sees you doing great things. The difference between a winner and a loser is that winners train and losers complain. As believers, we are winners in Christ Jesus!

Walt Disney once said, "The difference in winning and losing is most often not quitting."

101 DEVOTIONALS — PART TWO

STORY – WOMAN WITH THE ISSUE OF BLOOD

> "And he went with Him. And a great crowd followed Him and thronged about Him. And there was a woman who had had a discharge of blood for twelve years, and who had suffered much under many physicians, and had spent all that she had, and was no better but rather grew worse. She had heard the reports about Jesus and came up behind Him in the crowd and touched His garment. For she said, 'If I touch even His garments, I will be made well.' And immediately the flow of blood dried up, and she felt in her body that she was healed of her disease. And Jesus, perceiving in Himself that power had gone out from Him, immediately turned about in the crowd and said, 'Who touched my garments?' And His disciples said to Him, 'You see the crowd pressing around you, and yet you say, 'Who touched me?' And He looked around to see who had done it. But the woman, knowing what had happened to her, came in fear and trembling and fell down before Him and told Him the whole truth. And He said to her, 'Daughter, your faith has made you well; go in peace, and be healed of your disease.'"
> — Mark 5:24-34

This woman didn't quit. Despite twelve years of suffering and countless failed attempts, she found a way to win by having faith and reaching out to Jesus.

You were made to win. You are destined to win. God has given you everything you need to win, and He wants you to win at life through Jesus Christ. God's will is for you to succeed, and He is on your side, not against you. As 2 Peter 1:3 says, "His divine power has bestowed on us everything necessary for life and godliness through the rich knowledge of the one who called us by His own glory and excellence."

> "Brothers, I do not consider that I have made it my own. But one thing I do: forgetting what lies behind and straining forward to what lies ahead, I press on toward the goal for the prize of the upward call of God in Christ Jesus." — Philippians 3:13-14

We are destined to win. God made you a winner—a victorious person. You are unstoppable because He placed greatness within you. He created you to be an achiever and an overcomer in all things!

> "You were born to win, but to be a winner, you must plan to win, prepare to win, and expect to win." – Zig Ziglar

WINNING

> *"The victory will go to the one who doesn't quit." – Van Crouch*

The Difference Between a Winner and a Loser:

A winner says:
"I will find a way."
"I made a mistake."
"I'm getting better."
"I listen to sound counsel."
"I respect those in authority."
"I take ownership."
"I can become better."
"I see faith."
"I have self-control."

A loser says:
"There is no way."
"I never make mistakes."
"I don't have problems."
"I don't need to improve."
"I receive no counsel."
"I have no respect for authority."
"I cast blame."
"I see no need to change."
"I see fear."
"I have no control."

> *"No, in all these things we are more than conquerors through Him who loved us." — Romans 8:37*

You are a conqueror, a winner, and an overcomer! Don't ever forget that you are destined to win in Christ!

THINK ON IT

Winners aren't those who never fail, but those who never quit.

> *"But thanks be to God, who in Christ always leads us in triumphal procession…" — 2 Corinthians 2:14*

To win in life, you have to see it, believe it, and keep moving forward. The woman with the issue of blood (Mark 5:24-34) didn't quit after 12 years of suffering. She reached out in faith, and Jesus healed her. Similarly, we are called to persist, trusting that God will lead us to victory.

You were made to win in Christ! No matter what challenges you face, with God's help, you can overcome and emerge victorious. Keep pressing forward—victory is yours!

DAY 92
POSITIVE

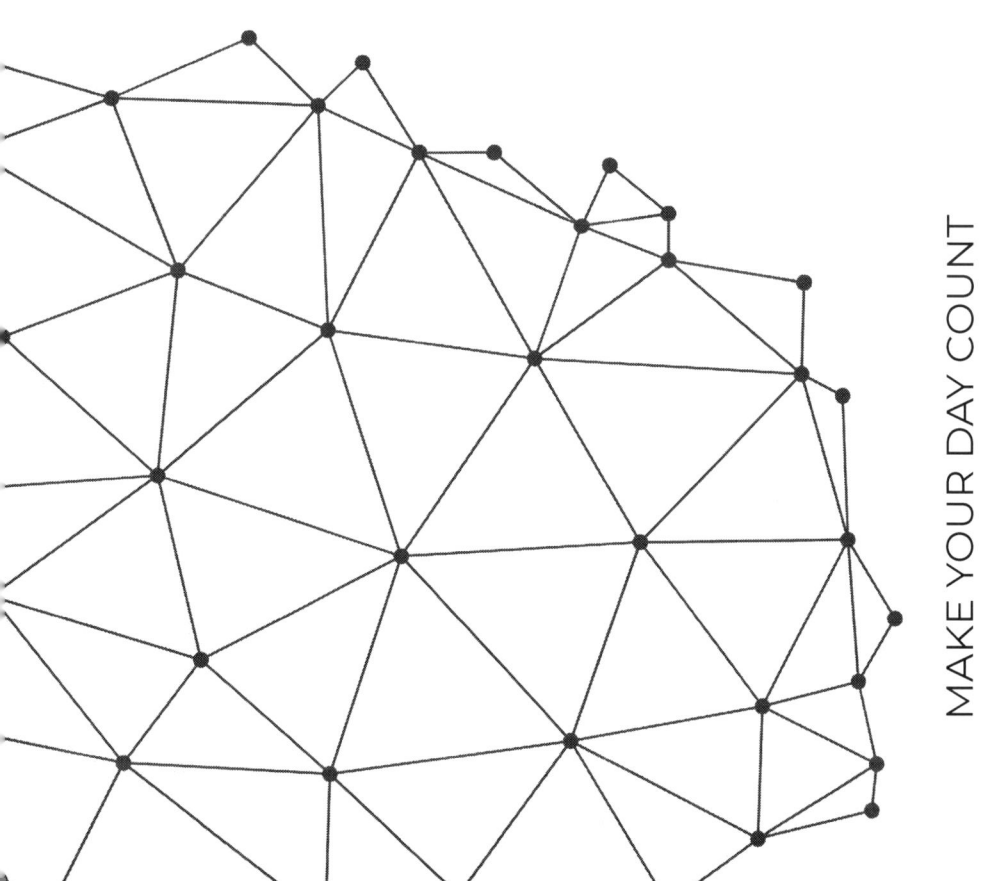

MAKE YOUR DAY COUNT

101 DEVOTIONALS — PART TWO

POSITIVE

BIG THOUGHT
How you look at things can make a world of difference. Having a positive outlook changes everything.

> "The positive thinker sees the invisible, feels the intangible, and achieves the impossible."—Winston Churchill

There's a story of a farmer who was feeling discouraged and decided to sell his land. A realtor came to prepare an ad describing a well-maintained property with sturdy barns, lush pastures, and a beautiful pond. After hearing the ad, the farmer had a change of heart. He realized he had always wanted a place like that, so he decided not to sell. His perception shifted, and his outlook changed.

The way you look at life can make a significant difference. Do you focus on the positive aspects of your life or only the negative?

The Bible tells us exactly how we should think: "Finally, brothers, whatever is true, whatever is honorable, whatever is just, whatever is pure, whatever is lovely, whatever is commendable, if there is any excellence, if there is anything worthy of praise, think about these things." — Philippians 4:8

We should commit this verse to memory and intentionally focus on the positive, rather than dwelling on negativity.

STORY – KING JEHOSHAPHAT GOES TO WAR
(2 CHRONICLES 20:1-25)

When the Moabites, Ammonites, and others came to attack Judah, King Jehoshaphat feared for his people. He called for a fast and prayed to God for help, admitting that they were powerless against this great army. But instead of succumbing to fear, he remained positive and sought the Lord.

The Lord responded with a message: "Do not be afraid or discouraged… The battle is not yours, but God's."

Jehoshaphat believed in God's promise and encouraged his people to praise the Lord. As they sang, God set an ambush against their enemies, leading to a miraculous victory. They didn't have to fight; they just had to stand firm, trust in God, and keep their eyes on Him.

Jehoshaphat's decision to stay positive, even when things looked impossible, led to success. His focus on God and his positive confession helped the people of Judah achieve victory. This story shows us how crucial it is to keep a positive outlook and to focus on God's promises rather than the negative circumstances around us.

Philippians 2:14-16 encourages us to do everything without grumbling or arguing, and instead, live with a positive spirit.

CONFESSION

- ◊ I will be positive.
- ◊ I will talk positive.
- ◊ I will live positive.
- ◊ I will walk positive.
- ◊ I will think positive.
- ◊ And positive things will happen.

Your mind is powerful. When you fill it with positive thoughts, your life will begin to change.

5 WAYS TO STAY POSITIVE IN A NEGATIVE WORLD

- ◊ Pray – Seek God and bring your concerns to Him.

- ◊ Read God's Word – Allow Scripture to encourage and uplift you.

- ◊ Spend time worshipping the Lord – Worship brings a fresh perspective.

- ◊ Be around positive people – Surround yourself with those who uplift and inspire you.

- ◊ Have a spirit of gratitude – Focus on what you have rather than what you lack.

PRACTICAL TIPS TO STAY POSITIVE

- ◊ Watch the content of the music you listen to.
- ◊ Be mindful of the movies you watch.
- ◊ Keep your self-talk and conversations positive.
- ◊ Get rid of any secret or destructive habits.
- ◊ Be cautious about the places you go.

The Bible tells us to take control of our thoughts: "We destroy arguments and every lofty opinion raised against the knowledge of God, and take every thought captive to obey Christ." — 2 Corinthians 10:5

THINK ON IT

How you look at life makes all the difference. A positive outlook changes everything.

> *"Finally, brothers, whatever is true, whatever is honorable, whatever is just, whatever is pure, whatever is lovely, whatever is commendable, if there is any excellence, if there is anything worthy of praise, think about these things." — Philippians 4:8*

In 2 Chronicles 20, King Jehoshaphat chose to stay positive even when faced with overwhelming odds. Instead of focusing on fear, he focused on God's promise and led his people to victory. When we choose to focus on the positive, trusting in God's faithfulness, we too will experience His power.

Our thoughts shape our lives. Let's fill our minds with God's truth and remain positive in every circumstance. God is with us, and with Him, we can overcome anything.

DAY 93
GIVING

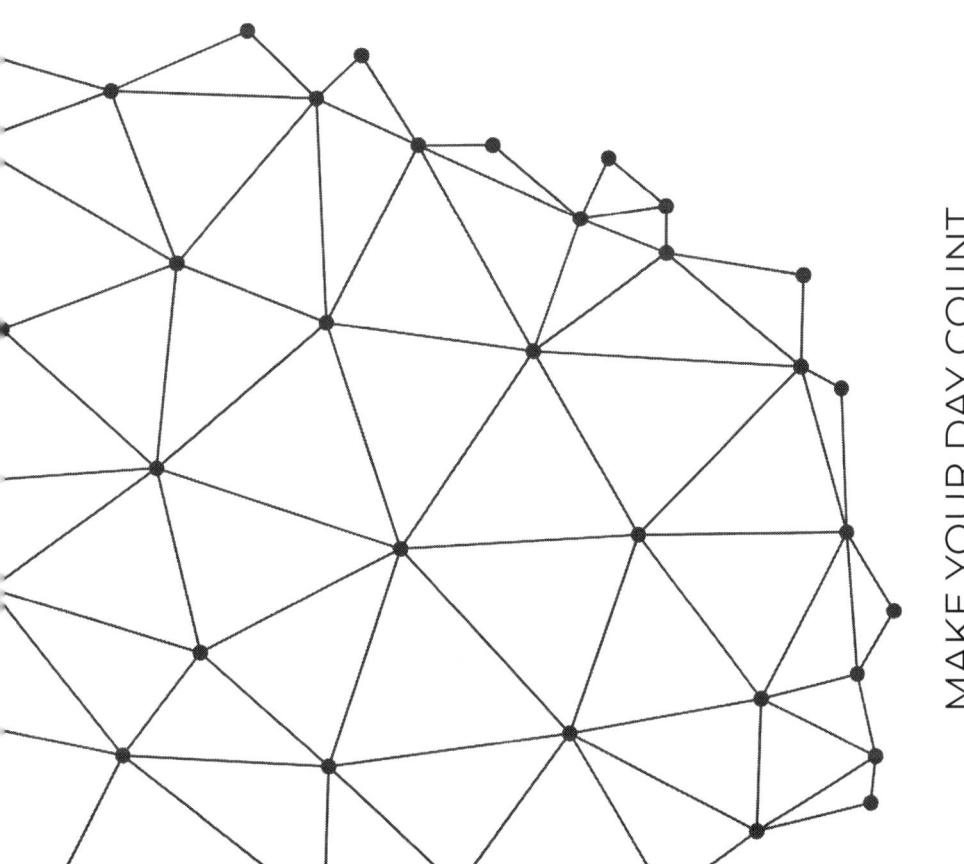

MAKE YOUR DAY COUNT

101 DEVOTIONALS — PART TWO

GIVING

BIG THOUGHT
Giving is living!

> "No one has ever become poor by giving." — Anne Frank

There's a story of a woman who served the Queen as her personal maid for 50 years. After the Queen passed away, the maid was dismissed and moved to a poor area of town, settling in a small shack. One day, a reporter noticed a plaque hanging in the window and asked the elderly woman about it. She shared her story, and the reporter told her that the plaque stated the Queen had given her a house and servants on her property—something she could have claimed but had never known.

When you serve and give to others, it opens doors for greater opportunities. Many people don't realize the potential that giving can unlock when done with a pure heart. God blesses those who give generously. The Bible says in Acts 20:35 that you are more blessed when you give than when you receive. Givers always have more than enough. Though our natural instinct may be selfishness, true giving requires a heart aligned with God's Word, understanding that Jesus is the greatest gift ever given to us.

> "Give, and it will be given to you. Good measure, pressed down, shaken together, running over, will be put into your lap. For with the measure you use it will be measured back to you." — Luke 6:38

This verse explains that the measure you use in giving will determine how much is returned to you—not just in money, but in every area of your life. Giving is an act of trusting God to take care of you in ways beyond what you can do for yourself.

TAKE A LOOK

> "In all things I have shown you that by working hard in this way we must help the weak and remember the words of the Lord Jesus, how he himself said, 'It is more blessed to give than to receive.'" — Acts 20:35

> "Do not be deceived: God is not mocked, for whatever one sows, that will he also reap." — Galatians 6:7

Generous giving brings many rewards:

- ◊ Increased happiness
- ◊ Better physical health
- ◊ Purpose in living
- ◊ Avoidance of depression
- ◊ Interest in personal growth

Having a generous spirit honors God and brings great rewards.

STORY // THE WIDOW (LUKE 21:1-4)

Jesus observed the rich giving large amounts into the offering box, but He also saw a poor widow who put in just two small coins. He told His disciples that the widow had given more than all the others, as she gave all she had to live on, while the others gave out of their abundance.

This story shows that even if you feel like you have little, what matters is the heart behind your giving. Faithfulness in generosity, no matter the amount, is what counts. Whether you have a lot or a little, God honors your faithfulness. Givers always have more than enough. Your worth is not in what you have but in what you give.

THINK ON IT

Generosity isn't just about giving material things; it's about having a heart that reflects God's love and trust in His provision. The act of giving, no matter how big or small, carries with it the promise of blessings—not just for the receiver, but for the giver as well. Jesus taught that true giving is measured by the heart behind it, not by the amount. When we give selflessly, we open the door to greater joy, peace, and fulfillment in our lives.

> *"Give, and it will be given to you. Good measure, pressed down, shaken together, running over, will be put into your lap."*
> *— Luke 6:38*

When you choose to give generously, trust that God will always provide more than enough for you in return.

101 DEVOTIONALS — PART TWO

DAY 94
BURN THE PLOWS, EMBRACE THE GREATER

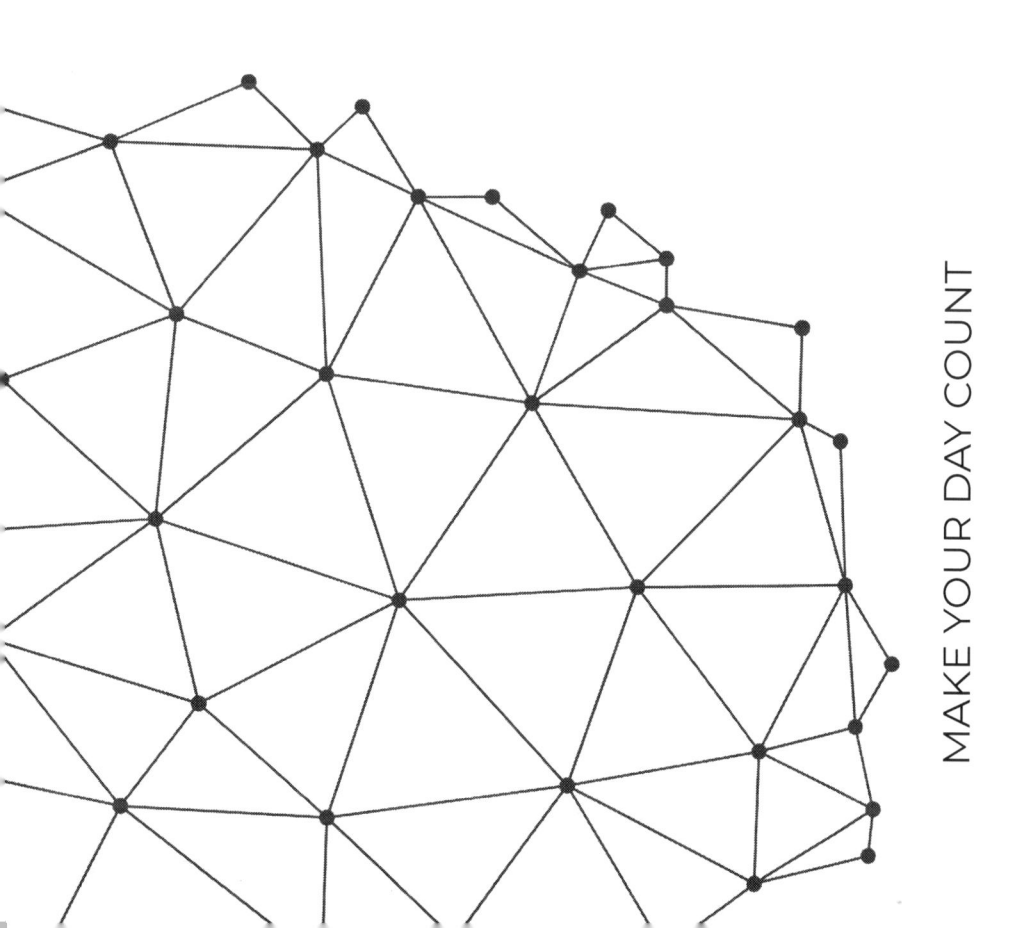

MAKE YOUR DAY COUNT

101 DEVOTIONALS — PART TWO

BURN THE PLOWS, EMBRACE THE GREATER

BIG THOUGHT

God's calling for you is not about staying in the comfort of the known but stepping boldly into the 'greater' He has prepared.

> **Jeremiah 29:11** – "For I know the plans I have for you, declares the Lord, plans for welfare and not for evil, to give you a future and a hope."

In 1 Kings 19:19-21, Elisha makes one of the boldest decisions in Scripture. He burns his plows, slaughters his oxen, and leaves behind his family's livelihood to follow the call of God. At a glance, this act may seem extreme, even reckless. But in reality, Elisha's decision is a powerful example of what it looks like to embrace God's greater calling. He didn't just step out of his comfort zone—he completely left behind the familiar to step into the unknown.

This act of surrender wasn't merely a symbolic gesture; it was a pivotal moment in Elisha's life, marking his total commitment to God's purpose. His bold choice challenges us to think about what we might need to "burn" in our own lives to follow God's call. Sometimes, to move forward, we must be willing to let go of the things that anchor us to our past.

God's plans for us are often far greater than anything we could ever imagine, but stepping into His greater purpose sometimes demands sacrifice. Are you ready to take that step?

THE CALL TO LET GO

When God calls us to something greater, the initial step is often the hardest: letting go. In Elisha's case, burning his plows was an intentional and irreversible act of releasing what was familiar. Plows were more than just tools for farming—they were his livelihood, his security, and the identity he had built for himself. By destroying them, Elisha made the choice to fully trust in God's call over everything he had known.

Similarly, God calls us to let go of what we rely on for security, comfort, and identity. It may not be a literal plow or oxen, but each of us has something we're holding onto—whether it's a career, a relationship, a comfort zone, or even our past mistakes and failures. Sometimes, we cling to the familiar because it feels safe, even though it's limiting us from experiencing the fullness of God's plan.

In John 14:12, Jesus speaks to His disciples, saying, "Very truly I tell you, whoever believes in me will do the works I have been doing, and they will do even greater things than these." The promise of doing "greater works" isn't just a lofty ideal; it's the reality of stepping into the purposes God has for us. But to embrace this calling, we must first let go of the things that hold us back.

Releasing the past—whether it's hurt, fear, or regret—is essential. As we release what has bound us, we make room for God to do a new thing in our lives. Just as Elisha could not follow God's call while holding onto his plows, neither can we fully step into God's greater purpose if we're tethered to our past.

THE PROMISE OF GREATER

In Jeremiah 29:11, God promises us, "For I know the plans I have for you, declares the Lord, plans for welfare and not for evil, to give you a future and a hope." This verse is a powerful reminder that God's intentions for our lives are filled with hope and good things. When we trust God and let go of the things that anchor us to the past, we open ourselves up to experience the "greater" He has in store for us.

Stepping into God's greater plan often means stepping into the unknown. It requires faith, courage, and a willingness to take risks. But the Bible assures us that God's plans for us are good. His promise is that His ways are higher than our ways, and His thoughts are higher than our thoughts (Isaiah 55:8-9). His plans will always exceed our expectations.

In the New Testament, Jesus talks about the "greater works" His followers will do. The truth is that God's work in us is always more than we could ask or imagine (Ephesians 3:20). The "greater" may not always look like what we expect, but it is always better than anything we could have planned on our own.

This is where we see the connection between sacrifice and blessing. As we lay down our plows and our past, we make space for God to fill our lives with something far greater. Our obedience becomes the key to unlocking God's provision, peace, and power in ways we could never have experienced had we stayed in our comfort zones.

PRACTICAL APPLICATION

So, how do we practically apply this in our lives? What does it look like to "burn the plows" and embrace God's greater purpose? Here are a few steps to consider:

- ◊ Identify What Needs to Be "Burned": Take time to prayerfully reflect on what might be holding you back from fully surrendering to God's plan. Is there an area of your life where you're unwilling to let go? It could be something as simple as a fear of failure or as significant as an unhealthy relationship or a past mistake. Whatever it is, identify it and make the decision to release it into God's hands.

- ◊ Commit to Prayer: The process of embracing God's greater calling begins with prayer. Ask God to reveal His purpose for your life and give you the strength to follow His lead. Prayer is not just about asking for what we want; it's about aligning our hearts with God's will and being willing to follow wherever He leads.

- ◊ Trust in God's Timing and Plan: Trust that God's plans are far greater than your own. His ways may not always make sense at first, but He is trustworthy. Step out in faith, believing that He has a good plan for you and will guide you every step of the way. Even if the journey feels uncertain, remember that God is already in your future, preparing it for you.

- ◊ Take Bold Steps of Faith: Elisha didn't just talk about following God; he acted. Taking bold steps often means moving without full visibility of the outcome.

It may require risk, but it's in those moments of bold obedience that God's power becomes most evident.

THINK ON IT

God's calling for your life requires faith, courage, and the willingness to surrender everything to Him. Like Elisha, we are called to "burn our plows"—to let go of anything that ties us to the past and hinders our future with God. The sacrifice may seem great, but the rewards are beyond measure. When we step out in faith, trusting God's greater purpose, He will lead us into a future filled with hope, blessing, and His presence.

> *"For I know the plans I have for you, declares the Lord, plans for welfare and not for evil, to give you a future and a hope."*
> *— Jeremiah 29:11*

Trust that as you step into the greater things God has prepared, He is already ahead of you, guiding you toward an extraordinary future.

DAY 95
STAND FIRM IN THE STORM

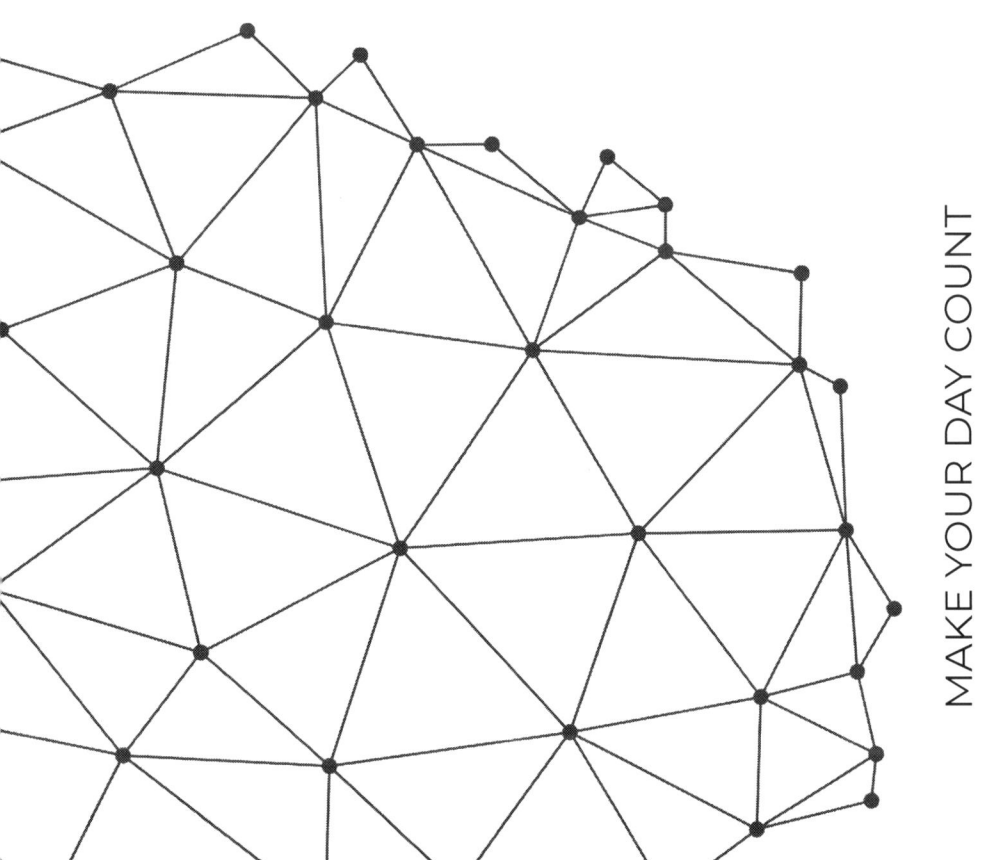

101 DEVOTIONALS — PART TWO

STAND FIRM IN THE STORM

BIG THOUGHT
Victory isn't for the fastest but for those who persevere and stand firm in faith.

> "Be sure you put your feet in the right place, then stand firm." —Abraham Lincoln

In Exodus 14, the Israelites found themselves trapped between the vast Red Sea and Pharaoh's mighty army. The situation seemed hopeless. The enemy was closing in, and the Israelites feared for their lives. It was in the face of this terrifying crisis that Moses gave them a simple, yet profound command: "Do not be afraid. Stand firm and see the deliverance of the Lord." (Exodus 14:13).

In the midst of this impossible situation, God was preparing to display His unparalleled power. The Red Sea would part, and the Israelites would walk through on dry land, escaping their enemies and experiencing the miraculous deliverance of God. This moment of crisis became the stage for God's mighty victory.

Like the Israelites, we too find ourselves facing storms and challenges in life. Whether it's relational struggles, financial burdens, personal loss, or fear about the future, we all experience moments when it feels like we're trapped between a "Red Sea" and an "army" that threatens to overwhelm us. In these moments, God calls us to stand firm in faith, trusting that He will fight for us, just as He did for the Israelites.

THE CALL TO STAND FIRM

Standing firm doesn't mean standing still. It's not a passive, resigned acceptance of our circumstances; it's an active choice to trust God even when the winds of adversity are fierce. Standing firm requires us to make a conscious decision to remain grounded in God's promises and His power, despite what our eyes may see.

When life gets tough, the temptation is to react out of fear, frustration, or self-preservation. We might want to fight back in our own strength or give in to anxiety. However, God calls us to a different response. He calls us to remain rooted in faith, knowing that He is always with us and that His plans for us are good. This is the essence of standing firm—holding on to God's Word, even when the storm rages around us.

In Ephesians 6:13, Paul encourages us to "put on the full armor of God, so that when the day of evil comes, you may be able to stand your ground." Victory comes not from our own strength but from God's power working in us. The armor of God equips us to stand firm against the enemy's attacks, protecting our hearts and minds with truth, righteousness, peace, faith, and salvation. We don't fight alone; we stand in God's strength.

THE POWER OF FAITHFUL PERSISTENCE

Standing firm also requires persistence. It's one thing to stand firm for a moment; it's another to stand firm through the duration of the storm. The Israelites faced more than a brief crisis. They were up against Pharaoh's army, a terrifying force, and they didn't know how long they would have to wait before God intervened. But Moses' words to them were clear: "The Lord will fight for you; you need only to be still" (Exodus 14:14).

The journey of standing firm in faith is not easy. It's a test of patience and trust. Proverbs 4:23 reminds us, "Above all else, guard your heart, for everything you do flows from it." Our ability to stand firm is rooted in the condition of our hearts. A heart that is filled with God's Word, anchored in His promises, and fully surrendered to His will can endure any storm.

Persistence in faith means trusting in God's timing and recognizing that He is at work, even when we don't see immediate results. It's about knowing that God's silence doesn't equate to His absence. The Israelites had to wait at the edge of the Red Sea, with Pharaoh's army closing in. It seemed like God had forgotten them, but He had not. And in your storm, God has not forgotten you either. His deliverance is coming.

THE POWER OF GOD'S DELIVERANCE

When the Israelites stood firm, they were able to witness God's miraculous power. In Exodus 14:21-22, God parted the Red Sea, allowing His people to walk through on dry land. It wasn't by their own strength, strategy, or speed that they gained victory—it was by God's power alone. God fought for them.

Similarly, in our own storms, God wants to show us His power and faithfulness. Standing firm doesn't guarantee that the storm will be over immediately, but it positions us to see God move in powerful ways. The waiting may feel long, but God's deliverance is sure. His timing is perfect, and His ability to bring us through any trial is beyond what we can comprehend.

Remember, sometimes standing firm is not about changing the storm—it's about allowing God to change us through the storm. As we remain steadfast in our faith, God strengthens us, deepens our trust, and reveals His character to us in ways that wouldn't be possible without the storm.

PRACTICAL APPLICATION

When we face life's challenges, it can feel overwhelming, but we are called to stand firm in faith. Here are some practical steps for doing just that:

- ◊ Choose to Stand Firm in Faith: In the midst of your storm, decide to trust God's promises. When fear and doubt arise, combat them with Scripture. Declare His Word over your life. Psalm 34:17 says, "The righteous cry out, and the Lord hears them; he delivers them from all their troubles." Stand firm on that promise.

- ◊ Guard Your Heart: Proverbs 4:23 teaches us that everything we do flows from our heart. Guard your heart by filling it with God's truth. When the storm is loud, it's easy to listen to the voice of fear. But we must actively choose to listen to God's voice through His Word, prayer, and worship. Keep your heart grounded in His promises.

- ◊ Put on the Armor of God: In Ephesians 6:13, Paul urges us to put on the full armor of God, so we can stand firm in battle. Take time daily to equip yourself with truth, righteousness, peace, faith, and the Word of God. The armor of God isn't just a metaphor; it's a powerful spiritual tool that helps you remain strong and steady in the face of adversity.

- ◊ Trust God's Timing: Just like the Israelites had to wait for God's command to part the Red Sea, sometimes we must wait for God's perfect timing. Trust that His plan is always for your good. His ways are higher than our ways, and His deliverance will come at just the right moment.

- ◊ Take One Step at a Time: The journey through the storm can be exhausting, but we don't have to face it all at once. Take each day one step at a time, relying on God's strength to carry you through. With every step of faith, you grow stronger and more equipped for the next.

THINK ON IT

Standing firm in the storm doesn't change the storm, but it changes us. It anchors us in God's truth and prepares us to witness His deliverance. Like the Israelites at the Red Sea, when we stand firm, we position ourselves to experience the power of God at work in our lives. Victory isn't about being the fastest, the smartest, or the most skilled; it's about those who persevere and trust in God's faithfulness.

> *"Blessed is the one who perseveres under trial because, having stood the test, that person will receive the crown of life that the Lord has promised to those who love him."*— James 1:12

As you face life's storms, stand firm in faith, knowing that God will fight for you. His deliverance is sure, His timing is perfect, and His power is more than enough to carry you through.

DAY 96
VISION FOR MORE

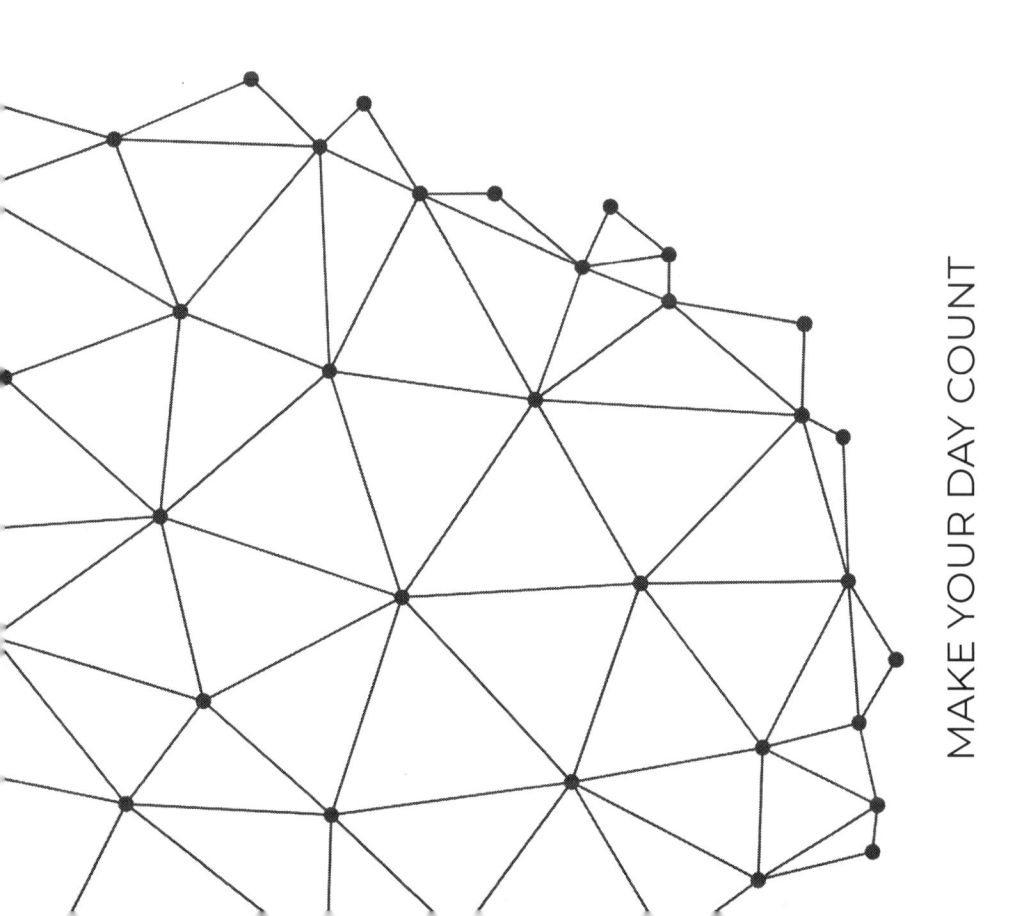

MAKE YOUR DAY COUNT

101 DEVOTIONALS — PART TWO

VISION FOR MORE

BIG THOUGHT
God's plans for you are far greater than you can imagine. Vision gives pain a purpose.

> "The only thing worse than being blind is having sight but no vision." —Helen Keller

---

God has a vision for your life—one that exceeds anything you could ever ask for or imagine. In Ephesians 3:20, Paul declares, "Now to him who is able to do immeasurably more than all we ask or imagine, according to his power that is at work within us." This verse reminds us that God's plans for us are limitless, far beyond our understanding.

Vision is not simply about setting personal goals or dreaming big dreams; it's about aligning our hearts with God's purpose for our lives. Vision allows us to look beyond our current circumstances and see the potential God has placed within us. It transforms ordinary moments into opportunities to fulfill His greater purpose. Through vision, even the hardest seasons in life gain meaning and purpose.

God's vision for us doesn't only shape our future; it gives purpose to our present. It helps us endure pain, setbacks, and struggles by reminding us that they are part of a bigger plan. When we embrace God's vision, we realize that every experience, good or bad, is an opportunity to move closer to the destiny He has prepared for us.

THE POWER OF VISION

Vision is the key that unlocks our potential. Without it, we are like a ship without a rudder—drifting aimlessly without direction. Proverbs 29:18 states, "Where there is no vision, the people perish." This isn't just about physical survival—it's about the vitality and purpose of our lives. Vision gives us clarity in the midst of chaos, direction when we feel lost, and hope when we face challenges. It helps us see beyond our current limitations and circumstances, to the extraordinary plans God has for us.

Vision also empowers us to persevere. Without a clear picture of the future God wants to bring us into, we might be tempted to give up when things get tough. But with vision, we can endure, knowing that the struggles we face today are preparing us for the greatness God has in store. The pain we experience now has purpose—it refines us, builds our character, and strengthens our faith.

In Habakkuk 2:2-3, God instructs the prophet to "Write down the revelation and make it plain on tablets so that a herald may run with it. For the revelation awaits an appointed time; it speaks of the end and will not prove false. Though it linger, wait for it; it will certainly come and will not delay." God's vision for us may not unfold immediately, but He promises that it will come to pass in His perfect timing. Vision requires patience, but it also fuels our persistence. It keeps us moving forward, even when the road ahead is unclear.

THE CALL TO ACTION

Vision is not passive—it demands action. God's call is not just for us to dream, but for us to step out in faith, trusting that He will guide us each step of the way. While vision gives us clarity, it is through obedience and action that we make that vision a reality. We must have the courage to take the first step, even when we cannot see the whole staircase.

Faith and obedience go hand in hand. In James 2:17, it says, "In the same way, faith by itself, if it is not accompanied by action, is dead." Vision without action is just a dream. It's the small, everyday steps of obedience that bring us closer to the fulfillment of God's promises.

Every step of faith, no matter how small, positions us to see God's greater plan unfold. As we walk out the vision, we begin to experience the "immeasurably more" that God has promised. We may not see immediate results, but as we continue to walk in faith, God begins to reveal His plans for us more clearly.

PRACTICAL APPLICATION

Here are a few practical steps to help you embrace and act on God's vision for your life:

- ◊ Write Down Your Vision: Take time to reflect on God's calling for your life. What are the dreams and desires He has placed in your heart? Write them down, making them clear and specific. Habakkuk 2:2 encourages us to "write the vision and make it plain." Having a written vision helps you keep your focus and reminds you of God's purpose, even when obstacles arise.

- ◊ Commit Your Vision to Prayer: Once you've written down your vision, bring it before God in prayer. Ask Him to align your dreams with His will. Seek His guidance, asking Him to clarify what steps you should take and when. Surrender your plans to Him, trusting that His vision for your life is better than anything you could have imagined. Remember, God's timing is always perfect.

- ◊ Take Small Steps of Faith: Action is the key to seeing your vision come to life. Start with small steps of faith. You don't need to have the entire path mapped out—just take one step at a time, trusting that God will lead you. Every act of obedience, no matter how small, brings you closer to fulfilling your vision. It's not about having everything figured out; it's about trusting God with each step you take.

- ◊ Trust God with the Process: Vision doesn't always unfold according to our timeline. Sometimes, the journey takes longer than expected, or we encounter obstacles that we didn't anticipate. But know that the waiting is not wasted. God is preparing you in ways that you can't yet see. Trust that He is working behind the scenes, even in the quiet moments. His timing is always perfect.

- ◊ Embrace the Pain with Purpose: Vision gives pain a purpose. If you're going through a difficult season, remember that God uses the challenges of today to prepare you for the greater things ahead. Just as the

Israelites had to go through the wilderness before they reached the Promised Land, sometimes our struggles refine us for something greater. Trust that God is using every part of your journey to fulfill His greater purpose.

THINK ON IT

God's plans for your life are far greater than anything you can imagine. Vision is not just a dream; it's a divine revelation that transforms how we live today. Vision gives pain a purpose by helping us see beyond the present struggles, knowing that God is using every challenge to prepare us for something greater. The key to stepping into God's purpose for your life is embracing the journey with faith and obedience, trusting that He will guide you every step of the way.

> *"Now to him who is able to do immeasurably more than all we ask or imagine, according to his power that is at work within us."*
> *— Ephesians 3:20*

Trust that even when the road ahead seems unclear, God is working behind the scenes. Keep moving forward, one step of faith at a time, knowing that the fulfillment of His vision will come in His perfect timing.

DAY 97
VISION BEYOND THE VISIBLE

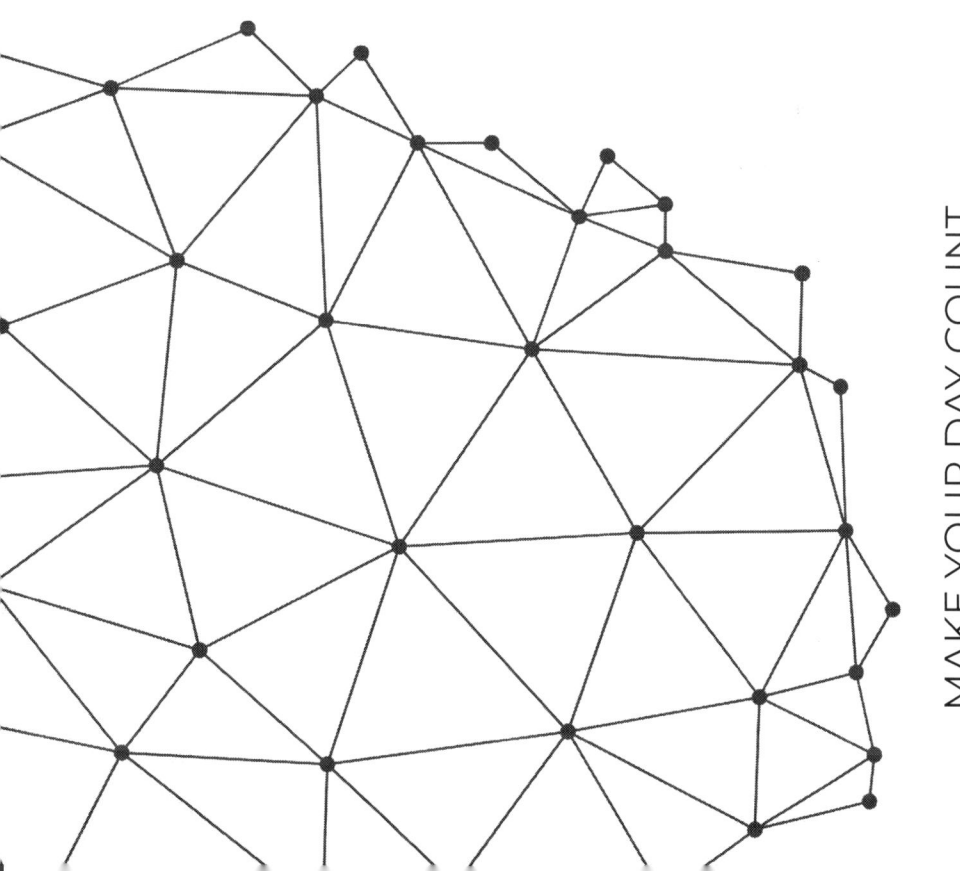

MAKE YOUR DAY COUNT

101 DEVOTIONALS — PART TWO

VISION BEYOND THE VISIBLE

BIG THOUGHT
Without vision, people perish; with vision, people thrive.

Proverbs 29:18 – "Where there is no vision, the people perish."

Vision is not just a nice idea—it is essential for a thriving spiritual life. Just as a city needs a roadmap to reach its destination, our lives need divine vision to guide us. Proverbs 29:18 tells us, "Where there is no vision, the people perish." Vision gives us direction, purpose, and motivation, especially during difficult seasons. It enables us to keep going when life is challenging, and it empowers us to grow into who God has created us to be.

Without vision, we often settle for mediocrity and complacency, missing out on the fullness of what God has for us. Vision calls us beyond what we can see with our natural eyes and opens our hearts to the incredible plans God has prepared for us—plans that give hope and a future (Jeremiah 29:11). With vision, we don't just survive; we thrive.

MAIN TEACHING: THE POWER OF VISION

Vision is not simply wishful thinking—it is seeing the world through God's eyes and pursuing His plans for our lives. Habakkuk 2:2-3 says, "Write the vision and make it plain on tablets, that he may run who reads it. For the vision is yet for an appointed time; but at the end it will speak, and it will not lie. Though it tarries, wait for it; because it will surely come, it will not tarry."

This passage teaches us that vision is both a process and a promise. God gives us a vision for our lives, and we must write it down, clarify it, and make it plain. The act of writing it down helps solidify our commitment to pursuing it with purpose. Vision requires us to step out in faith and believe that God's timing is perfect, even when we can't yet see the full picture. Sometimes it takes time for our vision to unfold, but we must trust that God is working in the unseen.

Ephesians 3:20 reminds us that God is able to do "immeasurably more than all we ask or imagine." The vision He gives us often challenges us to grow beyond our comfort zones and to dream bigger than we thought possible. His vision is always bigger than our own understanding. When we step out in faith, we position ourselves to experience God's power in ways we couldn't have anticipated.

THE POWER OF A WRITTEN VISION

Consider the story of a man who dreamed of opening a bakery. For years, he saved every penny, envisioning a welcoming space where his community could come together over fresh bread and pastries. Along the way, he faced numerous challenges—financial struggles, doubts from others, and moments of discouragement. But he had a written vision for his bakery, a clear picture of what he wanted to build. This vision became his motivation, fueling his persistence even when obstacles seemed insurmountable.

Eventually, after much hard work and determination, his bakery opened and became a local staple, a place where people gathered, shared stories, and experienced warmth and community. The man's dream was not easy, but his vision sustained him through the trials. His vision kept him focused on the bigger picture, and he was able to see the dream come to fruition.

Just like this man, we too need a clear vision for our lives—a vision that will drive us to push through challenges and pursue the future God has planned for us. A written vision becomes a constant reminder of what God is calling us to do, helping us stay on course when things get tough.

GOD'S PLAN AND FAITHFUL COMPLETION

Jeremiah 29:11 speaks directly to our hearts, reminding us that "I know the plans I have for you, declares the Lord, plans for welfare and not for evil, to give you a future and a hope." God's vision for our lives is always filled with hope and purpose. His plans are designed to prosper us, not harm us, and to give us a future that reflects His goodness.

Philippians 1:6 encourages us, "And I am sure of this, that he who began a good work in you will bring it to completion at the day of Jesus Christ." God doesn't just start the vision—He will finish it. No matter how impossible the vision may seem, He is faithful to complete the work He has begun in us. His timing is perfect, and His power is unstoppable.

LIVING OUT THE VISION

Having vision is one thing, but living it out is another. It takes intentional action, faith, and trust in God's timing. Here are some practical steps to help you pursue the vision God has given you:

- ◊ Write Down Your God-Given Vision for the Next Year: Take time to write down your vision for your life. What is God calling you to do? What are the dreams He's placed in your heart? It's important to make the vision clear and specific, so you know where you are heading. This vision should be God-sized—something that challenges you to grow and step out in faith.

- ◊ Pray for Clarity and Guidance: Seek God's direction through prayer. Ask Him to clarify the vision He has for you and to reveal any steps you need to take. Trust that He will guide you each step of the way. Even if the full picture isn't clear yet, trust that God's plan is unfolding. Ask for the courage to pursue it with faith.

TAKE ACTIONABLE STEPS TOWARD YOUR VISION

A vision without action is just a dream. Identify small, practical steps you can take toward your vision each day. Whether it's learning a new skill, making a new connection, or setting up a meeting, these steps build momentum toward fulfilling your God-given purpose.

- ◊ Share Your Vision with a Trusted Mentor or Spiritual Friend: Share your vision with someone who can encourage and pray with you. Sometimes, speaking it out loud gives you the accountability and support you need to move forward. A mentor or spiritual friend can help you see things from a different perspective, pray for you, and provide valuable guidance as you pursue your dreams.

- ◊ Trust God's Timing: Vision requires patience. Even when things seem to move slowly or when obstacles arise, trust that God is at work behind the scenes. Habakkuk 2:3 reminds us that the vision will not lie, and though it may tarry, it will come to pass at the right time. Trust that God's timing is always perfect, and His plans for you are worth the wait.

THINK ON IT

Vision is essential for thriving in every area of life. It's not just about seeing where you want to go, but about aligning with God's plans for your life. As Proverbs 29:18 warns, "Where there is no vision, the people perish." Without vision, we lose direction and purpose, but with it, we thrive, even through challenges. Vision unlocks our potential and fuels our perseverance, helping us stay focused on the greater purpose God has for us.

> *"Write the vision and make it plain on tablets, that he may run who reads it. For the vision is yet for an appointed time; but at the end it will speak, and it will not lie. Though it tarries, wait for it; because it will surely come, it will not tarry." — Habakkuk 2:2-3*

As you pursue the vision God has placed in your heart, remember that it requires action, faith, and patience. Trust that God's timing is perfect, and with each step, you move closer to seeing His plans unfold in your life. Stay focused, write down your vision, and trust that the journey is as important as the destination.

DAY 98
BREAK THE CYCLE

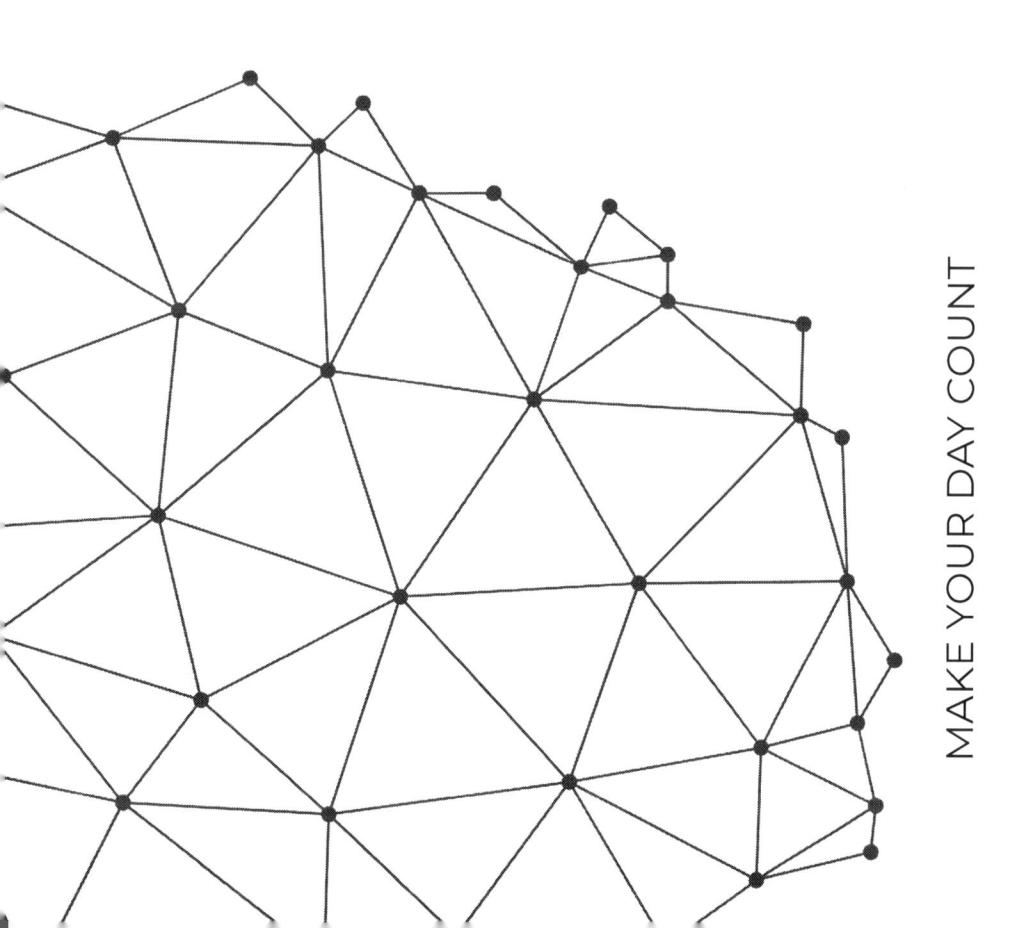

MAKE YOUR DAY COUNT

101 DEVOTIONALS — PART TWO

BREAK THE CYCLE

BIG THOUGHT

Real change comes not from behavior modification but from spiritual transformation.

> **Romans 12:2** – "Do not be conformed to this world, but be transformed by the renewal of your mind, that by testing you may discern what is the will of God, what is good and acceptable and perfect."

In John 5:1-9, we encounter a man who had been sick for 38 years, lying by the pool of Bethesda, hoping for healing. When Jesus approached him, He didn't immediately heal him. Instead, He asked a simple yet profound question: "Do you want to be made well?" This question challenges us deeply—how many of us, like the man at Bethesda, find ourselves stuck in cycles of disappointment, fear, or complacency? We may long for change but resist the steps required to experience it.

In this passage, Jesus doesn't just want to heal the man physically; He wants to help him break the cycle of hopelessness and despair. Real transformation comes from a renewed heart and mind, not just from external changes. Jesus calls us to take action and partner with Him in the process of change. Just like this man, we must evaluate whether we are truly ready for the change God wants to bring into our lives.

THE POWER OF SPIRITUAL TRANSFORMATION

Romans 12:2 calls us to "not be conformed to the pattern of this world, but be transformed by the renewing of your mind." Spiritual transformation begins from the inside out. True change isn't about modifying behavior—it's about the renewing of our hearts and minds through Christ. Behavior modification is surface-level. It's temporary. But when we allow God to renew our minds, we are transformed at the core, and this change becomes lasting.

The man at Bethesda had been stuck in a cycle of disappointment, repeatedly waiting for the waters to be stirred so that he could be healed. For 38 years, his expectation was rooted in a ritual. His pattern of thinking and hope had been shaped by an old way of viewing his situation. When Jesus asked, "Do you want to be made well?", it wasn't just about physical healing—it was about breaking his mental and spiritual cycle of resignation. Real change, Jesus was saying, requires more than a wish or a hope for improvement; it requires faith, trust, and action.

John 5:8 reveals Jesus' command to the man: "Get up! Pick up your mat and walk." The man had to take action in response to Jesus' invitation. He couldn't stay in the same mindset and expect different results. Similarly, when God calls us to break the cycles in our lives, it often requires a shift in thinking and a response of faith. We must be willing to take action, trust God's promises, and move forward even when the path seems uncertain.

THE YOUNG PROFESSIONAL'S BREAKTHROUGH

Consider the story of a young professional who felt stuck in a job that stifled his creativity and ambition. He dreamed of doing something more meaningful, but year after year, he stayed in a job that didn't align with his passions. One day, he prayed for breakthrough—asking God for a new opportunity or for change. However, despite his prayers, he wasn't actively taking steps to make a change. He didn't update his resume, he didn't expand his network, and he didn't pursue new skills that could have opened doors for him.

But then, God spoke to him clearly: change requires partnership. The young man had to take action, and only then would he see God's provision. He began updating his skills, reached out to people in his field, and actively sought new opportunities. Slowly, things began to shift. Within a few months, he landed a new role that allowed him to flourish and grow. It was a breakthrough, but it came only when he broke out of his cycle of inaction and chose to step out in faith.

Just like this man, sometimes we need to recognize that while we pray for change, we must actively cooperate with God's will.

Transformation isn't passive. It requires us to take tangible steps, even when they feel uncomfortable or unfamiliar.

SCRIPTURE CONNECTIONS: GOD'S STRENGTH AND PLANS FOR US

Philippians 4:13 reminds us, "I can do all things through Him who strengthens me." This verse speaks to the power of Christ to help us break free from cycles of defeat and despair. When we rely on God's strength, we can break patterns of sin, failure, or complacency and step into the new things He has prepared for us.

Jeremiah 29:11 assures us, "For I know the plans I have for you, declares the Lord, plans for welfare and not for evil, to give you a future and a hope." God's plans for us are good, and they are designed to give us hope and a future. If we are stuck in cycles that hold us back from living out His best for us, it's time to trust that His plans are better and take steps toward the future He has in store.

BREAKING THE CYCLE

Breaking cycles requires intentional steps and a renewed mindset. Here are practical actions you can take to experience spiritual transformation and break free from patterns that hold you back:

- ◊ Identify One Area Where You Are Stuck in a Cycle: Think about areas in your life where you feel trapped or where patterns of behavior or thinking have kept you from moving forward. This could be related to relationships, your career, finances, or even your spiritual life. Bring this area before God and ask Him to help you recognize the cycle you are in.

- ◊ Pray for Spiritual Transformation: Ask God to transform your heart and mind in this specific area. Prayer is a powerful tool for breaking cycles. Ask God to reveal any lies, fears, or past hurts that may be contributing to the cycle and pray for healing. Trust that He will give you the strength to overcome.

- ◊ Take One Faith-Filled Action Step: Identify one thing you can do today to break the cycle. It could be taking a step of faith in a new direction, having a difficult conversation, changing an old habit, or seeking help from someone who can encourage and support you.

God won't just do it for you; He calls you to participate in the process.

- ◊ Surround Yourself with Encouraging People Always: Transformation happens in community. Surround yourself with people who encourage your growth and hold you accountable. These individuals can provide wisdom, support, and prayer as you break free from old patterns and move toward the new things God has for you.

- ◊ Renew Your Mind with God's Truth: Romans 12:2 challenges us to renew our minds. Engage with God's Word daily to renew your thinking. Let His truth replace the lies and misconceptions that have kept you stuck. When your mind is aligned with God's truth, you can better discern His will and step into His purpose.

THINK ON IT

Real transformation doesn't come from simply changing your behavior; it comes from a spiritual renewal of the mind. In Romans 12:2, we are urged to "be transformed by the renewal of your mind." Just like the man at the pool of Bethesda, change requires more than a desire for improvement—it requires action, faith, and a willingness to shift our mindset. Jesus didn't just heal the man physically; He called him to break free from a cycle of hopelessness and take action. Similarly, God calls us to break the cycles of complacency in our own lives through the renewing of our minds and faith-driven actions.

> *"Do not be conformed to this world, but be transformed by the renewal of your mind, that by testing you may discern what is the will of God, what is good and acceptable and perfect."*
> — Romans 12:2

As you break free from patterns that keep you stuck, remember that God is with you, offering strength, guidance, and the wisdom to move forward. Trust Him to help you transform from the inside out and walk in the new things He has planned for you.

DAY 99
BETWEEN THE ROCKS

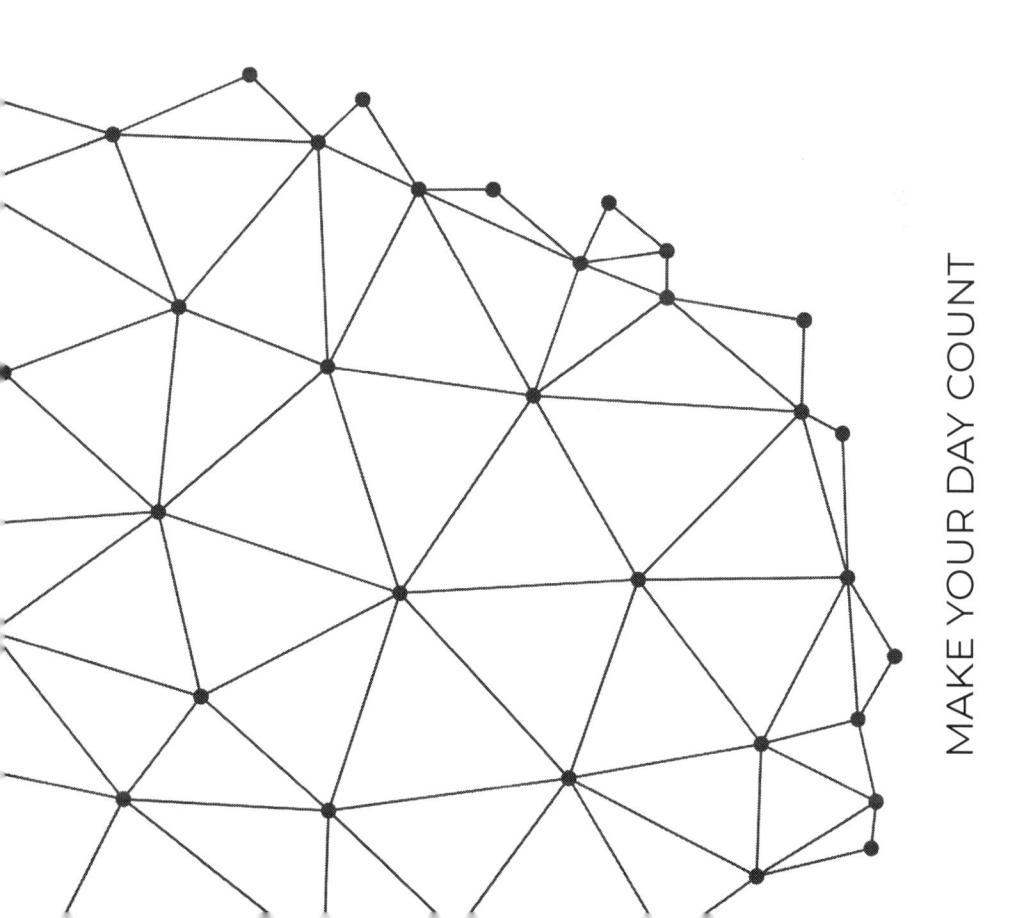

MAKE YOUR DAY COUNT

101 DEVOTIONALS — PART TWO

BETWEEN THE ROCKS

BIG THOUGHT
God uses hard places to prepare us for high places.

> "God never said that the journey would be easy, but He did say that the arrival would be worthwhile." —Max Lucado

Life is full of challenging moments, often placing us between a rock and a hard place. It's in these moments of pressure, difficulty, and uncertainty that God has the greatest opportunity to show His power and faithfulness. When faced with obstacles, we might feel trapped, discouraged, or overwhelmed, but God uses these times to prepare us for higher callings and greater victories. If we trust in His guidance and move forward in faith, He will lead us to new heights we never thought possible.

The Bible is full of stories where individuals faced what seemed like impossible circumstances. One such story is that of Jonathan in 1 Samuel 14. Jonathan's courage in the face of daunting obstacles teaches us that God's power is often revealed most profoundly in the hard places of our lives.

FAITH IN THE FACE OF OBSTACLES

In 1 Samuel 14:6, we read that Jonathan, the son of King Saul, faced the Philistine army, which was greatly outnumbering and outgunning Israel's forces. Jonathan and his armor-bearer stood before a seemingly insurmountable challenge—an army poised to destroy Israel. But rather than waiting passively or being consumed by fear, Jonathan took bold action. He declared, "Come, let's go over to the outpost of those uncircumcised men. Perhaps the Lord will act on our behalf." Jonathan believed that God's power was bigger than the obstacles they faced. While Saul remained in fear, Jonathan boldly stepped forward with faith in God's provision and power.

In life, we often find ourselves facing overwhelming challenges. We may be caught in circumstances that seem impossible to overcome—financial struggles, health battles, broken relationships, or personal failures. But the story of Jonathan reminds us that our faith in God can propel us forward. Even when the odds are stacked against us, God is with us, and He can turn the hardest places into platforms for His power to shine.

Jonathan's faith drove him to climb a literal cliff to reach the enemy, a clear metaphor for the "cliffs" of difficulty we sometimes face. This story challenges us to have the same daring trust in God, to look past the difficulty, and move forward with courage. When we take the first step in faith, trusting God's strength to climb, He shows up in powerful ways, often leading us to heights we could never have reached on our own.

FAITH AMIDST FINANCIAL STRUGGLES

A powerful illustration of faith in the midst of hardship comes from the story of a single mother named Emily, who faced overwhelming debt. Despite the financial pressure, Emily refused to let her circumstances define her. She believed that God was bigger than her debts and trusted that He would provide.

She started small—creating a strict budget, cutting unnecessary expenses, and seeking advice from financial counselors. The journey was long, and there were times when she felt discouraged, but she kept pressing forward, trusting that God would show her the way out. Eventually, her efforts began to bear fruit. Not only did she pay off her debts, but she also began to build savings and improve her financial literacy. Her story serves as a reminder that faith and action, even in the hardest places, can bring breakthroughs. Just as Jonathan climbed the cliffs with courage, Emily took small but faithful steps to climb out of her financial struggles.

Her story also highlights that breakthrough doesn't always come in one dramatic moment but is often the result of consistent effort, trust, and faithfulness. The difficult places we face are often stepping stones that lead us to higher ground when we keep our eyes on God's promises.

SCRIPTURE CONNECTIONS: GOD'S PROMISES IN HARD PLACES

Jeremiah 32:17 states, "Ah, Sovereign Lord, You have made the heavens and the earth by Your great power and outstretched arm. Nothing is too hard for You." This verse reminds us that no situation is beyond God's ability to intervene. Whether we are facing physical, emotional, or spiritual challenges, God's power is sufficient to handle it all. His strength is greater than any obstacle, and He is able to carry us through the toughest times.

Matthew 19:26 echoes this truth: "With man this is impossible, but with God all things are possible." When we encounter situations that seem hopeless or beyond our control, we can take comfort in knowing that God can make a way where there seems to be no way. His promises are trustworthy, and He will provide the strength we need to persevere.

2 Corinthians 4:8-9 speaks to the resilience that God gives us in difficult times: "We are hard pressed on every side, but not crushed; perplexed, but not in despair; persecuted, but not abandoned; struck down, but not destroyed." The Apostle Paul understood that hard places are inevitable in life, but he also recognized that God's sustaining grace allows us to endure and rise above adversity. Even when we feel pressed from every angle, God's power will not only sustain us but strengthen us to keep going.

CLIMBING THE HARD PLACES WITH FAITH

Here are some practical steps to help you break free from the cycles of hardship and experience God's power in difficult situations:

- ◊ Identify Your "Hard Place": Think about areas in your life where you feel stuck or overwhelmed. It could be a situation at work, a personal challenge, a health issue, or an emotional struggle. Name it and bring it before God in prayer. Acknowledging where you're struggling allows you to see how God can show up in that area.

- ◊ Pray for Strength and Courage to Climb: Just as Jonathan trusted God to help him overcome obstacles, ask God for the strength to face your challenges head-on. Pray for courage to take bold steps and for clarity in how to move forward. Trust that God is with you, no matter how difficult the climb.

- ◊ Meditate on God's Promises: Regularly reflect on scriptures like Jeremiah 32:17 and Matthew 19:26 to remind yourself that God is bigger than your problems. Fill your mind with His promises, and let His truth fuel your faith. When we renew our minds with God's Word, we are reminded that He can turn any hard place into an opportunity for growth.

- ◊ Take One Step Forward in Faith: Break down your challenges into manageable steps. Just as Jonathan didn't defeat the Philistine army in one move, you don't need to solve everything at once. Take one step at a time, trusting God to guide your path and strengthen you along the way.

- ◊ Look for the Higher Ground: When we face hardship, it's easy to focus on the difficulty of the climb. But as you move forward, look ahead to the higher ground God is preparing for you. Each step of faith brings you closer to the victory God has planned for you. Trust that the hard places you're in today are preparing you for greater heights tomorrow.

THINK ON IT

God often uses hard places to prepare us for higher purposes. In the story of Jonathan, we see how facing seemingly impossible obstacles can lead to greater victories when we trust in God's power. Jonathan's bold faith in the midst of adversity showed that God's strength is made perfect in our weaknesses. Just as Jonathan climbed a literal cliff to reach the enemy, sometimes we must step into hard situations with faith, knowing that God will provide the strength to overcome.

> *"Ah, Sovereign Lord, You have made the heavens and the earth by Your great power and outstretched arm. Nothing is too hard for You." — Jeremiah 32:17*

When we find ourselves between the rocks, facing difficulties, remember that God is bigger than any obstacle. With Him, all things are possible, and the hard places are often the very steps that lead us to higher ground. Keep pressing forward in faith, and trust that He will take you to new heights.

101 DEVOTIONALS — PART TWO

DAY 100
MADE NEW

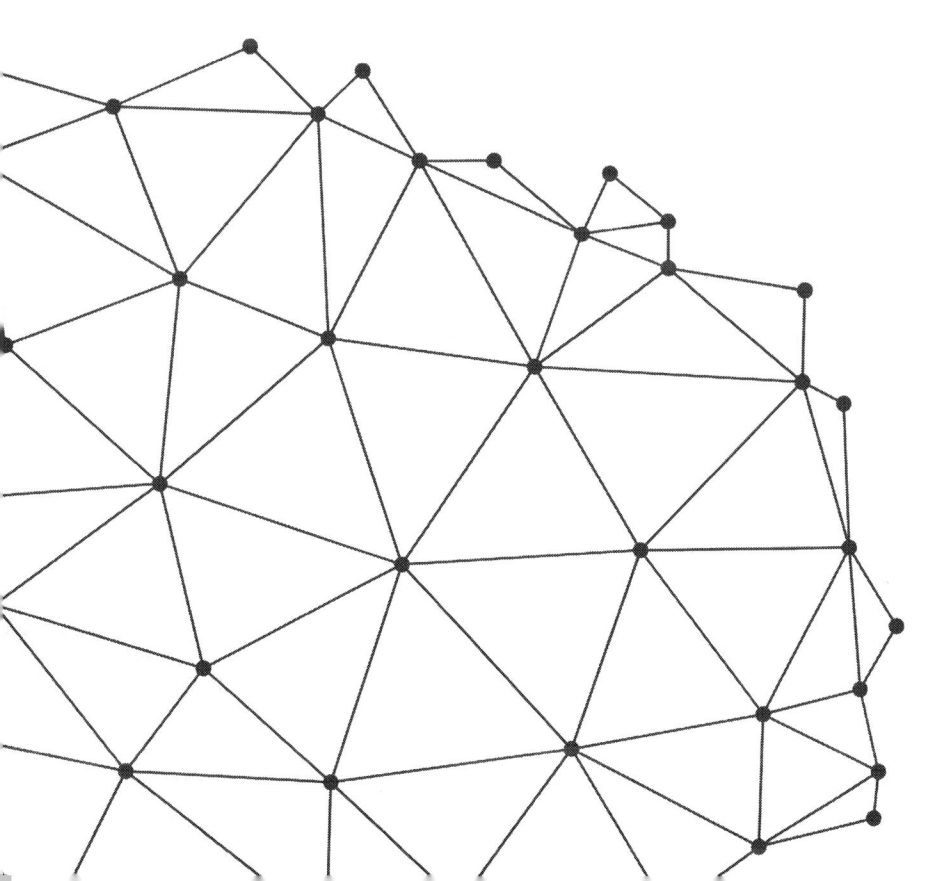

MAKE YOUR DAY COUNT

101 DEVOTIONALS — PART TWO

MADE NEW

BIG THOUGHT

God has the power to make you new.

> **2 Corinthians 5:17** — "Therefore, if anyone is in Christ, he is a new creation. The old has passed away; behold, the new has come."

In Christ, we are made new. This is the essence of the gospel message—Jesus came to restore us to our original purpose and design, offering us a fresh start. Our transformation into new creations begins with a deep, intentional pursuit of God. As we seek Him daily, we leave behind our old ways, thoughts, and habits, stepping into the fullness of His promises.

This renewal is not a one-time event, but a daily commitment to walk in the newness that Christ offers. It is a journey of transformation where we allow God's presence and power to shape us into who He created us to be.

SEEKING GOD FOR TRUE RENEWAL

Seeking God is not a passive or half-hearted effort. It is an active pursuit that involves time, energy, and focus. It means turning to Him in prayer, reading His Word, and allowing His Spirit to guide and convict us. Jeremiah 29:13 (ESV) offers us a promise: "You will seek me and find me when you seek me with all your heart." True renewal happens when we make God the priority of our lives, setting aside distractions and giving Him our undivided attention.

This process of renewal is not about achieving perfection but about continually turning our hearts toward God, allowing Him to work in and through us. In 2 Corinthians 5:17, the Apostle Paul declares, "Therefore, if anyone is in Christ, the new creation has come: The old has gone, the new is here!" When we come to Christ, we receive a new identity, one that is not defined by our past mistakes or failures but by the grace and love of God.

In Matthew 6:33 (ESV), Jesus gives us the key to finding true fulfillment and transformation: "But seek first the kingdom of God and his righteousness, and all these things will be added to you." This verse teaches us that renewal begins with aligning our lives with God's kingdom and prioritizing His righteousness. When we focus on God and His will for us, everything else falls into place.

THE POWER OF DAILY COMMITMENT

Consider the story of Michael, a successful businessman who had always prioritized his career. Over time, he realized that his focus on work had led him to neglect his spiritual life, and his relationships and personal well-being began to suffer. One day, he felt convicted to make a change. He decided to recommit his mornings to seeking God through prayer and Bible study.

At first, it felt challenging. He had to wake up earlier, shift his mindset, and put in the effort to stay consistent. But over time, Michael noticed a significant transformation. As he began his day with God, his perspective shifted. He found peace amidst the pressures of work, and his decisions became more aligned with God's will. His relationships with family and friends improved, and he became more aware of God's presence in every aspect of his life. Michael's renewed focus on God transformed not just his mornings but his entire life.

Michael's story highlights the truth that seeking God daily is transformative. The more we prioritize time with God, the more we begin to reflect His character and experience the renewal He promises.

SCRIPTURE CONNECTIONS

> *"I sought the Lord, and he answered me; he delivered me from all my fears."* — Psalm 34:4

This verse reinforces the promise that God answers those who seek Him. When we seek God, He is faithful to meet us in our need, bringing deliverance, peace, and guidance. The more we seek Him, the more we experience His presence and intervention in our lives.

> "Remember not the former things, nor consider the things of old. Behold, I am doing a new thing; now it springs forth, do you not perceive it?"
> — Isaiah 43:18-19

In this passage, God speaks to His people about His ability to make all things new. No matter what has happened in our past—whether it's failure, regret, or hurt—God promises to do a new thing in our lives. Renewal is not just a change on the outside but a deep, spiritual transformation that God is constantly at work in us. We can trust that God is always moving us toward something better.

> "Do not be conformed to this world, but be transformed by the renewal of your mind, that by testing you may discern what is the will of God, what is good and acceptable and perfect."
> — Romans 12:2

Transformation starts with the renewal of our minds. When we seek God, He changes the way we think and view the world, helping us to align our lives with His will. This kind of renewal leads to greater clarity and purpose in life, as we grow to understand God's good, pleasing, and perfect will for us.

SEEKING GOD DAILY FOR RENEWAL

- ◊ Dedicate Time Each Day to Seek God: Set aside time each day to seek God in prayer and through His Word. This can be as simple as starting your morning with a few minutes of focused prayer, reading a passage from the Bible, or reflecting on a devotional. The key is consistency. As you spend time with God, you'll begin to experience the transformation He promises.

    Scripture Reference: Matthew 6:33

- ◊ Identify One "Old" Thing to Leave Behind: Renewal involves both embracing the new and letting go of the old. Reflect on an area in your life where you need to release the old patterns or habits that are holding you back. This might be a mindset, an unhealthy relationship, or a past hurt. Trust God to help you move forward and leave behind the things that no longer serve His purpose for your life.

Scripture Reference: 2 Corinthians 5:17

- ◊ Celebrate Small Victories in Your Journey of Renewal: Renewal is a process. It takes time, and it's important to recognize the small steps of progress along the way. Celebrate the moments when you see growth—whether it's a new perspective, a more peaceful heart, or improved relationships. These small victories are evidence of God's work in your life.

Scripture Reference: Isaiah 43:18-19

THINK ON IT

Renewal is the work of God's grace, and it begins the moment we seek Him with all our hearts. Through intentional pursuit—spending time in prayer, immersing ourselves in His Word, and aligning our lives with His kingdom—we experience the transformation that God promises. As 2 Corinthians 5:17 reminds us, when we come to Christ, we are made new. The old has passed away, and the new has come!

> *"You will seek me and find me when you seek me with all your heart." — Jeremiah 29:13*

Seeking God daily leads to a renewed heart and mind, where we begin to think differently, act differently, and live in the fullness of God's purpose for us. This is a journey that requires consistent effort but leads to transformation and newness that only He can provide. If you desire change, begin today by seeking God wholeheartedly, trusting that He will make all things new.

DAY 101
GREATER THINGS

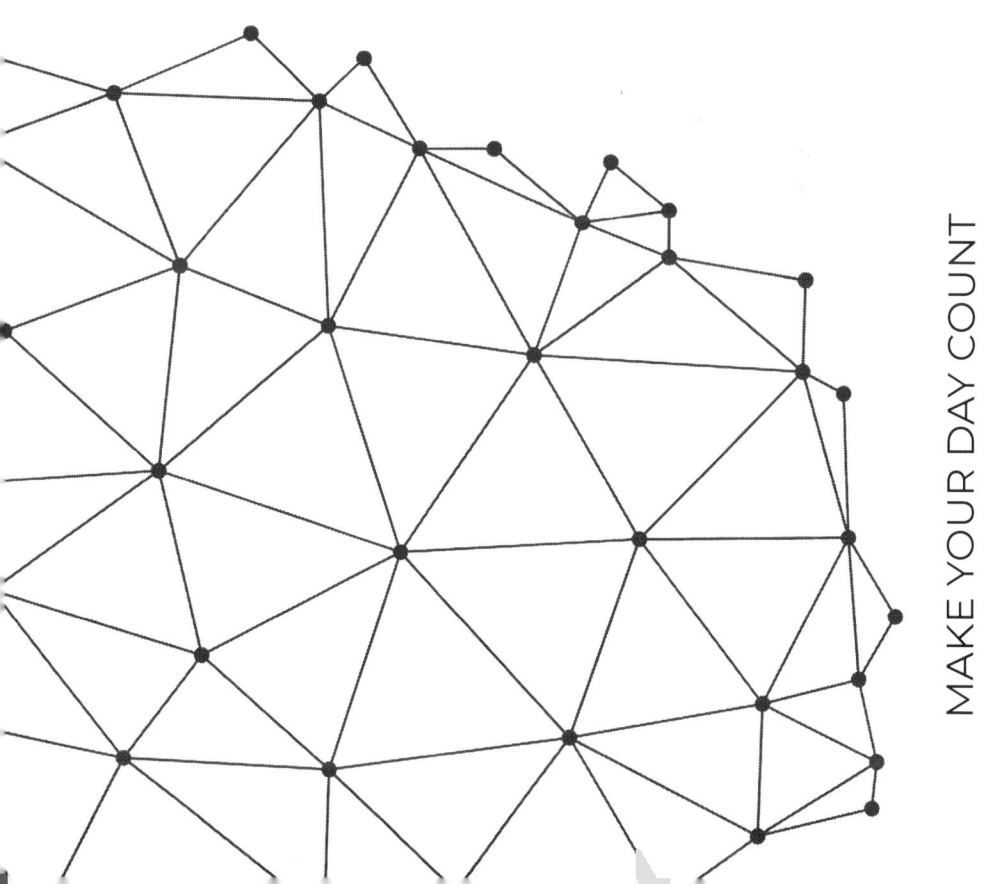

MAKE YOUR DAY COUNT

101 DEVOTIONALS — PART TWO

GREATER THINGS

BIG THOUGHT
You are called to do greater things through the power of Jesus.

> "What lies behind us and what lies before us are tiny matters compared to what lies within us."
> — Ralph Waldo Emerson

Jesus promised that those who believe in Him would do greater things than even He did. This bold statement is recorded in John 14:12 (ESV): "Truly, truly, I say to you, whoever believes in me will also do the works that I do; and greater works than these will he do, because I am going to the Father."

It's an incredible promise, isn't it? We often read this and wonder, "How could I, an ordinary person, do anything greater than what Jesus Himself did?" The key to understanding this is realizing that the "greater things" Jesus refers to are not about doing things bigger or more spectacular in our own strength. Instead, they are about God working through us, multiplying His power, love, and impact in the world.

When Jesus spoke these words, He was preparing His disciples for a time when He would no longer be physically with them. His departure through the ascension would open the door for the Holy Spirit to come and empower them—and empower us—to do greater things. The greater things are possible because of the Holy Spirit's presence within us, making us vessels of God's kingdom on earth.

THE PROMISE OF GREATER THINGS

What does it mean to do greater things? When Jesus made this declaration, He wasn't referring to miracles that would surpass His own, but rather, He was speaking of the multiplication of His works through His followers. The works of Jesus—healing the sick, loving the outcasts, preaching the gospel of salvation, casting out demons—were just the beginning. Through His disciples, and ultimately through every believer, these works would continue and spread across the world.

In John 14:12, Jesus tells us that whoever believes in Him will not only continue His works but will also do greater things. Why? Because Jesus' departure made way for the Holy Spirit to empower His followers to take His mission to the ends of the earth. The message of the gospel would spread to all nations, and through believers, the kingdom of God would expand in ways that Jesus' earthly ministry could never have achieved on His own.

It's important to note that these greater things aren't about seeking personal glory or fame; they are about bringing glory to God by doing His will on earth. The "greater things" refer to the spread of the gospel, the transformation of lives, and the advancing of God's kingdom.

THE POWER OF THE HOLY SPIRIT

Consider the story of a small church in a remote town that decided to step out in faith and make a difference in their community. This church was known for its prayer meetings, small gatherings, and a close-knit fellowship, but they felt called to do more. The pastor and the congregation believed that God wanted to do greater things in their midst.

They began reaching out to their neighbors, offering food to the hungry, and hosting free community events for children. Slowly, the town began to take notice. What started as a small group of believers, praying and serving, turned into a movement that reached hundreds. They were able to share the love of Christ with people who had never heard the gospel. One by one, families were healed, lives were transformed, and a community that had once felt hopeless was revived.

This small church was not doing greater things because of their own power, but because they were willing to step out in faith, believing that God would do more than they could imagine through the Holy

Spirit. Their willingness to follow God's leading multiplied the impact of their ministry and reached far beyond their expectations.

SCRIPTURE CONNECTIONS: BELIEVING FOR GREATER THINGS

> "Very truly I tell you, whoever believes in me will do the works I have been doing, and they will do even greater things than these, because I am going to the Father."—John 14:12

Jesus' words show that the power of the Holy Spirit, given after His ascension, would equip believers to continue and multiply His work on earth. We are not limited by our own abilities or experiences; we are empowered to do greater things because of the Spirit working through us.

> "Now to him who is able to do immeasurably more than all we ask or imagine, according to his power that is at work within us." — Ephesians 3:20

God is able to do immeasurably more through us than we can ask or imagine. When we align ourselves with His will, the Holy Spirit empowers us to accomplish things we never thought possible. The greater things are possible not because of our own strength, but because of God's power at work in us.

> "He replied, 'Because you have so little faith. Truly I tell you, if you have faith as small as a mustard seed, you can say to this mountain, 'Move from here to there,' and it will move. Nothing will be impossible for you.'"— Matthew 17:20

Even a small amount of faith can move mountains. The greater things Jesus talks about don't require perfect faith, but a willing heart and trust in God's ability to move through us. With faith, no obstacle is too great, and nothing is impossible for those who believe.

STEPPING INTO GREATER THINGS

- ◊ Step Out in Faith: The first step to seeing greater things is faith. Take a step of faith in an area where you feel God calling you to make a difference. Whether it's in ministry, relationships, or your career, trust that God can multiply your efforts for His glory. Don't wait for the perfect moment; start now, and watch how God shows up in extraordinary ways.

Scripture Reference: John 14:12

◊ Rely on the Holy Spirit: Greater things aren't achieved by human effort alone; they are the result of the Holy Spirit working through us. Every believer has access to the power of the Spirit, so don't try to do it in your own strength. Spend time in prayer, asking the Holy Spirit to empower you to do the greater works God has planned for you.

Scripture Reference: Ephesians 3:20

◊ Expect the Impossible: Begin to expect the impossible. Believe that God is capable of doing greater things in and through your life. Whether it's healing, restoration, or breakthroughs in your family or work, trust that God can do things beyond your wildest dreams. Let your faith align with His power, and expect to see Him move in mighty ways.

Scripture Reference: Matthew 17:20

◊ Be a Vessel of Change: God's greater works are not about us; they are about being vessels of His grace, love, and power. Each day, ask God how He can use you to bring His kingdom on earth. Whether it's through a kind word, a generous act, or a gospel conversation, be willing to be used by God for greater things.

Scripture Reference: John 14:12

THINK ON IT

Jesus promised that those who believe in Him would do greater things than even He did on earth. This isn't about achieving personal greatness, but about allowing God to use us to extend His work and impact the world for His kingdom.

> *"Very truly I tell you, whoever believes in me will do the works I have been doing, and they will do even greater things than these..."* — John 14:12

As we step out in faith, trusting the power of the Holy Spirit, we can expect God to do great things through us. Don't let fear or doubt limit what God wants to do in your life. Step into the greater things He has prepared for you—trusting that His power is at work within you.

101 DEVOTIONALS — PART TWO

PRAYER OF SALVATION

Have you ever made Jesus the Lord and Savior of your life? If you have not, then pray this prayer below and begin a new life in Christ:

> *"Lord Jesus, I believe You are the Son of God and ask You to come into my heart. Forgive me of all my sins and cleanse me of all unrighteousness. I believe that You took my sins when You died on the cross. I believe You rose again on the third day. I choose to serve You. Be the Lord and Savior of my life. In Jesus Name, Amen."*
>
> *"For everyone who calls on the name of the Lord will be saved."*
> — Romans 10:13

If you prayed this prayer for the first time, we would like to know. To send an email or share your testimony, connect with me on instagram @jeremy.d.baker or https://www.thenxtgeneration.com/

101 DEVOTIONALS — PART TWO

APPENDIX

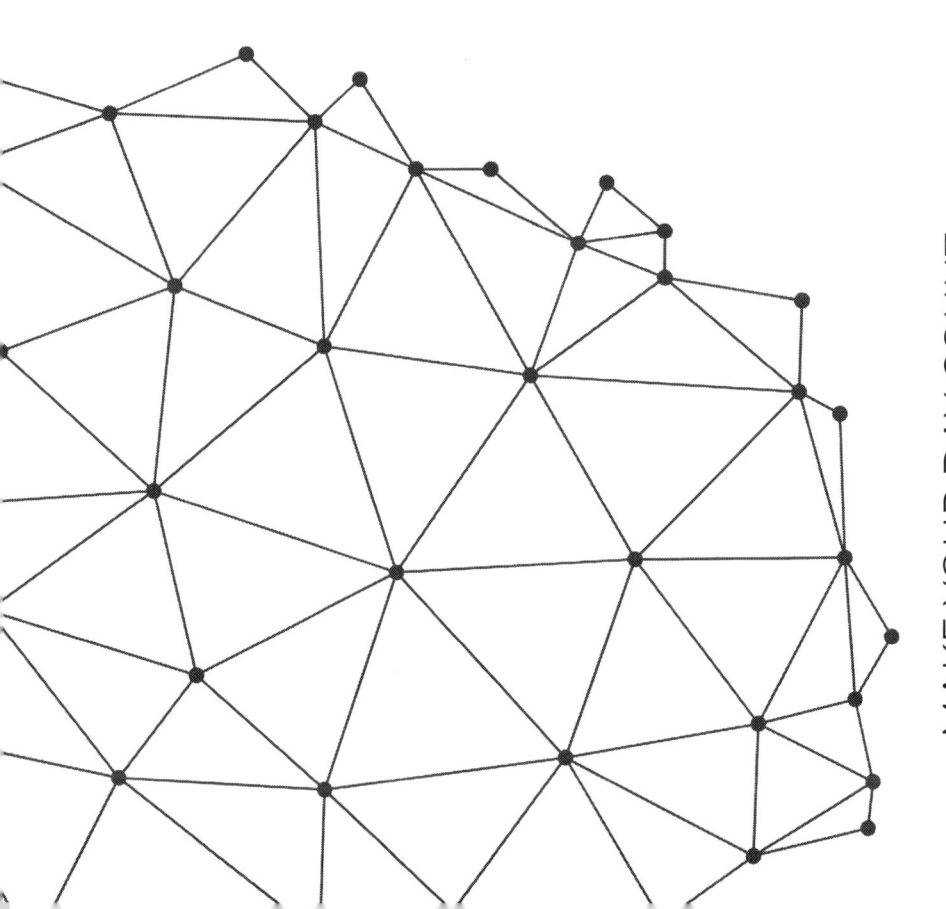

101 DEVOTIONALS — PART TWO

REFERENCES

ALL SCRIPTURES FROM THE ENGLISH STANDARD VERSION

"Scripture quotations are from The ESV® Bible (The Holy Bible, English Standard Version®), copyright © 2001 by Crossway, a publishing ministry of Good News Publishers. Used by permission. All rights reserved."

#creator, and #identity. "Facing The Music." Sermon Central, 19 Mar. 2012, www.sermoncentral.com/sermon-illustrations/81111/facing-the- music-by-curry-pikkaart.

Joseph, Georgy N. "Story : The Atheist Diver." Jesus Christ Wallpapers | Christian Songs Online, 16 Sept. 2010, www.turnbacktogod.com/story- the-atheist-diver/.

"One More Move Chess Art." One More Move Chess Art, www.one-more-move-chess-art.com/

"Marathon Man Akhwari Demonstrates Superhuman Spirit." International Olympic Committee, 15 Sept. 2016, www.olympic.org/news/marathon-man-akhwari-demonstrates-superhuman-spirit.

Wilma Rudolph: A Story of Determination, www.socialstudiesforkids.com/articles/ushistory/wilmarudolph.htm.

https://books.google.com/books/about/God_In_My_Corner.html?id=UEf5Al10M8wC

"The Axe." SermonSearch, www.sermonsearch.com/sermon-illustrations/4681/the-axe/.

Lidz, Franz. "There's a Giant Warehouse Full of Product Launches That Failed." Smithsonian.com, Smithsonian Institution, 1 Dec. 2017, www.smithsonianmag.com/innovation/where-to-go-to-buy-failed-prod- ucts-180967221/.

Sermon Illustrations, Quotes, Stories and Analogies by Kent Crockett,www.kentcrockett.com/cgi-bin/illustrations/index.cgi?topic=Trust.

"A Gold Doorstop." Ministry127, ministry127.com/resources/illustration/a-gold-doorstop.

"Courage Is Fear Holding on a Minute Longer." Ministry127, ministry127.com/resources/illustration/courage-is-fear-holding-on-a-minute- longer.

"Who Holds The Rope?" Our Daily Bread, 25 Nov. 2013, odb.org/1996/04/08/who-holds-the-rope/.

"Home." Speakingtree.in, 16 Feb. 2014, www.speakingtree.in/blog/hap- piness-280152.

#creator, and #identity. "God Will Make A Way." Sermon Central, 6 June 2005, www.sermoncentral.com/sermons/god-will-make-a-way- evie-megginson-sermon-on-descriptions-of-god-79896.

#creator, and #identity. "Popular Sermon Ideas & Illustrations for Biblical Preaching." SermonCentral.com, www.sermoncentral.com/ sermons/sermons-about-rose-crawford?keyword=Rose%2BCrawfor- d&ref=SermonSerps.

#creator, and #identity. "Get In Agreement With, 'Gods Word.'" Sermon Central, 24 Feb. 2011, www.sermoncentral.com/sermons/get-in- agreement-with-gods-word-charlie-roberts-sermon-on-grace-154663.

"Hope | Definition of Hope in English by Lexico Dictionaries." Lexico Dictionaries | English, Lexico Dictionaries, www.lexico.com/en/defini- tion/hope.

REFERENCES

Daily Inspirational Quotes. "Once You Choose Hope Anything Is Possible... (Motivational Quotes)." Daily Inspirational Quotes, 26 Feb. 2016, www.dailyinspirationalquotes.in/2012/09/once-you-choose-hope- anything-is-possible-motivational-quotes/.

#creator, and #identity. "The Perfect Storm." Sermon Central, 24 June 2013, www.sermoncentral.com/sermons/the-perfect-storm-ralph-juth- man-sermon-on-storms-of-life-177003.

"Baby Jessica." Biography.com, A&E Networks Television, 2 Apr. 2014, www.biography.com/people/baby-jessica-17175736.

"Vince Lombardi Quote." A-Z Quotes, www.azquotes.com/quote/664849.

"No Turning Back." SermonSearch, www.sermonsearch.com/sermon-illustrations/914/no-turning-back/.www.biography.com/people/jim-carrey-9542079.

"Forward." Merriam-Webster, Merriam-Webster, www.merriam-webster.com/dictionary/forward.

"Average Brain Has Up To 50,000 Daily Thoughts And 70% Of Them Are Negative." MessageToEagle.com, 1 Dec. 2017, www.messagetoeagle.com/average-brain-has-up-to-50000-daily-thoughts/. On site Source - Psychology Today

"Story: The Elephant Mindset." Story: The Elephant Mindset | Improve Your- self Daily, www.dailytenminutes.com/2012/06/story-elephant-mindset.html.

"Zig Ziglar Quotes." BrainyQuote, Xplore, www.brainyquote.com/quotes/zig_ziglar_617744.

"Faith." Merriam-Webster, Merriam-Webster, www.merriam-webster.com/dictionary/faith.

"Dwight L. Moody Quote." A-Z Quotes, www.azquotes.com/quote/1339842.

"One Prayer Week 2: God Is Able." NW OKC LifeGroup Leaders, 19 June 2009, 4nwleaders.wordpress.com/2009/06/12/one-prayer-week2-god-is- able/.

"Stabilizing The Leaning Tower Of ..." https://Www.sermoncentral.com, www.sermoncentral.com/illustrations/ser-mon-illustration-sermoncentral--stories-government-81903.

"Phobia List - The Ultimate List of Phobias and Fears." FearOf.net, 10 July 2016, www.fearof.net/.

PEGGY SENZARINO, Courier Lee News Service. "Little Girl Found Alive after Night Alone in Cornfield." Waterloo Cedar Falls Courier, 5 July 2006, wcfcourier.com/news/regional/little-girl-found-alive-after-night-alone-in-cornfield/article_ce2350b1-c3f8-56b4-b51f-5b0f2c49b6a8.html.

"'What Fueled The Great Chicago Fire.'" https://Www.sermoncentral.com,www.sermoncentral.com/sermons/what-fueled-the-great-chicago-fire-gerald-roberts-sermon-on-fire-207298?ref=SermonSerps.

Zenger, Jack, and Joseph Folkman. "The Ideal Praise-to-Criticism Ratio." Harvard Business Review, 27 June 2017, hbr.org/2013/03/the-ideal-praise-to-criticism.

"Horace Quotes." BrainyQuote, Xplore, www.brainyquote.com/quotes/horace_152507.

Levin, Michael. "Otherwise Indecipherable." Two Frogs in the Cream, 1 Jan. 1970, otherwiseindecipherable.blogspot.com/2009/08/frogs-in-cream.html.

Norman, P. "The Whole World Stinks." Positivity Post, 26 Jan. 2018, positivi- typost.com/the-whole-world-stinks/.

"Zig Ziglar Quotes." BrainyQuote, Xplore, www.brainyquote.com/quotes/ zig_ziglar_381975.

"Winston Churchill Quotes." BrainyQuote, Xplore, www.brainyquote.com/ quotes/winston_churchill_104164.

John C. Maxwell Quote." A-Z Quotes, www.azquotes.com/quote/556482.

"A Quote by Albert Camus." Quote by Albert Camus: "Life Is a Sum of All Your Choices". So, What ...", www.goodreads.com/quotes/405686-life-is-a-sum-of-all-your-choices-so- what.

REFERENCES

"Can't Make Decisions." SermonSearch, www.sermonsearch.com/sermon-illustrations/1478/cant-make-decisions/.

"Catherine Pulsifer Quotes." Art Quotes Categories, www.art-quotes.com/auth_search.php?authid=955#.WpsRmmaZPfY.

Hall, Dr. Kathleen. "Alter Your Life." https://www.google.com/books/edition/Alter_Your_Life/Kus5RUf1Ok8C?hl=es-419&gbpv=

Quote Investigator, quoteinvestigator.com/2011/08/05/lion-gazelle/.

"Newt Gingrich Quotes." BrainyQuote, Xplore, www.brainyquote.com/quotes/newt_gingrich_107062.

"Perseverance." Merriam-Webster, Merriam-Webster, www.merriam-webster.com/dictionary/perseverance.

"Henry Ford." Bible.org, bible.org/node/13258.

"Charles Spurgeon Quotes." BrainyQuote, Xplore, www.brainyquote.com/quotes/charles_spurgeon_143068.

"John C. Maxwell Quotes." BrainyQuote, Xplore, www.brainyquote.com/quotes/john_c_maxwell_383606.

"Praise - Get the Hell Out!" Google Books, books.google.com/books?id=hhVdDQAAQBAJ&pg=PT113&lp-g=PT113&dq=geese%2Bencourage%2Bone%2Banother%2Bto%2Bkeep-%2Bgoing&source=bl&ots=je4YTcl-nE&sig=ZiGFTRRn5RCl15Pk-lGin3P-kMLec&hl=en&sa=X&ved=0ahUKEwju5v2Go9HZAh UKZKwKHfOAC8E- Q6AEIPTAD#v=onepage&q=geese%20encourage%20one%20another%20 to%20keep%20going&f=false.

"Sermon - So You Will Never Forget." LifeWay, www.lifeway.com/en/articles/sermon-communion-lords-sup-per-cup-bread-1-corinthians-11.

"Maya Angelou Quotes." BrainyQuote, Xplore, www.brainyquote.com/quotes/maya_angelou_634520.

"In the Name of Jesus Stop! Telemachus' Story." Jesseleeproject.com, 8 Aug. 2011, jesseleeproject.com/2010/01/31/in-the-name-of-jesus-stop-telema- chus-story/.

"A Quote by Elsie De Wolfe." Quote by Elsie De Wolfe: "I Am Going to Make

 Everything around Me Beautif...", www.goodreads.com/quotes/51441-i-am- going-to-make-everything-around-me-beautiful--

"A Policeman Pulls Over 5 Old Ladies For Driving Too Slow And Their Explanation Is Hilarious." Reshareworthy, 15 Oct. 2017, www.reshareworthy.com/speeding-old-ladies-joke/.

"John C. Maxwell Quote: 'Leader's Potential Is Determined by Those Closest to Him.'." John C. Maxwell Quote: Quotefancy, quotefancy.com/quote/841786/John-C-Maxwell-Leader-s-potential-is-deter- mined-by-those-closest-to-him.

"A Quote by Jim Rohn." Quote by Jim Rohn: "You Are the Average of the Five People You Spen...", www.goodreads.com/quotes/1798-you-are-the-average-of-the-five-people- you-spend. www.linkedin.com/pulse/story-behind-picture-praying-hands-sons-of-is- sachar-concepts.

Ronca, Debra. "How Lion Taming Works." HowStuffWorks, HowStuffWorks, 16 Mar. 2009, entertainment.howstuffworks.com/arts/circus-arts/lion-tam- ing2.htm.

"Bruce Lee Quote, quotefancy.com/quote/78922/Bruce-Lee-The-successful-warrior-is-the-aver-age-man-with-laser-like-focus

"Les Brown Quotes." BrainyQuote, Xplore, www.brainyquote.com/quotes/les_brown_379155.

"Billy Graham Quotes." BrainyQuote, Xplore, www.brainyquote.com/quotes/billy_graham_382920.

Jelani Faraja. Rethink the Journey: "Reigniting the Spiritual Fire" (The Sin- cere Church). Kingdom Book and Gift Publishers and Booksellers, 2017.

Unknown. The Story of a Son - Who Will Take the Son?, www.jaredstory.com/story_of_a_son.html.

https://www.brainyquote.com/quotes/abraham_lincoln_383153

REFERENCES

"Thomas A. Edison Quotes." BrainyQuote, Xplore, www.brainyquote.com/quotes/thomas_a_edison_104931.

quotefancy.com/quote/980718/Bell-Hooks-People-with-healthy-self-esteem- do-not-need-to-create-pretend-identities.

"Identity." Merriam-Webster, Merriam-Webster, www.merriam-webster.com/dictionary/identity.

"Understanding Your Fingerprint Determines the Significance of Your Imprint." Keith Craft, keithcraft.org/understanding-your-fingerprint-deter- mines-the-significance-of-your-imprint/.

"Zig Ziglar Quotes." BrainyQuote, Xplore, www.brainyquote.com/quotes/zig_ziglar_72458

Furtick, Steven. "God Can't Bless Who You Pretend to Be. (See Luke 9:25) https://T.co/rpZZHxA8Glhttps://T.co/UoFEVrpFsr." Twitter, Twitter, 16 Jan. 2016,twitter.com/stevenfurtick/status/688445659741990912?lang=en.

"Trust." Merriam-Webster, Merriam-Webster, www.merriam-webster.com/dictionary/trust.

MY STORY." Bethany Hamilton - Bethany's Story, soulsurfer.com/story.html.

"Ferdinand Foch." Ferdinand Foch - Wikiquote, en.wikiquote.org/wiki/Ferdinand_Foch.

https://quoteinvestigator.com/2014/11/21/adventure/

"Georg Wilhelm Friedrich Hegel Quotes." BrainyQuote, Xplore, www.brainyquote.com/quotes/georg_wilhelm_friedrich_h_101479.

Pringle, Phil; Twitter, 10 June 2015, twitter.com/philpringle/status/608763140222894080.

https://bible.org/illustration/truth-or-fiction

"LastStand."SermonSearch,www.sermonsearch.com/sermon-illustrations/1183/last-stand/.

Einstein, Albert. "Albert Einstein Quote: 'A Ship Is Always Safe at the Shore, but That Is Not What It Is Built for.'." Albert Einstein Quote: "A Ship Is Always Safe at the Shore, but That Is Not What

It Is Built for." (24 Wallpa- pers) - Quotefancy, quotefancy.com/quote/6051/Albert-Einstein-A-ship-is- always-safe-at-the-shore-but-that-is-not-what-it-is-built-for.

"Mother Teresa Quote: Quotefancy, quotefancy.com/quote/869269/Mother- Teresa-It-s-not-about-how-much-you-do-but-how-much-love-you-put-in- to-what-you-do.

"Love." Merriam-Webster, Merriam-Webster, www.merriam-webster.com/dictionary/love.

"The True and Tragic Story of John Griffith and the Memphis Express." The True and Tragic Story of John Griffith and the Memphis Express. - Part One - Wattpad, www.wattpad.com/46594727-the-true-and-tragic-story-of-john- griffith-and-the.

"Edwin Louis Cole Quotes." BrainyQuote, Xplore, www.brainyquote.com/quotes/edwin_louis_cole_360107.

"Joyce Meyer Quotes." BrainyQuote, Xplore, www.brainyquote.com/quotes/joyce_meyer_565161.

"Dwight L. Moody Quote." A-Z Quotes, www.azquotes.com/quote/1412296.

"Defeated the Harlem Globetrotters." Bible.org, bible.org/illustration/defeated-harlem-globetrotters.

www.azquotes.com/quote/487359. (Walt Disney)

"Zig Ziglar Quotes." BrainyQuote, Xplore, www.brainyquote.com/quotes/zig_ziglar_381983.

"The Will To Win." https://Www.sermoncentral.com, www.sermoncentral. com/sermons/the-will-to-win-rob-yanok-sermon-on-power-126702.

"Winston Churchill Quote: (24 Wallpapers) - Quotefancy, quotefancy.com/quote/758984/Winston-Churchill-The-positive-think- er-sees-the-invisible-feels-the-intangible-and.

REFERENCES

"Anne Frank Quotes." BrainyQuote, Xplore, www.brainyquote.com/quotes/anne_frank_379577

"Fear Of The Unknown." Zechariah Newman, 21 Oct. 2014, zechariahnewman.com/2014/10/21/fear-of-the-unknown/.

"There Will Be No Peace." SermonQuotes, 8 Nov. 2016, sermonquotes.com/authors/9643-will-no-peace.html.

www.gracequotes.org, gracequotes.org/?topic=preaching-effectiveness&au- thor-quote=g-campbell-morgan&s=preaching

Jentezen Franklin, www.jentezenfranklin.org/daily-devotions/two-questions

https://www.google.com/books/edition/Rethink_the_Journey_Reigniting_the_Spiri/AC8qDwAAQBAJ?hl=es-419&gbpv=0

Tasler, Nick. "What Is Your Momentum Factor?" Psychology Today, Sussex Publishers, 30 Aug. 2012, www.psychologytoday.com/blog/strategic-think-ing/201208/what-is-your-momentum-facto

www.brainyquote.com/topics/quit.

101 DEVOTIONALS — PART TWO

Made in the USA
Columbia, SC
20 February 2025

5a592d40-aa3f-496f-8c5b-bbff7413d7b8R01